1.50

THE
National ⚾ Pastime
A REVIEW OF BASEBALL HISTORY

Our lead article in this issue, by David Jordan, Larry Gerlach, and John Rossi, definitively debunks a baseball myth created by Bill Veeck, one of the few owners who would probably get a favorable rating by SABR's membership. Veeck's reputation as an outsized, fully human promoter who loved the game will survive the truth. The wonder and lesson to researchers is less why Veeck did it than how this story became common baseball currency without ever having been verified.

Dick Thompson's appreciation of the late Tom Shea gives a glimpse of the impulses and dedication shared by the greatest SABR researchers. Dick usually gives us articles about little-known but fascinating players. Here he illuminates one of the best of our own.

My earliest baseball memory is of playing at my mother's feet as she ironed and listened to the Boston Braves on the radio. Somewhere in there I learned that "Spahn, Sain, and pray for rain" was the way to win a pennant. This is the fiftieth anniversary of the National League's last great year in Boston. Dixie Tourangeau brings us back, while Joe Marren recounts Spahnie's very first professional season in the minors. Of course, the '48 Braves lost to Veeck's Indians in the Series. And that's no myth.

—Mark Alvarez

A Baseball Myth Exploded .... *David M. Jordan, Larry R. Gerlach, John P. Rossi* 3
Cartwright's Trip West .... *Anne Cartwright* 14
Spahn, Sain, and the '48 Braves .... *Dixie Tourangeau* 17
Good Night .... *Bob Rives* 21
Bats and Saddles .... *Tim Wolter* 25
Know Them by Their Autographs .... *Tom Altherr* 29
A Nice Little Career .... *A.D. Suehsdorf* 32
Hey, Blue! .... *Beth Martin* 36
The Baseball Life of René Gonzales .... *Karl Lindholm* 46
A Yankee Fan—The Second Time Around .. *Lyle Spatz* 49
On the Silver Screen .... *Rob Edelman* 52
Jean Dubuc .... *Cappy Gagnon* 55
The First Charley Horse .... *Peter Morris* 59
Babe's Banyan Tree Grows in Hawaii .... *Frank Ardolino* 62
Baseball and Fidel Castro .... *Peter Bjarkman* 64
Baseball's Intriguing Couple .... *Larry Bowman* 69
Nick Altrock .... *Jim Blenko* 73
It's Time to Open the Door .... *Ted Williams* 78
John Coleman's 1883 .... *James D. Smith III* 80
A Photo, A Tour, A Life .... *David A. Hendsch* 82
Tex Sanner's Big Year .... *Joe Murphy* 85
A Happy Addendum .... *Viola Owen* 87
Remembering Mr. Brewer .... *David Davis* 88
It Happened in Brooklyn .... *Bob Gruber* 92
Tom Shea .... *Dick Thompson* 94
The 1921 AL Race .... *Paul Warburton* 103
Mr. Foster Comes to Washington .... *Lyle K. Wilson* 107
The Vulture .... *Tom Simon* 112
Spahn in the Bushes .... *Joe Marren* 116

THE NATIONAL PASTIME (ISSN 0734-6905, ISBN 0-910137-73-0), Number 17. Published by The Society for American Baseball Research, Inc., P.O. Box 93183, Cleveland, OH 44101. Postage paid at Birmingham, AL. Copyright 1998, The Society for American Baseball Research, Inc. All rights reserved. Reproduction in whole or in part without written permission is prohibited. Printed by EBSCO Media, Birmingham, AL.

Editor
Mark Alvarez

Copy Editor
A.D. Suehsdorf

D1401427

The Society for American Baseball Research

History

The Society for American Baseball Research (SABR) was founded on August 10, 1971, by L. Robert "Bob" Davids and fifteen other baseball researchers at Cooperstown, New York, and now boasts more than 6,750 members worldwide. The Society's objectives are to foster the study of baseball as a significant American institution, to establish an accurate historical account of baseball through the years, to facilitate the dissemination of baseball research information, to stimulate the best interest of baseball as our national pastime, and to cooperate in safeguarding proprietary interests of individual research efforts of members of the Society.

The National Pastime

The Society published its first issue of *The National Pastime* in 1982. The present volume is the eighteenth. Many of the previous volumes are still available for purchase (see page 120). The editorial policy is to publish a cross section of research articles by our members which reflect their interest in history, biography, statistics and other aspects of baseball not previously published.

Interested in Joining the Society?

SABR membership is open to all those interested in baseball research, statistics or history. The 1998 membership dues are $35 US, $45 Canada & Mexico and $50 overseas (US funds only) and are based on the calendar year. Members receive the *Baseball Research Journal*, *The National Pastime*, *The SABR Bulletin*, and other special publications. To join SABR, use the form found on the bottom of the publication order form found on page 120. For further information, contact the SABR office at the address or phone below:

SABR
Dept. TNP
PO Box 93183
Cleveland, OH 44101
216-575-0500
www.sabr.org
info @ sabr. org

A Baseball Myth Exploded

David M. Jordan, Larry R. Gerlach, and John P. Rossi

Baseball is a game in which the line between myth and reality is constantly blurred. The devotees of and participants in this most American of all sports delight in creating stories whose truth is often difficult to unravel: Abner Doubleday's invention of baseball, Pete Alexander's celebrated hangover in the 1926 World Series, Babe Ruth's "called shot" home run against the Cubs in 1932.

Another classic example of an enduring legend is the tale of Bill Veeck, lovable old Sportshirt Bill, the game's *enfant terrible*, arranging to buy the bankrupt Philadelphia Phillies franchise early in World War II. The story, first told by Veeck himself in his 1962 autobiography *Veeck—As In Wreck*, is that Veeck planned to stock the club with top-notch black ballplayers from the Negro Leagues but was cheated out of his opportunity by the last-minute chicanery of Judge Kenesaw Mountain Landis, the commissioner, and National League president Ford C. Frick.

The story has been told and retold so many times that it hardly needs citation to a source any more. It has become an article of historical faith, found in virtually every general history of black and white professional baseball as well as in studies of racial integration.[1] Veeck's most recent biographer goes into

David M. Jordan *is an attorney who has written biographies of Senator Roscoe Conkling, General Winfield Scott Hancock, and Hal Newhouser.* **Larry R. Gerlach** *is professor of history at the University of Utah.* **John P. Rossi** *is professor of history at LaSalle University in Philadelphia. His book on the relationship between baseball and developments in American society in the generation after World War II will be published by McFarland in 1999. This article grew out of Jordan's presentation to the 1994 SABR convention and independent work by Gerlach and Rossi.*

some detail about the alleged purchase of the Philadelphia club, although he includes some startling divergences from Veeck's own story.[2] A recently published work called *The Phillies Reader* reprints Veeck's tale verbatim without the slightest indication that there might be some question about its accuracy, except for a slight mixup in the year.[3] The *Los Angeles Times* columnist Jim Murray wrote a piece entitled "The '42 Phils That Weren't" which swallowed Veeck's story whole and even added embellishments of his own.[4]

The major difficulty with this oft-told story is that it is not true. Veeck did not have a deal to buy the Phillies. He did not work with Abe Saperstein and others to stock any team with Negro Leagues stars. No such deal was quashed by Landis or Frick. In fact, there was hardly any Veeck-Phillies connection at all.

This all becomes clear when we examine the record of what happened with and to the Phillies in the 1942-43 offseason. A review of the press coverage and what Veeck himself said at the time of his subsequent purchase of the Cleveland Indians furnishes further evidence, like Sherlock Holmes's nonbarking dog, of what did not happen in early 1943.

Let's start by examining the Phillies' situation in the 1942-43 offseason and what the National League, through its owners and its president, did about it, as well as what the baseball press wrote about the situation.

The pathetic Phillies—As the 1942 season came to an end, Gerald P. Nugent's Phillies were found in their customary spot, last place, for the fifth year in a row. With a record of 42 wins and 109 defeats, the Phils

Those dreadful Philadelphia Phils, 1942. Front row, left to right: Bragan, May, L. Waner, Culp, Lobert (manager), Murtaugh, Marnie, Northey, Naylor. Middle row, left to right: Pearson, Etten, Melton, Warren, Beck, Hoerst, Johnson, Koy, Miller (trainer). Back row, left to right: Litwhiler, Benjamin, Nahem, Podgajny, Hughes, Jones, Glossop, Klein (coach).

under manager John "Hans" Lobert finished 18-1/2 games behind the seventh-place Boston Braves and 62-1/2 behind the pennant-winning Cardinals. Home attendance for the season was a sad 230,183, and the wonder is that that many people came to see them in that first wartime season. On September 11, only 393 people showed up at Shibe Park to watch the Phils lose to Cincinnati. The pitching staff's earned run average was the highest in the National League, and the team's anemic .232 batting average was the worst in its history.

With the dreadful 1942 Phillies, the National League had finally had enough. For year after year the underfunded Philadelphia franchise had been a drag on the league. Most of the time a visiting club failed to make enough from a series in Philadelphia to cover its costs. Even the 1938 change from musty old Baker Bowl to Shibe Park had not improved the Phillies' fortunes.

Gerry Nugent was a savvy baseball executive, but he had no money and for years had performed feats of financial legerdemain simply to keep the club afloat. Now he had just about run out of options. He was in debt to the league, after an advance that had enabled the team to go to spring training in 1942, and in arrears for the rent owed to the Athletics, who owned Shibe Park. The Philadelphia *Inquirer*'s Stan Baumgartner calculated that the club owed a total of $330,000.[5] With an average attendance of fewer than 3,000 fans per game, there was little prospect of salvation. For years, Nugent had peddled whatever competent players he came up with in order to meet day-to-day expenses. He planned, in the '42-'43 offseason, to sell Danny Litwhiler, Tommy Hughes, and Ike Pearson, the best of the sorry lot of 1942 Phils, to the highest bidders. The National League, as his creditor, with a lien upon his assets, now restrained him from doing this.[6]

League action—Early in November the National League owners met, at Nugent's request, to hear the Phillies' problems laid out in detail. The Associated Press then reported that "sale of the…[club] now is certain this winter and possibly within a few weeks." League president Ford Frick denied that any definite action had been settled on, but when asked if the league would lend Nugent more money Frick replied, "Absolutely no."[7]

Early in December, at the major league meetings in Chicago, the National League devoted a full day to "threshing out its biggest problem, what to do with the Philadelphia Phils." Nugent and his lawyer sat out in the hall while his fellow moguls deliberated. Nothing was decided, and the problem was dumped back into Nugent's lap. He was told to go back to Philadelphia and find a well-heeled buyer. He said he was "willing to sell my stock to a suitable buyer who would have enough capital to build the Phils. As I understand it, no such potential buyer has been uncovered."[8]

On February 1, 1943, Nugent told the press that rumors of the league taking the team from him were unfounded. "Certainly," he said, "nobody can come in and take the club without buying it." His lawyer had assured him of that. Unfortunately, Nugent had been unable to find a qualified buyer. Another league meeting was called for February 9, at which it was expected some sort of resolution would be reached.[9]

At this meeting, things came to a head. The National League purchased "substantially all" of the club stock from Gerry Nugent and other stockholders for whom he acted "at an agreed price" of $10 a share for 2,600 shares, plus the assumption of the club's estimated $300,000 debt, more than a third of which was owed to the league itself. Although Red Smith in the Philadelphia *Record* said "the Phils were sold out from under" Nugent, and Ed Pollock in the Philadelphia *Evening Bulletin* said the league had given him "what amounts to a dignified 'bum's rush'," the Phils' owner himself said he was "entirely satisfied" with the league's action. A week or so later, a syndicate put together by lumber broker William D. Cox, a wealthy New Yorker out of Yale, purchased the Phillies from the National League for approximately $250,000. On paper, Cox and his group looked like just the sort of well-endowed ownership that the Phillies had long needed, but within a year Cox himself had been booted from the game by Judge Landis.[10]

This resolution of the Nugent-Phillies problem was obviously not a hasty action on the part of the National League. At least since November, 1942, if not earlier, the groundwork was being laid for Gerry Nugent to sell his franchise back to the league if he was unable to locate a qualified purchaser. Nugent knew it, the other owners knew it, and the members of the press covering the Phillies knew that such a step was a likely outcome of a situation that had become impossible.

Veeck's story—It was during this period that Veeck, at the time the flamboyant owner of the minor league Milwaukee Brewers, later claimed he attempted to purchase the team with the intent of breaking Organized Baseball's long-standing color barrier. In his autobiography, Veeck says he made an offer to Nugent to buy the club, planning to "stock it with Negro players," and that "he [Nugent] had expressed a willingness to accept" the offer. The players, Veeck says, "were going to be assembled for me by Abe Saperstein and [A.S.] "Doc" Young, the sports editor of the Chicago *Defender*, two of the most knowledgeable men in the country on the subject of Negro baseball." He goes on to say that with performers like Satchel Paige, Roy Campanella, Luke Easter, Monte Irvin, and many others "in action and available, I had not the slightest doubt that in 1944, a war year, the Phils would have leaped from seventh place to the pennant."

Veeck says he "made one bad mistake." Out of respect he told Judge Landis what he was planning to do. "Judge Landis wasn't exactly shocked but he wasn't exactly overjoyed either. His first reaction, in fact, was that I was kidding him...The next thing I knew," Veeck says, he learned that the National League had taken over the team and that Frick found a buyer who paid half what Veeck was offering.

Veeck asserts that "the CIO was ready and eager to give me all the financing I needed. The money, in fact, was already escrowed." Unfortunately, the CIO official with whom Veeck was dealing did not want his name to "enter into any of the publicity," and twenty years later Veeck, with rare delicacy, was still respecting that desire for anonymity, even at the cost of frustrating those who might want to check out his story. He had "another potential—and logical—backer, Phillies Cigars." This was, presumably, the Bayuk Company, which manufactured the cigars, but this organization, too, lost out on its chance to help Veeck buy the Phillies.[11]

There are many problems with Veeck's recital. The main one is that it has never been corroborated by anyone else. Although the story shows up in many accounts of the eventual racial integration of baseball, the source always turns out to be either the two pages from Veeck's autobiography or an interview with Veeck himself.[12] Another is that it defies economic logic. If such an offer had been on the table, Nugent would certainly not have yielded up his franchise to Frick and the National League, saying he was "entirely satisfied," to get half of what Veeck later claimed he had offered. Nugent was quite aware that the league could not legally take his team away from him, and Nugent's livelihood depended on the Phillies. If he sold the club, he needed to get the best price possible. In fact, Nugent was given the period from November to early February to develop just the kind of offer Veeck claims to have made him, and he was unable to do so.

The Veeck-Nugent meeting—During the '42 World Series, a reporter with some space to fill concocted a rumor, denied immediately by Nugent, that Veeck had offered to buy the Phils. Veeck said this report gave him an idea. He, with Rudie Schaffer, his righthand man, stopped to see Nugent in Philadelphia after the Series. "We talked about his club," Veeck told the Milwaukee *Journal*. "He quoted some large figures, of course, but that was all." Schaffer has told one of the authors of this article that the meeting "wasn't a very productive one." He and Veeck went back to Milwaukee, and Schaffer knew of no further contacts between Veeck and Nugent. In fact, that *was* all.[13]

In November, 1942, Stan Baumgartner had asked Nugent about Veeck. The Phillies' owner, after saying, "Any person who comes to me with a worthwhile bid and has money to back it up can have the club, or at least my share in it," went on to say:

> During the past year it was published that Bill Veeck, head of the Milwaukee club, had, or would make an offer for the Phils. Veeck stopped in to see me on his way [sic] to the World's Series and did not mention buying or even being interested in the club. When he got back home I saw a clipping from a Milwaukee paper which quoted Veeck as saying he had stopped in to see me because he had read that he was interested in buying the club—and he wanted to see what it was all about.[14]

One can certainly see in this simply another version of the same meeting that Veeck described to the Milwaukee writers and that Rudie Schaffer described: casual conversation with Nugent about the Phillies ball club but nothing more.

Veeck's October meeting was mentioned in the November 12 *Inquirer*, but never again, from that time to the unveiling of the new owner on February 20, 1943, did Veeck's name appear again in the Philadelphia papers in speculation about a possible buyer. Branch Rickey was mentioned, until he took a new job with the Dodgers. Former Postmaster General Jim Farley was mentioned. Several Philadelphia prospects were mentioned, including the brickwork mogul, John B. Kelly, father of future movie queen and Monagasque princess Grace Kelly. A couple of groups from Baltimore, who wanted to move the franchise there, were mentioned. Bill Veeck was not mentioned once in this connection.

The African American media—Significantly, the Philadelphia *Tribune*, the city's leading black newspaper, never wrote a word about the sale of the Phillies in this period, either before or after the departure of Gerry Nugent, indicating by its silence that the fate of the ball club was a matter of indifference to its readers.[15] The *Tribune*'s silence also indicates, of course, that its editors and reporters had never picked up anything about Veeck's alleged intentions, although the CIO and the Bayuk people and Young, at least, supposedly knew of them. Nor did the usually garrulous Veeck say anything further about the Phillies' situation to his sportswriters in Milwaukee.[16]

The silence of the Philadelphia *Tribune* and other leading black newspapers on a possible sale of the Phillies to Veeck and its frustration by Landis and/or Frick is significant. By 1942 African American sportswriters had become increasingly vocal and persistent in pressing for the racial integration of Organized Baseball as part of the overall assault on segregation in America. Led by Wendell Smith of the Pittsburgh *Courier*, Sam Lacy of the Baltimore *Afro American*, Joe Bostic of New York's *The People's Voice*, and Fay Young of the Chicago *Defender*, they were pointedly critical of Commissioner Landis as the personification of the racism that consigned such talented players as Satchel Paige and Josh Gibson to the separate and decidedly unequal world of black baseball. Given the relentless campaign for the integration of the national pastime, the silence of the black press on the alleged effort of Veeck to buy the Phillies in order to integrate the team—and the interference of Landis—is deafening.[17]

If Veeck was lining up money for his purchase, if Saperstein and Young were lining up players for the team, it is inconceivable that Veeck's Phillies project would not have become a matter of public currency, at least within the world of Negro baseball. That the black press refrained from reacting with great vehemence to the betrayal of Veeck by the white authorities, especially in light of its campaign for the integration of baseball, is simply not believable.

The lone black writer to comment on the sale of the woebegone Philadelphia franchise was Joe Bostic of *The People's Voice*, a self-described "militant paper" for "the New Negro," and his report made no reference to Bill Veeck as a possible buyer of the club. An uncompromising and scathing critic of Landis and the moguls of white baseball, Bostic wrote that "the officials of the National League are the most relieved men in the world now that they have unloaded the phutile Phillies…Giving the Phillies to a group of businessmen will hardly solve the problem of making a ball team out of them. They should have been turned over to a group of magicians…." Not a word about Veeck or his alleged plans.[18]

Nat Low, the white sports editor of the Communist Party's *Daily Worker*, was the lone sportswriter to raise the issue of integration with regard to the sale of the Phillies, but the name of Bill Veeck is conspicuously absent from his column, too. Low issued a caustic "goodbye and good riddance" to Nugent for his "attitude toward Negro stars. For a comparatively small price he could have gotten the best stars in the game from the Negro leagues." Low noted that the only place where Bill Cox, the new owner of the team, "can look for first rate players is among those Negro stars who have never been given a major league chance."[19]

Is it possible that the black press either did not know in 1943 about Veeck's plans or decided to avoid making a major issue of the ill-fated scenario so as not unduly to alienate the baseball establishment and thus compromise the ongoing effort to promote the signing of black players by one or more of the existing owners? Perhaps, but it is very improbable. Those constraints, for example, certainly did not apply when Veeck, hard on the heels of Jackie Robinson's signing with Brooklyn in October, 1945, succeeded in purchasing the Cleveland Indians on June 22, 1946, heading up a ten-man syndicate which put up a reputed $2 million for the club.

Cleveland events—Cleveland's daily newspapers, the *Plain Dealer*, the *Press*, and the *News*, covered Veeck's negotiations and his plans to improve the team's fortunes in minute detail. Every aspect of club operations was subjected to analysis and speculation. There was fascination with Veeck himself, a brash 32-year-old ex-Marine with a history of building attendance with amusing and sometimes bizarre stunts. Veeck regaled reporters with his plans to revitalize the club, intending to buy at least three new players at the first opportunity and to undertake a major rebuilding job for 1947. During the weeks and months following his purchase, Bill talked incessantly to the press about every conceivable aspect of club operations—resumption of radio broadcasts, reorganization of the front-office, increased ticket outlets, a final move from old League Park to mammoth Municipal Stadium. One thing he never mentioned was an earlier attempt to buy the Phillies, let alone the possibility of signing Negro Leaguers.[20]

Similarly, with one interesting exception, none of the leading dailies in other major league cities made any reference to a prior effort to buy the Phillies or even remotely hinted that Veeck might be interested in signing black players. The July 3, 1946, issue of *The Sporting News* contained extensive coverage of the sale of the Cleveland franchise along with several profiles of Veeck, all without reference to the Phillies or racial integration, a curious omission if, as Veeck says in his book, Ford Frick had bragged *"all over the baseball world…about how he had stopped me from contaminating the league"* back in 1943.[21]

The exception was the New York *Herald Tribune*, which printed a column by Red Smith in which the former Philadelphia *Record* writer commented: "Hardly anyone knows how close Veeck came to buying the Phillies when the National League was forcing Gerry Nugent to sell. He had the financial backing and an inside track, but at the last moment he decided the risk was too great to take with his friend's money." Smith, who had been in Philadelphia at the time of the Phillies' sale, obviously knew of Veeck's interest resulting in his meeting with Nugent in October '42. This was a matter of public record. The rest of the tale he evidently got from Sportshirt Bill, and it hardly matches the actual course of events as they occurred in the winter of 1942-43. Significantly, again, even Red Smith's recollection never mentions any plans for racial integration of the Phillies, and it was Veeck himself, in Smith's version, who ended his pursuit of the Philadelphia franchise, not Landis or Frick.[22]

While black newspapers elsewhere ignored Veeck's purchase of the Indians, it was of special interest to Cleveland's black newspaper, the *Call and Post*, which had long promoted the Negro Leagues generally and the local Buckeyes of the Negro American League specifically as a potential source of major league ballplayers. On July 20, 1946, the paper featured sports editor Cleveland Jackson's interview with Veeck under a banner headline reading "INDIAN OWNER WOULD HIRE QUALIFIED NEGRO PLAYERS." Stating that he had "absolutely no objections to playing Negro baseball players on the Cleveland Indians," Veeck told Jackson that "in my opinion, none of the present crop of Negro players measure up to big league standards."

Indeed, Veeck's purchase of the Indians by itself argues against the existence of an earlier attempt to acquire the Phillies. Although Rickey had breached the color line in Organized Baseball by signing Jackie Robinson, who was performing well with the Montreal Royals in the International League during the summer of 1946, the racial integration of major league baseball itself remained uncertain. Given the widespread and adamant opposition to integration and the unhappiness within the game with Rickey's course, why would the owners permit the sale of the Indians to Veeck if his intention to sign black players was known to them, as he claimed it was? Most of the men who had owned major league clubs in 1943 were still around in 1946. Contemporaneous accounts stressed that Veeck's acquisition of the Indians was consummated precisely because of his long-standing close ties with powerful figures in the baseball establishment, including the late Judge Landis.[23]

Reaction to real integration—On July 3, 1947, Veeck's Cleveland club purchased Larry Doby from the Newark Eagles, thereby making Doby the first black player in the American League. Veeck explained his acquisition by saying, "Robinson has proved to be a real big leaguer. So I wanted to get the best of the available Negro boys while the grabbing was good. Why wait? Within ten years Negro players will be in regular service with big league teams."[24]

But in all the press comment that followed the historic signing of Doby—by Veeck, by other baseball figures, by white sportswriters, by black sportswriters—no one suggested that this action might have been foreseen from an earlier attempt by Veeck to buy the Phillies or to stock the team with blacks. And in praising Veeck for signing Doby, no one, including such ardent advocates of integration as Sam Lacy, Wendell Smith, and Fay Young, even hinted at an earlier attempt with the Phillies. Silence from Young and Smith is especially instructive, because Veeck at various later times named them as parties to his planned purchase of the Phillies. Telling, too, is the failure of Lou Boudreau, player-manager of the Indians during Veeck's ownership, and Hank Greenberg, vice-president and second largest stockholder in the club, to mention in their books that racial integration of a big league team had been Veeck's longtime if deferred goal. Then-commissioner Albert B. "Happy" Chandler candidly discussed in his memoirs the Negro Leagues and Landis's opposition to racial mixing without reference to Bill Veeck. Finally, even Abe Saperstein never corroborated Veeck's story.[25]

A year later Veeck signed the legendary Satchel Paige to an Indians contract. Long the best-known Negro League performer and the personification of black baseball, Paige was bitter that he had not been the first to breach the color line. How natural it would have been for Veeck to share the story of his aborted purchase of the Phillies, with Paige as one of his intended trailblazers, to assuage Satchel's wounded pride. But no such reference ever appeared in either the black or white press after Paige's signing, and there are no mentions of the story in either of the pitcher's autobiographies, indicating that Veeck never told the story to Paige. The same is true of Orestes "Minnie" Minoso, who discussed his signing with Cleveland in the context of being among the first wave of blacks in the majors but did not mention any particular commitment to integration on the part of the Indians' owner.[26]

Curiously, Veeck in his book says that he was "almost sure" when he bought the Indians that he would sign a black player but that he moved "slowly and carefully, perhaps even timidly" because he "wasn't that sure about Cleveland."[27]

An odd comment, indeed, for a man who was determined to sign black players in 1943, and to introduce them into Philadelphia, widely perceived as among the most racist northern cities, a city which suffered a crippling transit strike in 1944 over the issue of employing black trolley drivers. Besides, Cleveland was in the forefront of integrated sports, its football Browns having signed the African American stars Bill Willis and Marion Motley before Veeck bought the Indians. Although not cellar-dwellers, the Indians, who limped home to a sixth-place finish in 1946, were surely in need of an infusion of new talent. Yet Veeck made no attempt to sign Negro Leaguers *en masse,* signing only Doby in '47, followed by Paige and Al Smith in 1948, and Luke Easter, Minoso, and Harry "Suitcase" Simpson in 1949.[28]

Even after the "revelation" in Bill Veeck's 1962 book, Doc Young, a sports journalist and historian of African Americans in sport, wrote an article in *Ebony* on the signing of Larry Doby back in 1947, in which Young mentions Veeck extensively but makes no reference whatever to any earlier attempt to integrate the Phillies. Young's silence is significant because, as sports editor of Cleveland's black newspaper during Veeck's tenure with the Indians, Young said he "spent countless hours" with Satchel Paige after his signing. If Paige had any inkling of the aborted Phillies' integra-

tion, he would surely have passed it on to Doc Young. Moreover, it is significant that no Negro League player has *ever* recorded having been contacted by Saperstein for Veeck's Phillies.[29]

The Wendell Smith article—Pittsburgh *Courier* sports editor Wendell Smith appears to be the only major black sportswriter to mention Veeck's autobiography. Smith recommended the book, noting that readers "will be exposed for the first time…to all the hypocrisy and chicanery" of "Frick and his ilk" when they learned that "Veeck contemplated buying the Philadelphia Phillies and signing Negro players."[30]

Wendell Smith had written several months earlier about Veeck's aborted purchase of the Philadelphia club in a series of articles on Abe Saperstein, the white founder and owner of the legendary all-black Harlem Globetrotters basketball team. He says that Veeck and Saperstein became "partners" in the scheme to purchase the Phillies and turn the club into an all-black team, that they offered Nugent some $250,000 for the franchise, but that because "baseball's hierarchy"—specifically Landis and Frick—"would not tolerate Negro players in the majors," Nugent sold the club to Cox for $85,000 in order to "keep the majors lily-white."[31]

Smith's report is of major significance inasmuch as it is the only known published account of the plan not taken from those written by Veeck himself. We quickly notice that the details of Smith's story differ greatly from those set down at about the same time in *Veeck—As In Wreck.* Yet, although Veeck later identified Smith as one of his "confidants" in his plan to buy the Phillies, the account in the *Courier* is not based upon Smith's first-hand knowledge but on an interview with Veeck in early March, 1962, at his home in Easton, Maryland. What becomes painfully clear from this interview, from the passage in Veeck's book, and from several accounts Veeck gave later to others is that he had a singularly cavalier attitude toward the details of this story—or that he couldn't remember from one time to the next how he had told the story.

Internal inconsistencies—The errors contained in Veeck's autobiography are further evidence that the account is a latter-day construction. Doc Young, described as sports editor of the Chicago *Defender,* was not. The sports editor's name was Fay Young. Veeck talks of the Phillies leaping from seventh place to the pennant in 1944, but the sale of Nugent's club took place before the 1943 season. He mentions as among the black players "in action and available" both Monte Irvin, who was in the military service, and Luke Easter, who would not even begin his professional career until 1946. Beyond these errors, Veeck in subsequent years gave other versions of the story—to Donn

Rogosin, to Jules Tygiel, and to Shirley Povich—that contradict what he said in his own book. In fact, when Jules Tygiel asked if Landis had in fact prevented him from buying the Phillies, Veeck replied, "I have no proof of that. I can only surmise."[32]

Not only did Bill Veeck contradict himself in subsequent accounts, he even did so before his autobiography appeared. In the summer of 1960, he wrote an article about blacks in baseball for *Ebony* magazine. Toward the close of the article, he wrote:

> Back in 1942, I suggested that the only reservoir of players still untouched during the war was the Negro leagues. As a matter of fact, I wanted to buy the Philadelphia ball club to put in an all-Negro team. It wasn't really aimed at being an all-Negro team, but it would have worked out that way. I was going to add 15 Negro players who were better than anything that Philadelphia had and would have won the pennant by 30 games. I could have gotten Robinson, Paige, Don Newcombe, a pretty fair catcher named Roy Campanella, and we had the club put together. That plan was done away with.[33]

Veeck, in telling this story to a black sportswriter, never mentions any involvement of Abe Saperstein or any black writers in his plan, not even Doc Young, a frequent contributor to *Ebony*, or Fay Young of the Chicago *Defender*. There is no mention of any concrete offer to Nugent, the location of financing for a purchase, or any interference in a deal by Landis or Frick. Veeck probably came closer to the truth in this article than in anything he said later about the proposed Phillies deal: he did want to buy the club and he thought about getting black players for it. But nothing came of it after his one meeting with Gerry Nugent. "That plan was done away with," he says, rather quaint phraseology that appears to mean, "Nothing more came of it. That was all." Clearly, the story was embellished and changed for the autobiography a couple of years later.

External considerations—How about the Saperstein connection? Many of the players Veeck suggests Abe had lined up for him in '42-'43—Paige, Campanella, Easter, and Irvin in *Veeck—As In Wreck*; and Paige, Campanella, Robinson, and Newcombe in the *Ebony* article—were not available at the time, though they looked good from a 1960-62 perspective. Besides, had Abe Saperstein actually made arrangements with any Negro League players, nothing would have prevented Veeck from signing them to Milwaukee Brewer contracts when the rug was allegedly pulled from under him with the Phillies. Surely the solidity of the American Association, as a foothold in Organized Baseball

just one step below the majors and with scheduling and financial stability far superior to anything the Negro Leagues could offer, would have appealed to Saperstein's recruits, if they had really existed.

How about Veeck's own nature? Can we really believe that Bill Veeck, baseball's great iconoclast, would have suffered a betrayal and double-cross of the nature described in his book without saying a word to anyone? That thought boggles the mind. But no one, in Philadelphia, in Milwaukee, in Chicago, or anywhere else, heard a peep out of Veeck when the league bought the franchise from Nugent and then sold it to Cox.

How about Gerry Nugent's economic realities? Can we really believe that Gerry Nugent, not a man of independent means, would have accepted without a murmur the league's payment of half of what Veeck was establishing as the market value of the franchise—a value that he was, according to Veeck's story, expecting to receive?

How about Veeck's economic realities? It is not impossible that Veeck, who was accustomed to operating on a shoestring, could have gotten financing for such a purchase, but it is unlikely. A bankrupt baseball team seems an odd investment for the CIO to make during the war, when it was focusing on maintaining its peacetime gains and coping with the stresses of a wartime economy, and no evidence of such intention has been found. However, representatives of the CIO, at the major league meetings in December, 1942, did make a fruitless request that Landis conduct a hearing on integrating baseball; this may well have been what later got the CIO into Veeck's story.[34]

How about the time frame? The timing of Veeck's yarn is completely different from the November-to-February span that actually occurred. Veeck met with Nugent in October, after the World Series. But in December, at the major league meetings in Chicago, Nugent admitted that no bona-fide potential buyer could be found.

Why didn't Ford Frick rebut the story? Some suggest that the failure of Frick, baseball commissioner in 1962 when Veeck's book appeared, to react publicly to being charged with scuttling the purchase of the Phillies may at least be negative corroboration of Veeck's story. It seems more likely, however, that since Sportshirt Bill took numerous potshots at Frick throughout his book the commissioner decided that his best course would be to ignore Veeck's work altogether. The baseball press generally gave the volume short shrift, so there was little pressure on Frick to respond to any of Veeck's charges. He probably ignored Veeck at the time because no one else seemed to give much credence to the Phillies-integration story, and he made no mention of it in his own autobiography.[35] This was the tactic evidently pursued by other frequent targets in the book like George Weiss and Del

their frustration were known to writers and executives "all over the baseball world," the remarkable fact that not one of them ever revealed the secret meant that for the first time in history these individuals—not one of them but *all* of them—took an historically significant story to their graves. *Everybody* knew about it, but not one man of them ever came forward and said, "This is what old Bill Veeck tried to do back in nineteen and forty-two."[37]

Why would Veeck manufacture the story?—Obviously something caused Veeck to include this story in his book twenty years after the fact. There are several possible reasons, though we will never know for sure.

• Early in 1942, Joe Bostic wrote a column entitled "Dreamin'" in *The People's Voice*. In his dream Bostic was a broker selling black ballplayers as replacements for major leaguers away in the military. After describing a couple of individual sales, he says, "I set up a deal to sell Jerry [sic] Nugent the entire Homestead Grays club as a unit to replace the Phils..."[38] We do not know that Veeck was aware of Bostic's column, but it was illustrative of the speculation commonplace at the time about the possible impact of Negro League talent on weak major league clubs—particularly a club like the Phillies.

Several months later, Satchel Paige mused in *The*

Philadelphia owner Gerry Nugent knew the game, but his team was losing money and he was in debt to the league, which forced him to sell the club. He had a casual conversation with Bill Veeck, but there was never even an offer to buy, let alone an agreement on a sale of the Phils.

Webb.[36]

There is one other curious feature pertaining to Veeck's story, a feature which serves to invalidate the whole tale. As we have seen, Veeck says in his book that after the Phillies were sold elsewhere, "word reached me soon enough that Frick was bragging all over the baseball world—strictly off the record, of course—about how he had stopped me from contaminating the league." If this were so, and his plans and

Sporting News about what would happen if a squad of top Negro League players were entered in one of the major league races. No doubt Veeck *did* see this item, and it piqued his fertile imagination. *He* would put together such a team! Rudie Schaffer confirms that Veeck talked with Saperstein, a power in black baseball in the Midwest, about procuring players. He even had the idea of holding two separate spring training camps, one, as a blind, for the white players he was *not* going to use, the other for the blacks who would constitute his team when the season started.[39]

When the opportunity to talk about purchasing the Phillies came up, Veeck jumped at it, only to have the idea dashed by Nugent's insistence on "large figures." Sportshirt Bill may have followed up with some efforts to secure financing, although no evidence of any has been found, but it is clear that nothing further transpired with Nugent, and Veeck went back to thinking up ways to jazz up attendance for his Milwaukee club.

There was no acceptance of an offer by Nugent and no interference in a Veeck-Nugent deal by Landis or Frick. The baseball executives *might* have acted in the way described by Veeck, had the situation come up, but it is manifestly unfair to convict them of something they never had a chance to do. Veeck, nothing if not a storyteller, seems to have added these embellishments, putting black hats on the commissioner and league president, simply to juice up his tale. Because of Landis's well-known aversion to integrated baseball, Veeck's tale found believers, which was unfair to Frick, who, flawed though he may have been, was not in the judge's class in his attitude toward black players.[40]

• Clearly, by 1962, Bill Veeck had wearied of hearing about Branch Rickey as the breaker of baseball's color bar, when Veeck himself had had it in his heart and mind to shatter that bar four or five years earlier. It is obvious from Veeck's book that he was no great admirer of Rickey, and we may be sure it galled him that the Brooklyn president got the credit for baseball's integration—a step, Veeck felt, that Rickey took only for business reasons. Moreover, Veeck always took pride in the fact that he behaved honorably in purchasing Doby's contract from the Newark Eagles, in contrast to Rickey, who refused to compensate the Kansas City Monarchs for Robinson. In order to make what he had *wanted* to do more plausible, Veeck added the fictitious details which made it seem that only the nefarious, racist actions of baseball's leaders kept him from his crusading role, not something as mundane as his own inability to raise enough money.

• Another possible reason for the creation of the story of his frustrated attempt to buy the Phillies was Veeck's belated consciousness that he *could* have integrated the Milwaukee Brewers in the American Association but made no effort to do so. If Bill Veeck had signed prominent black stars to his minor league club, Judge Landis, who had in any event no administrative authority over the minor leagues, could no more have forbidden such signings as "detrimental to baseball" in the midst of World War II than he could have if Veeck had signed them to major-league contracts. ("With Negroes fighting in the war," Veeck wrote, "such a ruling was unthinkable.") After his black signees made good at the Triple-A level, Veeck could presumably have sold them to major league clubs for big dollars, a course of action always dear to his hustler's heart. There is no evidence that he considered signing black ballplayers for the Brewers, another sign that the crusading zeal recalled in 1962 may have been *ex post facto*.[41]

• Finally, this story may have resulted from Bill Veeck's ill health at the time he sat down with Ed Linn to do his book, Seriously ill, Veeck sold the White Sox in 1961 on doctors' orders. When he went to Easton, he probably felt that this book was to be his last chance to poke the baseball powers in the eye, to steal some credit from Rickey, and to polish up his own place in baseball history. The Phillies story, with its exaggeration and embellishment, was not the only tall tale in the book, but it was the one that became Historical Truth.

The question remains, of course, as to why Veeck's story has been accepted so unquestioningly, without even the most rudimentary research to see if it checked out. It is especially surprising that academic historians failed either to verify Veeck's claim or to investigate more fully a story of major significance for both baseball and social history, although in many instances, to be fair, the Veeck story was peripheral to the events being written about. Still, *no one* ever looked into it. Perhaps the canons of professional research were set aside in this instance because Veeck and his yarn fit in nicely with personal preconceptions and values. Kenesaw Mountain Landis has been held up as the principal villain (along with Cap Anson, who was no longer around) in the long-successful conspiracy to keep Organized Baseball lily-white.

Veeck, on the other hand, has been a favorite of historians as the irreverent, unconventional antithesis of the stuffy and bigoted rulers of baseball. Given the cast of characters—Landis, the crusty and biased keeper of the bar against blacks, and Veeck, the iconoclastic employer of midgets, demolisher of disco records, creator of exploding scoreboards, and spokesman for "the little guy"—and the cause—racial justice in the national pastime—it is hardly surprising that historians have wanted Veeck's tale to be true. Bill Veeck is a more appealing crusader than the sanctimonious Branch Rickey, and his story has the added fillip of letting us believe that his plan was thwarted by the guardians of privilege and racism.

Nonetheless, we must face the fact that Bill Veeck falsified the historical record. This is unfortunate. His *actual* role in advancing the integration of major league baseball is admirable and can stand on its own merit.

Notes:

1. See, for example, Bruce Kuklick, *To Every Thing A Season: Shibe Park and Urban Philadelphia* (Princeton, N.J.: Princeton University Press, 1991), 146; Jules Tygiel, *Baseball's Great Experiment: Jackie Robinson and his Legacy* (New York: Oxford University Press, 1983), 40-41; Geoffrey Ward, *Baseball: An Illustrated History* (New York: Alfred A. Knopf, 1994), 283; G. Edward White, *Creating the National Pastime: Baseball Transforms Itself 1903-1953* (Princeton, N.J.: Princeton University Press, 1996), 147; Benjamin G. Rader, *Baseball: A History of America's Game* (Urbana and Chicago: University of Illinois Press, 1992), 150; Charles C. Alexander, *Our Game: An American Baseball History* (New York: Henry Holt, 1991), 194; David Q. Voigt, *American Baseball*, v. II, *From the Commissioners to Continental Expansion* (Norman: U. of Oklahoma Press, 1970). 297, and *America Through Baseball* (Chicago: Nelson-Hall, 1976), 116; Harvey Frommer, *Rickey and Robinson: The Men Who Broke Baseball's Color Barrier* (New York: Macmillan, 1982), 98; Mark Ribowsky, *A Complete History of the Negro Leagues, 1884-1955* (New York: Birch Lane Press, 1995), 265; Neil Lanctot, *Fair Dealing and Clean Playing: The Hilldale Club and the Development of Black Professional Baseball, 1910-32* (Jefferson, N.C.: McFarland, 1994), 18; Jim Overmyer, *Effa Manley and the Newark Eagles* (Metuchen, N.J.: Scarecrow Press, 1993), 236-237; Janet Bruce, *The Kansas City Monarchs: Champions of Baseball* (Lawrence: University Press of Kansas, 1985), 109; Donn Rogosin, *Invisible Men: Life in Baseball's Negro Leagues* (New York: Atheneum, 1983), 196-97; Robert W. Peterson, *Only the Ball Was White* (Englewood Cliffs, N.J.: Prentice-Hall, 1970), 180; Joseph Thomas Moore, *Pride Against Prejudice: The Biography of Larry Doby* (Westport, Ct.: Greenwood Press, 1988), 39; Arthur Ashe, *A Hard Road to Glory: A History of the African American Athlete Since 1946* (New York: Warner Books, 1988) v. 3, 9; and Mark Ribowsky, *Don't Look Back: Satchel Paige in the Shadows of Baseball* (New York: Simon & Schuster, 1994), 245.

2. Gerald Eskanazi, *Bill Veeck: A Baseball Legend* (New York, McGraw-Hill, 1988), 25-26. According to Eskanazi, Veeck tried to buy the Phillies in 1945, apparently after the season (the author cites the statistics of the '45 Phils to show what Veeck proposed to correct with his influx of black players), but was frustrated by Judge Landis, who had of course passed away in November, 1944.

3. Richard Orodenker, ed. (Philadelphia: Temple University Press, 1996), 53-55.

4. *Los Angeles Times* (undated clipping, Natl. Baseball Library). Murray even has Veeck showing Landis his roster of proposed Phillies, "all signed and collected by Saperstein, Veeck and a Chicago newsman named 'Doc' Young." Murray's version of the 1942 Phils (which of course missed the actual time of the sale by a year) included, along with Paige, Campanella, and Irvin, such additional Negro League luminaries as Cool Papa Bell, Theolic Smith, Buck Leonard, and Josh Gibson. Murray's column is replete with factual errors, which tend to lessen the reader's confidence in his conclusions.

5. Philadelphia *Inquirer*, Feb. 8, 1943.

6. Tommy Hughes, a promising young pitcher, was drafted into the army, so Nugent could not have sold him even if permitted to do so. Over the course of the ten years in which he ran the Phillies, Nugent traded or sold such players as Pinky Whitney, Spud Davis, Chuck Klein, Don Hurst, Dick Bartell, Kiddo Davis, Al Todd, Ethan Allen, Curt Davis, Dolph Camilli, Bucky Walters, Claude Passeau, Max Butcher, Morrie Arnovich, and Kirby Higbe. A shrewd judge of talent, Nugent often picked up valuable but unsung players in return, many of whom he then sold for more cash. .

7. Philadelphia *Record*, Nov. 12, 1942.

8. Philadelphia *Inquirer*, Dec. 3, 1942.

9. Philadelphia *Inquirer*, Feb. 1, 1943.

10. Philadelphia *Record* and *Evening Bulletin*, both Feb. 10, 1943. The new owner, Cox, meddled constantly in baseball affairs he knew nothing about, attracted more media attention than his team did, fired manager Bucky Harris because he wouldn't talk baseball with him at all hours, thereby stirring up a players' revolt, and was thrown out of baseball after the '43 season for betting on his team's games.

11. Bill Veeck, with Ed Linn, *Veeck—As In Wreck* (New York: G.P. Putnam's Sons, 1962), 171-172.

12. Daniel Cattau wrote an article in the April 1991 Chicago *Reporter*, "Baseball Strikes Out With Black Fans," in which he recites the story of Landis frustrating Veeck's plan to buy the Phillies, based on the recollection of Veeck's widow, Mary Frances. That sounds authoritative, until one recalls that Bill and Mary Frances did not meet until the fall of 1949 and were not married until April 29, 1950. So, whatever knowledge Mary Frances had of the aborted purchase of the Phillies traced back to the same source as all the other stories: Sportshirt Bill and his tales.

13. Milwaukee *Journal*, Oct. 18, 1942; phone interviews with Rudie Schaffer, Aug. 24, 1994, and Gerald P. Nugent, Jr., May 21, 1994. "You have to remember Veeck was a showman," Nugent's son said.

14. *The Sporting News*, Nov. 19, 1942.

15. The following African American newspapers were researched for all aspects of this paper: the Philadelphia *Tribune*, Pittsburgh *Courier*, Baltimore *Afro American*, Chicago *Defender*, the Cleveland *Call and Post*, Kansas City *Call*, the *Amsterdam News* (New York), the New York *Age*, *The People's Voice* (New York), the New Jersey *Afro American* (Newark), the Philadelphia *Afro American*, the St. Louis *Argus*, Los Angeles *Sentinel*, and the Washington *Afro American*.

16. Philadelphia *Inquirer*, Nov. 12, 1942. Careful review of the Philadelphia and Milwaukee papers for the time from that date to February 20, 1943,

shows no further references to Bill Veeck as a possible buyer of the Phillies, although many other names were mentioned.

17. See Tygiel, *op. cit.*, 30-41, and David K. Wiggins, "Wendell Smith, the Pittsburgh *Courier-Journal* and the Campaign to Include Blacks in Organized Baseball, 1933-1945," *Journal of Sports History*, 10 (Summer 1983), 5-29.

18. *The People's Voice*, Feb. 27, 1943.

19. *Daily Worker*, Feb. 11 and 26, 1943.

20. Cleveland *Plain Dealer*, Cleveland *Press*, the Cleveland *News*, and the Cleveland *Call and Post*, the city's black newspaper, from June to December 1946.

21. Emphasis added; Veeck and Linn, *op. cit.*, 172.

22. New York *Herald Tribune*, June 25, 1946. Curiously, too, "his friend's money" hardly sounds like backing from the CIO.

23. See, for example, the Cleveland *Plain Dealer*, June 23, 1946, and *The Sporting News*, July 3, 1946. As an instance of the owners' displeasure with Rickey, see Red Smith's story, quoted in Ira Berkow, *Red: A Biography of Red Smith* (New York: Times Books, 1986), 109, of an interview with Connie Mack, the "Grand Old Man of Baseball," during the 1946 spring training. When asked what would happen if the Dodgers brought Robinson to a scheduled exhibition game with the Athletics, "Mack, recalled Smith, 'just blew his stack. "I have no respect for Rickey," Connie said. "I have no respect for him now." He went into a tirade.' "

24. Cleveland *Plain Dealer*, July 4, 1947.

25. Baltimore *Afro American*, July 5, 12, 19, 1947; Chicago *Defender*, July 12, 19, 1947. See also the Kansas City *Call*, July 11, 1947; New Jersey *Afro American* (Newark), July 12, 1947; New York *Age*, July 12, 1947; *Amsterdam News* (New York), July 12, 19, 1947; Philadelphia *Afro American*, July 12, 1947; Pittsburgh *Courier*, July 12, 1947; and Washington *Afro American*, July 7, 1947. Lou Boudreau with Ed Fitzgerald, *Player-Manager* (Boston: Little, Brown, 1949), 77-81, 105-08, 161-64; Lou Boudreau with Russell Schneider, *Lou Boudreau: Covering All the Bases* (Champaign, Ill.: Sagamore Publishing, 1993), 11-14, 95-98, 143ff; Hank Greenberg, *Hank Greenberg: The Story of My Life* (New York: Times Books, 1989), 198-207, 216-17, 248-49; Albert B. Chandler with Vance Trimble, *Heroes, Plain Folks, and Skunks: The Life and Times of Happy Chandler* (Chicago: Basic Books, 1989), 224-29; Dave Zinkoff with Edgar Williams, *Go, Man, Go* (New York: Pyramid Communications, 1971), 46. Saperstein wrote the foreword to this "official" history of the Harlem Globetrotters, originally published in 1953 as *Around the World With the Harlem Globetrotters*.

26. Leroy (Satchel) Paige, as told to Hal Lebovitz, *Pitchin' Man* (Cleveland: n.p., 1948); Leroy (Satchel) Paige, as told to David Lipman, *Maybe I'll Pitch Forever* (New York: Doubleday, 1962); Minnie Minoso with Herb Fagen, *Just Call Me Minnie: My Six Decades in Baseball* (Champaign, Ill.: Sagamore Publishing, 1994), 32-46.

27. Veeck and Linn, *op. cit.*, 175.

28. Obviously, the number of blacks who *were* signed by Veeck was higher than that for most other clubs. Yet while he owned the St. Louis Browns, who certainly needed whatever help they could get, talent-wise, Veeck acquired no Negro Leaguers at all (except, of course, Paige again).

29. A.S. Young, "A Black Man in the Wigwam," *Ebony*, February 1969. Also, Young's column of May 10, 1962, in the Los Angeles *Sentinel*.

30. Pittsburgh *Courier*, July 21, 1962.

31. Pittsburgh *Courier*, March 14, 31, 1962. The $85,000 purchase price for Cox is clearly wrong, of course, an example of Veeck's careless attitude toward the "facts" of his story.

32. Tygiel, *op. cit.*, 41. Veeck told Rogosin that he hatched the plan "with only three confidants," Rudie Schaffer, Wendell Smith, and Saperstein, that he told Landis of his plan in Chicago on his way home from wrapping up the deal with Nugent, and that "when he arrived home the next morning he discovered that the Phillies had been sold to the National League overnight." Rogosin, *op. cit.*, 196-97. Finally, Veeck told Povich, the veteran sportswriter for the Washington *Post*, that he had gone to Landis with his plan *after* the National League had taken over the team, that Landis referred him to Frick, and that Frick "wouldn't talk business with us. Instead, he sold the Phillies to William Cox...." Bill Gilbert, *They Also Served: Baseball and the Home Front 1941-1945* (New York: Crown, 1992), 220-22.

33. Bill Veeck, as told to Louie Robinson, "Are There Too Many Negroes in Baseball?" *Ebony*, August, 1960. Neither Robinson nor Newcombe (16 at the time) had started a professional career in 1942.

34. A check of the CIO archives at Wayne State University reveals no mention of Bill Veeck or the possible financing of his purchase of the Phillies.

35. Ford C. Frick, *Games, Asterisks, and People: Memoirs of a Lucky Fan* (New York: Crown, 1973). In describing his own support of Jackie Robinson, Frick mentions earlier attempts at integration and the opposition of Landis without a line about Veeck's alleged attempt in 1942-43; *ibid.*, 93-102. Of course, Ford Frick's failure to put in a good word for Bill Veeck is hardly startling. The reviews of Veeck's book do not mention the story of his attempted purchase and integration of the Phillies. See reviews in *Time*, July 27, 1962; *Newsweek*, July 30, 1962; Chicago *Daily News*, July 2, 1962; Chicago *Sun-Times*, July 2, 1962; Chicago *Tribune*, June 30, 1962; *Los Angeles Times*, July 24, 1962; New York *Herald-Tribune*, July 15, 1962. Alfred Wright of *Sports Illustrated*, reviewing Veeck's book in the New York *Times*, said that reading it "is much like sitting with Veeck...through a few long nights in a saloon." New York *Times* (Book Review), July 29, 1962. The book was ignored by the two major Philadelphia papers, the *Inquirer* and the *Evening Bulletin*.

36. When portions of Veeck's book appeared in *Look* magazine in early 1962, Webb responded with good-natured quips to Veeck's charges against him; Philadelphia *Inquirer*, June 8, 1962.

37. Veeck and Linn, *op. cit.*, 172.

38. *The People's Voice*, March 12, 1942.

39. *The Sporting News*, August 13, 1942; old Satchel pointed out that there was no way such a team could afford *him*! Interview with Schaffer for Veeck's plans. One wonders how eager Veeck's backers would have been to finance *two* training camps instead of the usual one!

40. David Pietrusza, studying the life of Judge Landis, came across a letter which Veeck wrote to the commissioner from the South Pacific on May 22, 1944. Friendly in tone, the letter talks of Veeck's Marine Corps experiences, which he says are "somewhat different from the last time I saw you, and, I can't say nearly as interesting or enjoyable." This hardly sounds like the writing of a man who was double-crossed as described in *Veeck—As In Wreck*.

41. Veeck and Linn, *op. cit.*, 171. There is a strange statement in an essay Roger Kahn wrote on Jackie Robinson in *The Baseball Hall of Fame 50th Anniversary Book* (New York: Prentice-Hall, 1988), 215: "Once Bill Veeck told me that he tried to sign a few blacks for the minor league franchise he ran in Milwaukee and was told by Commissioner Kenesaw Mountain Landis to go no further. If he went ahead, Landis said, Veeck himself would be barred from baseball." Obviously, Sportshirt Bill was getting his stories crossed by this time, but it is still incredible that a reporter like Kahn would simply accept such a statement without digging a little deeper, like asking, "On what authority, Bill?" In the same book, incidentally, on p. 204, appears a paragraph about Veeck's frustrated attempt to buy the Phillies.

Cartwright's Trip West

Anne Cartwright

Our family (Cartwright) is the original Baseball family in America. My late husband, William E. Cartwright (1913-1989) was born in the Territory of Hawaii. He was the great-grandson of Alexander Joy Cartwright, Jr., "Father of Modern Baseball," who, as a leading member of the pioneering Knickerbocker Baseball Club, is often credited with setting down the basic rules of the game.

Alexander Joy Cartwright, Jr., was born on Lombardy Street in New York City on April 17, 1820. His father, Alexander Joy Cartwright ,Sr., a retired captain of the ship *Enterprise*, maintained a shipping business in New York. In 1812, returning from a journey to Spain and unaware that war had broken out between Britain and the United States, he had been captured by the British and, with his crew, imprisoned for eight months.

In the spring of 1845, the year the Knickerbockers published their rules, young Cartwright was a bank teller with the Union Bank in New York City. He later headed a bookstore and stationers with his brother Alfred DeForest Cartwright. Most of his fellow Knickerbockers were also young businessmen.

Cartwright was an extraordinary-looking man—6'3" tall, with dark eyes and hair. He was, by all accounts, a devoted husband and father, and an unselfish community volunteer.

A few years after the founding of the Knickerbockers, Cartwright heard of the discovery of gold in California, and decided to set out for the West to make his fortune. He left on March 1, 1849, from Newark, New Jersey with the following party: Captain Thomas W. Seely, Captain Benjamin F. Woolsey, Caleb D. Boylston, John W. Schaff, and General Darcy. In Pittsburgh they were joined by S. Harris Meeker, William Kinney, Dolph Pennington, Mr. Baldwin, and others. They purchased their outfits and shipped them to Independence, Missouri. They followed to St. Louis by train, arriving on April 11, and made their way overland to Independence. There they joined the wagon train of Colonel William Henry "Owl" Russell, an ex-army officer and a wild, woolly and dissipated frontier character. They moved to "Boundary"—the trailhead—and camped there for a week to rest up, fix the wagons, and add supplies, weapons, and whatever else was needed for the long and arduous journey overland. The wagon train consisted of 110 men and 32 wagons pulled by mules. Cartwright kept a diary of his trip. A few of the entries:

April 23rd, 1849

During the past week moving to "Boundary" fixing the wagons, store away our property, etc., varied by hunting and fishing, swimming and playing Base Ball. I have the ball and rules with me that we used back home. Tonight we held a council and decided to strike out to California tomorrow along the Santa Fe Trail until we reach the Oregon Trail, then follow that to the South Pass and then North of the Great Salt Lake in the lands of the Utes through the Sierra Nevada Mountains to California....

Anne Cartwright *is the widow of William E. Cartwright. She is continuing the work of her late husband to help preserve the origins of baseball.*

Alexander J. Cartwright,

General Agent for
Equitable Life Ass'r. Soc'y. of the U.S.
Imperial Fire Insurance Co. of London.
Commercial Union Fire Assurance Co.
N.Y. Board of Underwriters.

No 3 Kaahumanu St.,
Honolulu, _____ 188_0_

Tuesday, 24th April 1849

The weather being clear and warm and all nature smiling propitiously, at 7 o'clock we started under the guidance of Colonel Russell. The company consisted of 32 wagons and 110 men. We were off for the "Gold Diggins" of California. Our trail lay over the prairie on the Santa Fe route. A cover of luxuriant grass covers the prairie, dotted here and there with clumps of gaudy wild flowers. At 12 o'clock we arrived at "Lone Elm," a poor solitary tree in a wide expanse of prairie, miserable and weathered. Here we watered our animals and refreshed the inner man! After resting for 1/2 hour, we started for "Bull Creek" where we intended to camp for the night. At 3:30 o'clock, we came to a frog-pond where we decided to make our first camp. We supped on coffee and cold ham. We travelled 28 miles, all of which I walked.

April 25th, 1849

Ned Townsend stood watch from 11 o'clock to 2:30 o'clock, but was not relieved until 3:30 which caused a little grumbling. We had a little "flare-up" on the road today between Tom and a "sucker" from Illinois. Things looked serious but the "sucker" apologized. Our train travelled 15 miles today, all of which I walked.

June 2, 1849

We "Catched up" and "rolled" at 6 1/2. Weather clear and fine. Tom, Mr. Emery and myself started ahead of the train to hunt. We took our way over the bluffs and after 3 hours hard travel, seeing numerous antelope, elk etc. going over the hills, gulches and ravines, we concluded to strike out for the trail as 'twas impossible to get a shot at anything. About 2 o'clock we came upon a party of "Crow" Indians numbering 18 men and 2 women. They were seated in a buffalo-skin tepee on one side

of the trail. Several of us who were ahead of the train rode up and dismounting accepted their invitation to smoke. They smoked dried sage and I found it so pleasant that I smoked the pipe out. We conversed with them by signs until the train came when after exchanging a pocket kerchief for a necklace of beads made by the Indians from the clay deposit of "Soda Springs"...These Crows were the finest specimens of mankind I ever beheld; tall, wellformed and very muscular. They were on a hunting party and were in apparent dread of meeting any of the "lords of this particular soil," the "Sioux," or as they called them—by signs—"Cut Throats." We came to camp on a stream running from "Willow Spring." Lafferty train camped right back of us. About 8 o'clock we were aroused from our slumbers by the reports of fire-arms and the whoop of Indians. A number of shots were fired from Lafferty's camp, but as there was no one we could see to shoot at, we held our fire and finding after a short time the fight was over. Distance 24 miles.

The train struggled to the South Pass in Wyoming, to Fort Hall and Soda Springs on the Snake River in Idaho, and entered California near Reno, Nevada, south of Lake Tahoe, arriving in the "Green Valley" on August 4, 1849. Their journey was exceedingly hard. They went often without food and water, were attacked by Indians and lost all their mules. They were obliged to abandon their wagons and most of their clothing and when they finally reached Green Valley in California they were in a weakened, half-starved condition, plagued by dysentery.

In a letter dated August 20, 1849, Cartwright's brother Alfred DeForest, who had come around Cape Horn on a ship to San Francisco, wrote to his wife, Rebecca: "Alick arrived here on 10th August. They had what they had upon their backs, a cup and a spoon apiece left, his journal, the original rules of the

Knickerbocker Base Ball Club, his rifle and ammunition, and that was all."

On to Hawaii—Most of the arriving party turned their attentions to mining, but after Cartwright looked over the fields he wisely decided that other openings offered greater inducements. Charles Robinson, a friend of his brother who had previously lived in Honolulu, Hawaii—then the Sandwich Islands—gave a glowing account of the people of the Islands and advised him to go there.

Cartwright sailed from San Francisco on August 15, 1849, on the Peruvian brig *Pacifico*, and arrived in Honolulu on August 28, 1849. He, his brother, and Robinson pooled all their money, bought fruit and vegetables (especially potatoes), chartered a ship, and sent their goods off to San Francisco. It was a profitable enterprise and Alexander J. Cartwright, Jr. fell in love with the friendly people of Hawaii and stayed there. He established himself in business as a representing agent of the whaling ships, and as a commission merchant. He organized the volunteer Honolulu Fire Department, the Honolulu Library and Reading Room, the Chamber of Commerce, the Seamen's Institute, the Iron Works, the Masonic Lodge No. 21, now known as the Grand Lodge of Free and Accepted Masons of Hawaii. He served several years as the fire chief, and our son, Alexander J. Cartwright, IV, can proudly show the silver speaking trumpet engraved with the dates as fire chief of his great-great-grandfather.

Cartwright's love for baseball never died. He taught the children of Hawaii how to play the game, and it was a commonplace to see the goodhearted Cartwright drawing diagrams in chalk on some grammar school blackboards. As early as 1852, he passed Makiki Park in Honolulu one day, stopped on impulse and paced out the dimension of Hawaii's first baseball diamond. He organized teams and taught the game all over the Islands.

On July 12, 1892, Alexander Joy Cartwright, Jr. passed away suddenly. He is buried in the family plot at Nuuanu Cemetery in Honolulu.

Organized Baseball decided to have a "Centennial Celebration" in 1939 at Cooperstown to open the new Baseball Hall of Fame, to honor Abner Doubleday as the founder of baseball, and to celebrate what it was calling the 100th Anniversary of the game.

My father-in-law, Bruce Cartwright, Jr., wrote from Hawaii to refute the Doubleday legend and to put the more historically accurate case for his grandfather and the Knickerbockers as the founders of the game. The Centennial Committee declared some days as "Cartwright Days" as an apology for their "historical mistake!"

Bruce Cartwright also commissioned two plaques to commemorate his grandfather as "The Father of Modern Baseball." On June 12, 1939, one was unveiled at the old Honolulu Stadium, the same day that the other was placed at the Hall of Fame. The Honolulu plaque, presented by my late husband, William E. Cartwright, was then mounted in the rotunda of City Hall. It remained there for 56 years, noticed less and less, before it was returned to me at my request to be held by the Alexander Joy Cartwright, Jr. Baseball Foundation, Inc.

The Alexander Joy Cartwright, Jr. Baseball Foundation, Inc.

This nonprofit foundation was incorporated on September 30, 1996 in the State of New Jersey. The purpose of this foundation is to preserve baseball's history, artifacts, memorabilia, photos, uniforms, etc. for the establishment of a permanent museum, probably near Hoboken, New Jersey, the birthplace of baseball.

Collector Barry Halper is the president, Mrs. Anne E. Cartwright, vice-president, our son and daughter, Alexander Joy Cartwright, IV and Anna B. Cartwright, Directors.

The Foundation would greatly appreciate donations. These donations can be sent to Mr. Halper at Nottingham Road, Livingston, NJ 07039.

Anybody who is interested in facts about our ancestor and his life or his family genealogy can write to me at:
alex@mr.baseball.com
or
P.O. Box 713
Agoura Hills, CA 91736

Spahn, Sain, and the '48 Braves

Dixie Tourangeau

When Boston's crazed baseball fans inspected their half-dozen morning newspapers on September 1, 1948, there must have been a mixture of wonder, joy and anxiety bouncing around every Hub breakfast table and corner diner. Both the Red Sox and their neighbors a mile west, the Braves, were in first place.

Owner Tom Yawkey's Sox, World Series heartbreak losers in 1946, had fought for four months to reach and maintain the American League's top spot, and a 19-10 August record had propelled them to it. Manager Billy Southworth's Braves, in first place since mid-June, were nudged out for a few days in late August (14-17), but were tied (70-55) with Brooklyn (68-53) as the National League's stretch run for the pennant began that day. The Braves' owners since the 1944 season began, construction business associates Lou Perini, Joe Maney, and Guido Rugo—the "Three Little Steam Shovels"—were getting big dividends from the money they had spent on a few player acquisitions, such as Bob Elliott from the Pirates, former Indian star Geoff (also Jeff) Heath and rookie Alvin Dark, the former LSU footballer.

Braves rooters loved their upper Commonwealth Avenue boys, but the team's track record had been woeful since its "Miracle" 1914 pennant and shocking World Series sweep over Connie Mack's stellar Athletics. Things turned brighter in 1947 as the Braves, with MVP third sacker Elliott and 20-win sensations Warren Spahn and Johnny Sain, drove to third place. While al-

Richard Dixie Tourangeau *has been a SABR member since 1980 and has authored the* Play Ball! *calendar since 1981. He is a National Park Service ranger in Boston with an office a pop up away from the* USS *Constitution.*

lowing the fewest runs, the Braves led the NL in hitting (.275) and doubles, and were second in ERA to the St. Louis Cardinals. Boston repeated those offensive feats in '48, and with a great September surpassed the Cards on the mound, leading the NL with a 3.38 ERA.

But when September 1 dawned, Brooklyn and St. Louis—noted powers and winners of six of the previous seven NL pennants—were right with the Braves. No one could have guessed how spectacularly the month would unfold or that a thirteen-day string of games and a bit of simple newspaper doggerel would make two members of the Braves mound corps legends forever.

Sept. 1. That Wednesday afternoon Boston hosted the lowly Porkopolitan Reds from the Ohio River's Queen City. The clubs split a twin bill as Spahn lost to Johnny Vander Meer, 3-1, while Glenn Elliott, just called up from the Braves' Triple-A American Association affiliate Milwaukee Brewers, bested the Reds, 11-1. Elliott pitched his only three NL innings of 1948 before colliding with big Ted Kluszewski while running to first as a batter. The Association's ERA winner (3.76) left leading 4-1, and got a victory from the official scorer even though reliever Clyde Shoun pitched six scoreless frames.

Sept. 2. Day off No. 1.

Sept. 3. Allowing just three hits, Johnny Sain won his 17th game beating Philadelphia, 3-1, thanks to Heath's circuit blast.

Sept. 4. Bill Voiselle lost, 4-3, to Phillie Schoolboy Rowe, but Vern Bickford won the nightcap, 8-1, with Vern and Tommy Holmes each getting two RBIs.

Sept. 5. Charley "Red" Barrett five-hit Philadelphia, 5-1, behind Frank McCormick's three RBIs.

Sept. 6. If there was a day that Braves' fans really started to believe they were headed toward the pennant it was after Spahn beat Brooklyn reliever Joe Hatten and company, 2-1, in 14 innings on an Earl Torgeson single. Warren picked Jackie Robinson off first base twice in his five-hitter. Sain won the seven-inning "Wigwam dusk-beater," 4-0, as 40,000 watched Boston's lead increase to four games over dangerous Brooklyn. Boston eclipsed 1.3 million in attendance, its all-time high.

Sept. 7. Day off No. 2.

Sept. 8. Day off No. 3.

Sept. 9. Rained out in Philadelphia.

Sept. 10. Rained out again.

Sept. 11. Before fewer than 5,000, Sain won, 3-1, over host Philly's Rowe on Bob Elliott's three-run homer, while Spahn breezed to a 13-2 win helped by his own first career roundtripper (off Charlie Bicknell, 0-1 lifetime) in the nightcap. Rookie Robin Roberts took

the loss. At this point both Boston teams had three-game leads, their combined high mark.

Sept. 12. After Barrett lost the opener, 6-4, in Philly, Nelson Potter, obtained in June after his release by the Athletics, rescued Bickford by escaping a bases-loaded, none out, tenth-inning crisis in the second game (two Ks). Catcher Bill Salkeld's sacrifice fly knocked home Dark, who had scratched an infield hit and sped all the way to third on a sacrifice bunt, for a 2-1 victory in thirteen innings. Sibby Sisti scored the other run.

Sept. 13. Day off No. 4. Rookie Dark (.322, 3 homers, 48 RBI, 85 runs, and a 23-game hit streak broken by Cub rookie hurler Bob Rush) was pictured in the morning papers congratulating Phillie phenom Richie Ashburn (.333, 2 homers, 40 RBI, 78 runs, 32 steals) for being named *The Sporting News* Rookie of the Year. Dark, who had played in fifteen games with thirteen at bats in 1946, was ineligible. Edward Burns, president of the Baseball Writers Association of America, and Ken Smith, treasurer, met in conference with a view to-

Spahn and Sain.
They want you to remember Nelson Potter, Bill Voiselle, and Bobby Hogue, but we remember Gerry Hearn's rain.

Transcendental Graphics

ward changing the rule to allow rookies with less than 25 games to be eligible in another year. When the change was made after the season, the writers elected Dark as their best rookie, giving him 27 votes to 8 for Cleveland's Gene Bearden and 7 for Ashburn. Dark was the only righthanded hitter among the top nine NL batters who played at least 90 games. It was baseball's last vote for a single rookie star for both leagues.

Sept. 14. Chicago invaded Beantown and lost badly to Sain, 10-3, mainly because of hits by Dark, Torgeson and Johnny himself, who captured his 20th, reaching that plateau for the third consecutive season. That Tuesday morning Boston *Post* sports editor Gerry Hern published his poem:

First we'll use Spahn, then we'll use Sain,
Then an off day, followed by rain.
Back will come Spahn, followed by Sain,
And followed, we hope, by two days of rain.

Boston fans quickly shortened the original lines to, "Spahn and Sain and pray for rain," which was quicker and easier to recite. Although Hern's simple rhyme reflected the Braves' previous week, it was not true of September as a whole. Nonetheless, Bostonians and many others repeated the famous lines for years after the pennant was a distant memory, and they remain the best-known artifact of the 1948 season.

Sept. 15. Spahnie twirled another gem whipping the Cubs, 5-2, behind the offense of Torgeson, Heath, and Mike McCormick.

Sept. 16. Day off No. 5.

Sept. 17. Six Braves including Sain knocked in runs as the crafty righthander marched to his 21st win, 6-2, over visiting second-place Pittsburgh.

Sept. 18. Spahn kept up the incredible pace by one-hitting the Pirates through eight innings (a Johnny Hopp single) before settling for a 2-1 win over Fritz Ostermueller. Warren got slugger Wally Westlake with two on to end the game. Spahn and Elliott scored Boston's tallies, while Frank McCormick tripled home the winner.

Sept. 19. Barrett and relief winner Shoun combined to put down the Reds, 4-2, behind twelve hits, including Elliott's solo blast. Pepperpot Eddie Stanky pinch-hit a single to aid a seventh-inning rally. It was his first appearance since breaking an ankle on July 8 in Brooklyn. The Cardinals and the Dodgers now trailed by six games with twelve to play. The Pirates were eight behind.

Sept. 20. Rained out of last scheduled game with seventh-place Cincinnati.

Sept. 21. Scoring two runs and knocking in two, Sain won his own game beating St. Louis, 11-3. Bickford tossed a four-hit shutout in the second game for a 4-0 win before 24,320. McCormick had two RBIs

and scored a run. Boston needed one win for the NL flag.

Sept. 22. Spahn was finally beaten as Stan Musial slammed five hits and Al Brazle handled the starter and four relievers, 8-2. Boston's eight-game win streak ended. Cards' baserunner Enos Slaughter was badly hurt by a batted ball.

Sept. 23. Day off No. 6.

Sept. 24. Day off No. 7.

Sept. 25. New York Giant Sheldon Jones out dueled Sain, 3-2, despite allowing 12 hits, including a solo homer by Heath. Jones' two hits plated two of New York's runs. Only 15,377 patrons showed up.

Sept. 26. Vern Bickford copped the pennant by preserving Elliott's opening frame, three-run homer off Giant Larry Jansen for a 3-2 win before 31,172. Potter provided two innings of relief for what today would have been a save. During September only St. Louis, of the three other contenders, managed to play above-.500 ball. The Pirates were at .500 and Brooklyn fell below.

Sept. 29. While playing out the string in Brooklyn, Heath (.319) broke an ankle sliding home during a 4-3 Braves triumph for Sain's 23rd victory. His offense (eighth in NL hitting, second on the team with 20 homers and second to Musial's top NL slugging percentage) would be sorely missed in the World Series against the Cleveland Indians, the team Geoff starred with for eight years. His .582 slugging mark was the third highest of his career.

In the first twelve days of September (plus an August 31 win) the Braves pitching corps gave up 10 runs in as many wins. Half were either 3-1 or 2-1 victories. For the remainder of the month until the flag was secured, the staff gave up 15 runs in 8 wins. Nine times the Braves gave up but a single run—four of those were on solo home runs. Sain, Spahn, Bickford, and Barrett each pitched two single-run efforts. In each of Sain's wins Philadelphia shortstop Eddie Miller whacked solo homers to prevent shutouts.During those twenty-six September days the '48 Boston Braves compiled a 17-5 record, intermingling ten regular games, six doubleheaders (they swept three and split three), seven days off, and three rainouts. From the 6th through the 18th, Spahn and Sain started eight of ten games, winning them all. There were four scheduled off days scattered among those starts.

In a *Boston Globe* interview in January, 1993, Spahn and Sain reiterated their feelings that Hern's innocent rhyme was an injustice to their fellow hurlers Bickford (4-0), Potter, Voiselle, and Bobby Hogue, who all played crucial roles in helping Boston regain the NL lead and maintain a safe cushion in the final two weeks. Of course, the Braves never got to play an intracity World Series as the Red Sox were thrashed in their playoff game by Cleveland, an event that baseball researchers still find filled with odd decisions and circumstantial intrigue. Cardinal hero Musial missed the Triple Crown by one home run, but captured the NL MVP. "The Man" got 303 MVP votes, Sain 223, and Dark 174.

Though Braves hurlers had center stage, Boston's position players provided just as much excitement, especially in September. Of the eleven players with the bulk of the daily at-bats for those twenty-two crucial games several players topped their season's stats:

Player	September	Final
Tommy Holmes	.337	.325
Alvin Dark	.337	.322
Frank McCormick	.323	.250
Phil Masi	.310	.253
Geoff Heath	.328	.319
Clint Conatser	.385	.277

In total, eleven Braves batted .298 for that period to .275 for the season. Though Elliott (.283) hit only .241, he topped the Braves with 13 runs and 14 RBIs in those twenty-two games. Heath was particularly dangerous when Sain was on the hill. In eleven of Sain's last fifteen starts in which he played, Geoff hit .425, with 5 homers, 9 runs, and 12 RBIs. Sain was 8-3 when backed by Heath, 7-1 in September. Ironically, it was in John's final start that Heath slid into Ebbets Field's home plate and broke his ankle ending his season, his chance to play in the Series and, for all productive purposes, his career, which lasted only thirty-six games into 1949. While still on the ground in terrible pain after the sixth-inning tragedy all he could say was, "Why did I slide?" There were only four meaningless games left in the campaign.

Quick facts—In mid-June the Braves climbed into a tie for first place with New York after a great 10-4 Western road trip. They split with Pittsburgh and Cincinnati, but swept Chicago and St. Louis, averaging nearly nine runs per game in their last nine contests.

Mid-June marked three other notable baseball events. First, Babe Ruth wore his Number 3 for the last time before a roaring crowd at Yankee Stadium, then the uniform was sealed in his locker. Second, a rarely irate Connie Mack made headlines by yelling at and firing 36-year old reliever Nelson Potter after he blew a 5-1, eighth-inning lead to the Browns. Potter won his first NL game on July 18 at Forbes Field as his inseparable friend, Heath, banged out four hits including a grand slam, to beat Pittsburgh, 10-2.

Finally, infant WBZ-TV decided to televise the first game in the history of Boston baseball and chose what turned out to be the game that put the Braves into first place alone for the first time. How many Philco, RCA Victor, and Motorola television sets were owned within the forty-mile broadcast radius is unknown, but thousands at home and in evening establishments were said to have watched the June 15 night game that Boston won, 6-3, over Chicago. Usual radio voices, Jim Britt and Tom Hussey, were at the microphones, exchanging radio-television seats at midgame. Britt received kudos for not over-announcing during the fans' new television experience.

Outfielder Jim Russell, then 29, had come to Boston from Pittsburgh in November 1947 for Johnny Hopp and Danny Murtaugh. Switch-hitter Russell was enjoying a solid 1948 season, leading the Braves with 52 RBIs and running second to Elliott in homers (10 to 9), when in mid-July his health failed and he was diagnosed with a heart problem. He played a few more games but was never a factor after July and the Braves lost an important offensive cog. Mired in a horrid 3-for-39 hitting quagmire, Russell's last hurrah was a grand slam in Brooklyn that provided a 7-4 victory in the game when Stanky broke his ankle. When Heath went down in late September, it all but destroyed any chance of Boston having a multiple slugging attack for the World Series. Though the Braves scored 11 runs in Game 5, they averaged one run in the other five Series contests. Torgeson (.389), Elliott (.333), and Stanky (.286) proved to be the offensive heroes in defeat.

Bsseball Player Is Traded For Box of Mammoth Prunes
SAN FRANCISCO, March 25 (AP).—The question is, "Who got the better of the deal?"
The San Francisco Seals traded a case of mammoth Santa Clara prunes today to Memphis of the Southern Association for Jack Fenton, first baseman.
President Tom Watkins of the Memphis club telegraphed he was satisfied. Vice President Charles Graham of the Seals replied he was, too. Fenton formerly played with Oakland. (New York Times.)
—Joe Murphy

Good Night

Bob Rives

Ron Vance was a 170-pound 20-year-old when at 7:45 P.M. on April 30, 1930, in Independence, Kansas, he put his full weight on his right foot.

Behind him and to his right, Mark (Marty) Purtell bent his knees slightly in the manner of countless men who made their livings as he had done since 1909. Purtell was 41 and bending was tougher than in some earlier summers.

Just over 60 feet in front of Vance, Hardy Buff took his stance. Fresh from the University of Oklahoma, he was shortstop for the Muskogee (Oklahoma) Chiefs, playing only the fourth game of his professional career. Sherman Walker, 23, had been director of religious education for the First Presbyterian Church in Independence. He also had a year of minor league baseball experience and was squatting behind Buff.

The pitcher Vance was the newest at his craft. His move on the mound was his first in organized baseball. Back home in Wichita he had won 34 games and lost only 5 as a semipro the previous summer. His 507 strikeouts had earned him a contract with Independence of the Class C Western Association.

Rookie and veterans, what the four men had in common was at that moment they became a footnote in the long history of organized professional baseball.

Vance, pitching for the Independence Producers, was preparing to throw the first pitch ever made under artificial light in a regular season game of an organized league. Buff would watch it go by; Walker would catch it.

Purtell, while with Montreal in 1914, already had

become the subject of a footnote to the baseball records. He was the first professional to face a pitch from Babe Ruth. That night in 1930 he was managing at Independence and playing shortstop. The preceding summer he had led the league in fielding at age 40.

While their place in the record books may be obscure, the effect of lights on baseball was not. *The Official Encyclopedia of Baseball* says electric lights saved the minor leagues from extinction during the Great Depression. In 1935, armed with the minor league experience and facing the same economic pressure, the big leagues began to use them at Cincinnati. By World War II, ten more major league teams had lighted parks.

Today Shulthis Park in Independence sits where Producers Park was in 1930. A rubber-surfaced track turns where home plate was and a goal post stands at first base. The field now hosts high school and community college track meets and football games. Veteran baseball fans are most likely to remember the park as the field where Mickey Mantle played his first professional season. In 1949 he was the Independence shortstop, batting .313 in 89 Class D KOM League games and earning $400 for his summer's work.

Still, a bronze plaque above the stadium entrance does remind visitors of the site's lighting significance. In 1930, it points out, the first night game in organized baseball was played there.

When the lights went on for league play in 1930, the *Independence Reporter* used only one sentence to describe the event. It began the third paragraph of its game story by noting, "Last night's game was notable for the fact it was the premier night exhibition in orga-

Bob Rives *lives in Wichita, Kansas.*

nized baseball." The paper was far more concerned with the Producers' 13-3 loss to Muskogee, the second defeat in a disappointing three-game weekend series.

It was not the paper's lack of enthusiasm for lights or for baseball that led to its low-key report, however. Two weeks earlier, the Producers twice played the House of David, which arrived fresh from games with five major league clubs. Those games were heralded as the first in which any organized baseball team had played at night on its own diamond.

So big was that story that the *Reporter* made it the lead on Page One. Its three-line headline was bigger than any used in the first half of 1930 except when a local bank failed.

Achieving critical mass—While lights were new in organized baseball, they had been in sporadic exhibition use for half a century by 1930. An exhibition game in 1880 near Boston was perhaps the first. Even in Kansas, a town team-college game had been played under the lights of a gas flame in 1906. In the month before the Independence–House of David games, the New York Giants and Chicago White Sox played a lighted exhibition in Houston.

Further, if the lights hadn't gone on as scheduled in Independence, they would brighten the night days later in Muskogee. On March 27 Chiefs president S. C. Ellis announced that his club, too, would have lights for the home opener.

In Des Moines, Iowa, E. Lee Keyser and Minneapolis Millers manager M. E. (Mike) Kelly owned the class A Western League Demons. Keyser had announced at baseball winter meetings in Chattanooga that he would light his diamond. On May 2 Des Moines opened its home season against the Wichita Aviators in a night game that attracted 12,000 fans. Among them were American League president E. S. Barnard and Branch Rickey of the St. Louis Cardinals. (The Yankees drew 16,000 that afternoon in New York for a game with the White Sox.)

While the Demons had to settle for second place in the race for lights, the team did have the first nationwide radio broadcast of a night minor league game. NBC carried the last half of the contest, won by Des Moines, 13-6. But because the network could not pick up the game until midnight eastern time, Des Moines sportswriter Sec Taylor worried that it would be called on account of sunrise.

A Wichita newspaper gave NBC poor marks for its coverage. "The announcer evidently was not familiar with the teams and his hesitancy in recognizing the performance kept the affair from reaching the thrilling stage," a columnist wrote.

The game itself earned higher grades. The Associated Press account began, "Baseball can be played as well under artificial light as under the rays of the sun in broad daylight."

Later in the story, the news service said, "Sparkling fielding, fine hitting, good pitching—elements of the game which go to make up the sport—all were present.

"But to sports writers in particular and to a large portion of the minor league executives in attendance there arose the question of the public's reaction.

"Without a dissenting opinion, they felt that the game could be adopted to artificial lights, that balls could be handled as well in the field at night as in day light and that the hitting was as good if not a trifle better."

An artistic success—While Independence beat Des Moines to turning on the lights, there was no great rivalry with the Iowa city. Keyser had congratulated Independence backers when they announced lighting plans. And when the Producers' home season opened on Friday, April 27, business manager Ray K. Hart left the lights off. He scheduled it as a day game.

Lights were to be first used for the season's second game Saturday night. But even though Kansas and its neighbors were suffering from the drought that produced the Dust Bowl, there was a wet spring in 1930. Saturday's lighting inaugural was rained out and the Producers and Chiefs played on Sunday afternoon as scheduled. Thus it was Monday, April 30, before the night debut. The *Reporter* estimated that 1,000 persons watched, many of them women, the paper said, because it was Ladies' Night.

A larger crowd of 1,200 had seen the lights used for the first time when the Producers beat the Davids, 9-1.

Most fans went home from that game persuaded lights were good. Mrs. Purtell announced, "I think it's a keeper." She believed it would be easier for players to work at night rather than under the sun of summer.

A fan, Mrs. Ed Hatcher, called the lights "a grand success. Everything's so pretty. There are people here that probably haven't seen a baseball game for years."

Mrs. F. W. Shelton said the lighted game was not only much better than she expected, but added, "I heard someone say that they could see the lights 20 miles away. That's wonderful if it's true." And, if it was correct, one of the viewers could have been Walter Johnson whose home was only 15 miles from the park.

Problems? Very few. A blown fuse caused a 10-minute delay late in the game. Some fans were cold, unused to April air at night. Still, pitchers mentioned no problems keeping arms warm between turns on the mound. Outfielders described the ball as easy to see and catcher Walker said artificial lights created no problem for him.

"The light, as it falls on the field, bathes the field in a soft glow which resembles sunlight except that the distribution is better. In fact, the lights are so thoroughly distributed by the giant projectors that shadows are eliminated entirely," the newspaper said. Batters had no trouble finding balls to hit. Independence had 16 hits in the 9-1 win.

Fans may have had more trouble with their night vision than did players, according to the news writer:

"An unusual feature of the night game is the misleading (to the fans) vision when a high fly is hit to the out field. The first time it happened, several called 'pop-up,' and they couldn't understand why Slick Osburn in right field had turned his back to the plate and was racing toward the fence.

"A chorus of 'Oh's' and 'Ah's' greeted the player when he made the catch, and they settled down in their seats again.

"The fans never could seem to get settled down to the fact that the ball, traveling away from the stands was held so true by the illumination of the floodlights that it appears to be hanging in midair."

The paper did report that animals in a zoo adjacent to the ball park had an extended day. The *Reporter*'s headline said the animals played late along with the baseball team, thinking it still was daylight. Pete Endres, zoo superintendent, voiced concern. But Mayor Charles Kerr, who helped promote the lights, felt experience would teach animals to observe normal bedtime. If they couldn't sleep with the lights on, he promised, screens would be built to shield their eyes.

(In Des Moines, ball park neighbors claimed chickens laid more eggs than usual because the lights made them think there was more daylight. Construction employees reported trouble testing the lights because large flocks of birds were attracted.)

It might have been logical to expect more problems, particularly at Independence, where the lighting system was partly homemade. While the lights were produced by Giant Manufacturing Company of Council Bluffs, Iowa, the six 60-foot towers were built locally from oil-field pipe after the mayor asked for donations. Lights were tested only the day before the game with the House of David. Cost was estimated at $8,000.

No ordinary small town—Why was Independence the world leader in baseball field lighting? Among cities in the 1930 Western Association—Springfield and Joplin, Missouri, Fort Smith, Arkansas, and Muskogee and Shawnee Oklahoma—Independence with 12,500 residents was by far smallest.

But it was no ordinary small town. Its baseball team was called the Producers because of the region's oil industry. Local residents included men like Alf Landon, who won a seat on the Independence Chamber of Commerce board in 1930 and the 1936 Republican presidential nomination, although he could not defeat Franklin Roosevelt. Harry Sinclair, owner of the great race horse Man O' War, founded Sinclair Oil Company there. While he had moved to New York, he called Independence friends to cheer them after a local bank failed. William Inge, who grew up there, set his Putlitzer Prize-winning play, *Picnic*, in his old hometown.

But most important to the lights was oil man Marvin Truby. He operated a royalty company, was president of the baseball association, and a longtime friend of Dale Gear, of Topeka. Gear was president of both the Western League—which included Des Moines—and the Western Association. He also was an advocate of night baseball as a way to bolster minor league attendance. And the minor leagues were faltering. There had been 29 leagues in 1929. Only 24 remained in 1930. By 1931 just 16 would be in business.

It was Truby who advanced the money to buy the lights in Independence.

In February the city park board announced that lights were being considered. By March contracts for the lights were signed by Mayor Kerr for the city; Truby for the team; L. E. Losey for the high school athletic association, and B. H. Woodman for the board of education which wanted lights for football. C. B. Smith, president of Giant Manufacturing Company, signed for his firm.

By April 5, Mayor Kerr said two of the towers had been built and all would be by April 17. The lights would make the diamond lighter than indoor basketball courts of the 1920s, the paper reported.

Further, parking lot lights would keep fans safe. "This is merely a preventive measure," Mayor Kerr said. "It has been my observation that the average person who attends baseball games is not the type who promiscuously borrows other persons' property."

Still, there were skeptics. Independence pitcher Lefty McCutcheon was wary until shown a diagram of tower locations. He had believed there would be poles in the center of the diamond which would interfere with play.

Pete Lightner, sports writer for the *Wichita Eagle*, wrote, "This column predicts that night baseball as a novelty will stimulate the game but when the newness wears off it very likely will not prove as popular as the daylight variety."

But by summer's end, there was little novel about playing at night. Thirty-eight teams in fourteen leagues had lights. One was Los Angeles in the Pacific Coast League.

Lights out—Independence team members who played in that first night game would gain less than did baseball as a whole. None would escape the minor leagues in his career. The pitcher who started it all—Vance—did come to be called "Dazzy" after a more famous pitcher. His 16-8 record was the league's fourth best even though he left that first game in the fourth inning.

Purtell led Independence to the Western Association

championship and the newspaper described the late August-early September playoffs with Joplin as the first ever played under the lights. Before midsummer Purtell replaced himself at shortstop with Bill Lewis, who later played parts of three seasons with the St. Louis Cardinals and Boston Nationals. Lewis hit .397 at Independence in 1930. Walker, nicknamed Parson because of his church work, hit 10 home runs and batted .286 for Independence that summer.

By 1932 the ability of even lights to ward off the Depression was dimming. The Western Association folded in midseason. While it would revive in 1934, Independence was not a member. The city stayed out of organized baseball until 1945 when it entered the Class D KOM League. There it remained until again turning off the lights on professional baseball, perhaps for good, in 1952.

Getz gets a hit, or a tale of one city

While there is no records category for fewest hits allowed, one day, one city, multiple teams, perhaps September 9, 1915, will have to do until someone does more extensive research. On that day Ernie Shore of the Red Sox and Lefty Tyler of the Braves each threw one-hitters, giving Beantown opponents precious little to use for offense. Strangely, this pitching perfection only resulted in a split for Boston's teams.

Shore's work was the most clear cut. Only Jimmy Walsh's (.206) first-inning single for the disintegrating Philadelphia A's stood between Shore and what would have been another no-hitter for the Tarheel. The hit was early, and it was clean. No problem there.

Tyler's game against Brooklyn was another matter. Matched against Jeff Pfeffer, Tyler pitched even better than Shore but managed to lose his one-hitter, 1-0. Brooklyn's hit understandably helped contribute to its run, but its questionable nature raised howls in the Boston press, and was even called a "rank scratch" in Gotham journals. Hy Myers led off the Brooklyn second with a walk., Third baseman Gus ("Gee Gee") Getz grounded to Charley Schmidt at first. Schmidt stumbled while fielding the grounder, fell to his knees, and attempted to force Myers at second. His throw hit the sliding Myers in the back, with all hands safe. Getz was given a hit by a charitable scorer. Both runners advanced on a double steal, and Myers scored when the next batter grounded to Johnny Evers. Evers fumbled the ball, but recovered to get the runner at first while Myers crossed the plate. Pfeffer allowed only two hits himself to the defending World Champions.

One day, one city, two hits allowed, one win, one loss. Can any other city do better?

—Phil Bergen

Bats and Saddles

Tim Wolter

There are few if any figures in American history who excite opinions of greater diversity and fervor than George Armstrong Custer. Depending on your point of view he was either a paragon of martial gallantry or a power-mad agent of genocide. Partisans of both viewpoints have been prolific, to the point that it has been estimated that there have been more books written about Custer than Lincoln! A remarkable volume of minutiae has been unearthed about the man and the Seventh Cavalry with which his name will forever be linked—including a few fleeting glimpses of baseball, as it was played on the western frontier of the mid-1870's.

It should not surprise us that the troopers of the Seventh played baseball. From the Civil War onward it was a common pastime for soldiers. The military hierarchy encouraged it to some extent, feeling that it fostered physical fitness and a sense of unit camaraderie. And it was something to do during the long stretches of inactivity endemic to military life.

The first baseball team that I can document among the troopers of the Seventh Cavalry was in fact probably organized out of boredom. The winter of 1873 found the various companies of the regiment scattered across the vanquished South, engaged in the "unsoldierly duty" of suppressing the Ku Klux Klan and breaking up illegal distilleries.[1] Company H was stationed at Nashville, Tennessee. In an account written three years later by a remarkable soldier named Theodore Ewert, it is recalled that it was resolved to

"organize a club with the view of having games, sports and exercise to be known as the 'Benteen base ball and gymnasium club'."[2] It was named for Frederick Benteen, the captain in command of Company H, who, along with the other commissioned officers, was elected an honorary member.

Supplies were obtained, including "two sets boxing gloves, two pairs kehoe clubs, three pairs dumb bells, one pair broadswords, one pair foils and masks, 1/2 dozen base ball bats, one dozen base balls, one set chessmen and board, two sets domino games, three foot balls and one property chest." Scant time was to be afforded them for practice, as the reunited Seventh Cavalry was ordered to Dakota Territory at the end of the month. But the Benteens did find the opportunity to play three games, two in Nashville against a team known as the Clippers (losing the first, 27-25, and winning the second, 32-16), and a third at Louisville against a "picked nine of citizens and soldiers (winning, 36-12).

The cavalry pulled into the Territorial capital of Yankton on April 9, 1873—just in time to have their temporary encampment buried under a massive late-season blizzard. The regiment stayed on in Yankton about a month, during which time the weather seems to have improved sufficiently for a game to be played between the Benteens and a local nine known variously as the Yanktons, or more poetically, the Coyotes. The Benteens triumphed, 22-6.

The Seventh Cavalry had been ordered to the frontier to escort a railroad survey of the Yellowstone region, a task that occupied much of the summer of 1873. Amid much marching and some skirmishing with

Tim Wolter *hopes one day simultaneously to hold the posts of Surgeon General and Commissioner of Baseball. Biding his time, he practices medicine and coaches Little League in Chippewa Falls, Wisconsin.*

hostiles the Benteen club managed to find time for two more games, one against a picked nine from an infantry regiment, the other against a team called Aspinwall, presumably in the fashion of the day named after its commanding officer, but otherwise a mystery to my research. So far the Benteens had tallied a respectable 4-2 record against a variety of foes.

On the Black Hills expedition—Company H spent the winter of '73-'74 at Fort Rice, a notoriously desolate post near modern-day Bismarck, North Dakota. Springtime found them preparing for another expedition, a reconnaissance of the mysterious Black Hills, from which rumors of gold had been filtering out for some years. This was no mere scouting trip, but basically an invasion, with some 1,500 soldiers and officers, 60 Indian scouts, 130 teamsters, a post trader, a photographer, 275 wagons, and an assortment of miners, newspaper correspondents, and scientists. It was generally felt that the Hills were a sacred land for the Sioux, and that serious fighting would be encountered. But that did not prevent the cavalrymen from packing their baseball equipment in amongst their more warlike supplies!

It is the good fortune of later historians that Ewert kept a literate and detailed diary of the Black Hills Expedition of 1874.[3] As he was also the secretary of the Benteen base ball club he had a special interest in describing the two games played during the course of the expedition.

The first was played on the 31st of July, in an open field referred to as "Custer's Park," about 10 miles from Harney's Peak. The teams involved were

the "Actives" of Fort Lincoln, made up of members of the band and the companies of the right wing, versus the "Athletes" of Fort Rice, with a membership drawn from the companies of the left wing, but essentially comprising the Benteen club.

To a latter-day observer it seems strange that with the continued threat of possible lurking Indians, and the distraction of recently discovered traces of gold in nearby creeks, virtually the entire command would turn out to watch two amateur teams play ball. But play they did, under the supervision of a veterinary surgeon named Tempany who agreed to umpire the contest. Ewert felt that Tempany was shamelessly partial, and that the Actives did not deserve the 11-6 victory. He also mentions that the Athletes sorely missed the presence of a standout player named Cunningham, who had died a few days earlier, victim of illness and incompetent Army doctors.

George Armstrong Custer as commander of the Seventh Cavalry, engaged in his favorite sport.

Eleven days later, at another clearing dubbed "Genevieve Park" (at the site of present day Nemo, South Dakota) there was a rematch. Ewert relates that "The weather was splendid and the field good and the attendance large. The game was worthy of professional clubs, closely contested and well played. Score: Athletes-17, Actives-10. Time of game 3 hours and 3 minutes. One of the engineer party acted as umpire...The game was an excellent one for amateurs...." This is, by the way, the only baseball game at which it is reasonably certain that Custer was in attendance. During the previous Athlete-Active contest he had taken a party off to climb Harney Peak. And it seems unlikely that he attended any of the other games played by the Benteen club. Benteen and Custer disliked each other intensely.

The Black Hills Expedition returned home in the late summer of 1874, having accomplished its unofficial objective: proving that there was gold in the Hills. An account in the Bismarck *Tribune* describes a rubber game between the two teams that played in the hills, now referred to as the Actives and the Benteens. The Benteens won handily.

Soon thereafter Company H was among the units detailed to New Orleans to help suppress civil unrest. Here too the Benteens found opportunities to play ball, prevailing against teams from the 22nd Infantry, and against a "picked nine" not otherwise identified. Tensions in the carpetbagger days of Reconstruction may have been too high for play against local civilian nines.

1875—This was to be a banner year for the baseball teams of the Seventh. There were no major campaigns to be undertaken, outside of half-hearted patrols to try to stem the tide of miners flooding into the Black Hills. Spring of that year found the Benteens back in Yankton, taking another game from the Coyotes, then moving up-river to defeat a nine from the 1st infantry stationed at Fort Randall. At unspecified locations they also defeated the "McDougal" team from E Company of Seventh Cavalry, split additional games against the Fort Randall nine and played what seems to have been their final game back in the Black Hills against a "picked nine of citizen teamsters." Ewert's tally, recorded in February, 1876, gives the Benteens' cumulative record as 12 and 5, and shows them outscoring their opponents 464 to 230.

Meanwhile, back at Fort Abraham Lincoln where the Seventh Cavalry was headquartered, other shadowy teams made brief appearances. August 1 saw a contest between teams known as "Nameless" and "Alerts," with the Alerts carrying the day 25-10.[4] About two weeks later the Alerts were again victorious over a team known as the "Modocs," apparently named after the Indian tribe that had fought a brief war against the U.S. Army earlier in the 1870s.[5] A crowd of about 200 persons was said to be on hand.

The Little Bighorn—Of course, every modern reader approaches the story of the Seventh Cavalry with full knowledge of the disaster that overtook them in the summer of 1876. The story of how they came to be campaigning along the Little Big Horn river in June of that year is complicated, and does little credit to either military or civilian authorities. Suffice it to say that it was a fiasco that has become synonymous with catastrophe.

Custerphiles debate the most minute point of the Little Big Horn battle with hammer and tongs, but a fairly noncontroversial summary follows. Approaching

an Indian encampment of unknown size Custer chose to split his command into detachments. Perhaps to keep his detested subordinate from a share of the anticipated glory, Custer sent Benteen on an unproductive scouting foray, thereby saving the lives of his disliked subordinate and the three companies under his command. Meanwhile, Major Marcus Reno attacked the Sioux encampment from one side, only to be thrown back in disarray. Custer, and the 264 men in the five companies under his direct command, were confronted by several thousand Sioux warriors and were wiped out to a man.

Captain Benteen emerged as the hero of the day. Returning from his futile mission he encountered the fleeing survivors of Reno's command. Benteen seems to have rallied the troops to a spirited defense until a relief column could reach them two days later.

The various ball teams all suffered losses to one degree or another. No roster exists for the Modocs, so their fate is unknown. The members of the McDougals are likewise anonymous, but as it seems to have been based in the unfortunate E company, it is likely that all perished on Last Stand Hill. The roster of the Alerts suggests that they were mostly from the permanent infantry garrison of Fort Abraham Lincoln, and with the exception of a Private Charles Ramsey, who survived the fight, were not at Little Big Horn. The Nameless team lost four of their starting nine.

Thanks to Theodore Ewert we know the players of the Benteen Club a bit better. In his account written some four months before Little Big Horn he describes each member of their first nine.

Joseph McCurry—"Captain and pitcher of the nine. Delivers a swift and correct ball, generally to suit the batter, is a sure base runner…and is a gentlemanly player withal…He is undoubtedly the stay and prop of the club, as also the best player…Leaves the army next winter and will no doubt be engaged in some professional, or first-class amateur nine in the east in 1877, and I have no doubt but you will hear from Joseph in the 'diamond arena'."

Sergeant McCurry was wounded in the arm at Little Big Horn, and perhaps as a consequence never played professionally.

Wm. Rafter—"Catcher…The only man who could stand up to Mc's pitching, a sure catch, heavy batter and good runner."

Peter McCort—"First base. A No. 1 in any position, small but full of ambition, good catch, swift runner but middling batter."

"Fatty" Williams—"Second base, a reliable player, sure catch, swift runner, good and accurate thrower, full of ambition, ready to cry for vexation if the umpire called 'three strikes and out' which was often the case as the bat is 'Fatty's' weak point. He is improving, however. From Pittsburgh, Pennsylvania, where he signed papers to play in 1877; is 26 and a 'good boy'."

This appears to have been a certain George Williams, who sustained a minor wound at Little Big Horn. I can find no record of a Williams playing for Pittsburgh in 1877, but I would not rule out the possibility altogether. Not a few of the soldiers of the era were "on the lam" in one way or another, and there are numerous instances of them using aliases to enlist.[6]

William Davis—"Third base, from 'Porkopolis,' [Cincinnati] a sure catch, poor thrower, fair at the bat, slow runner, and he has the worst fault imaginable, wishing to play 'fancy,' thereby weakening his already very weak place. Age 24. In base ball he is scarcely 14."

Although a member of the Benteens, Davis' home company was E. He died with Custer.

Charles H. Bishop—"A boy from the capitol. 'Good as wheat.' Plays a remarkably fine game anywhere, though needing continually the sharp eye of the captain, not being exactly lazy, but born woefully tired."

Bishop was wounded in the arm and evacuated on the steamer "Far West."

Alonzo Plumb—"Right field, the 'funnyman,' don't profess to play base ball, but thinks he can keep the 'nine' in a good humorous vein, thus in a good working condition."

Alex Bishop—"From Brooklyn, New York, a neat little player, sure catch, fair batter, good runner. Considering that he intends to become a minister of the gospel in the future he loves base ball as a nigger does roast possum. He will be one of the best in the coming seasons."

This Bishop was also wounded and evacuated after the battle.

James H. Curly—"From Pennsylvania, a, or rather THE, heavy hitter of the club, generally clears all the bases on one of his distant field liners, tricky base runner, fair catcher, leaves the service this spring."

His timing in this regard seems to have been good.

With respect to the Benteen club in particular, or the base ball players of the Seventh in general, I cannot improve upon the words Ewert wrote in 1876. "Taking into consideration the fact that constant movings, expeditions, fatigues and there [sic] military duties prevented practice games or anything like a gymnastic training, one cannot help but admire the grit and pluck that caused these 'ball tossers' to continue in the face of so many discouraging obstacles...."

Notes:

1. *Boots and Saddles.* Memoir of Custer's widow, Libby Custer.

2. *Daily Press and Dakotian,* Feb. 26, 1876.

3. *Private Theodore Ewert's Diary of the Black Hills Expedition of 1874.* CRI Books, 1976.

4. *Bismarck Tribune,* Aug. 4, 1875.

5. *Bismarck Tribune,* Aug. 25, 1875.

6. Even our trusty correspondent Ewert was under a sort of nom de guerre. Enlisting at age 15 early in the Civil War, he signed on as Theodore rather than his true name of Augustus. On his retirement from the military years later he reverted to his given name.

Correction

My article in last year's *National Pastime* on the Rochester Hop Bitters stated that Joe Simmons was the manager of that team who absconded with the team payroll in late 1880. Additional information has come to light establishing that the blackguard was actually a Horace B. Phillips. On the slight chance that a Methuselan Joe Simmons is still on the run somewhere we feel bound to tell him it is safe to come out of hiding.

—*T.W.*

Know Them by Their Autographs

Tom Altherr

Baseball historians are familiar with the tricks and stratagems managers have and will continue to play on the opposition. Some managers, of course, have been deadly dull tacticians, but most have looked for the ace-up-the-sleeve, twinkle-in-the-eye maneuver to catch the opposite skipper napping. According to a July 1997 article in *Sports Illustrated*, sign-stealing, fakes and decoys, and counterespionage of all sorts constitute a busy industry within the national pastime. Belief in superstitian and ritual is abundant. How many managers have carefully stepped over the baseline to and from the mound? How many have perched on a certain spot in the dugout? John McGraw had his Charles "Victory" Faust; Casey Stengel spoke his Stengelese to mask his shrewdness; Tommy Lasorda employed his ebullient cheerleading to pump up the Dodgers.

Charlie Metro was a longtime minor league pilot who got his first chance to run a big league team as a member of the Cubs' "College of Coaches" revolving managerial scheme. Seeking any advantage he could find, Charlie dusted off an old plan to learn how to throw his voice to distract fielders and baserunners. Metro couldn't get the hang of ventriloquism from the two Chicago-area voice-throwers who gave him lessons, but he had another exotic idea that he thought might give him an edge.

"In 1962," he later wrote, "as manager of the Chicago Cubs, I had a handwriting expert analyze the signature of all the National League managers to learn as much

Tom Altherr *is professor of history and American Studies at Metropolitan State College at Denver, where he teaches baseball history, and a member of the Frank Haraway Chapter of SABR and the SABR Rattlers vintage baseball team.*

about my competition as quick as I could. It worked real well." (For a fuller treatment of all this, see Charlie Metro and Tom Altherr, "Nostalgia: Tricks of the Trade," *Baseball Weekly*, January 17-23, 1996, 25.)

Charlie collected the autographs of the other nine National League managers and sent them, along with his own, to someone in California who knew a graphologist. The California contact submitted them to the handwriting analyst, who was not a baseball fan, and thus probably did not know any of the ten managers. The graphologist wrote a page or so on each field general and sent them back to Charlie, who studied them and employed them in game situations. Here are those analyses, with their original spelling and sentence structure intact.

SABR readers won't need to be reminded not to put too much stock in these endeavors. The Cubs finished ninth that year, ahead of only the endearingly awful '62 Mets!

Charlie Metro, Chicago Cubs

"Objective, matter-of-fact and efficient. Knows and likes his material, and is master of it. Purposive —pursues goal without interuption. Steady, quiet. Strong effective personality. No showmanship. Not decorative except order and arrangement. Inclined to be serious. Conservative. Is exact. Likes simplicity. Needs enthusiasm and persuasiveness. Appeals too much to the player's reason should appeal more to their values (personal) and ideals. Very observative. Conservative—dislikes change. Possibly narrow-minded but very good insight. A good leader in times of peace but not in times of war. He is sane and soberminded. Best balance of all the managers."

Herman Franks

profound or scientific often inaccurate. Look for errors in judgement due to too casual an attitude. Be opportunistic with this man. When emotional not so reliable. Thinks with continuous associations—not very original however. Will repeat often. Favors long hitting and throwing. Over optimistic. Loves the game. A generous, obliging soul not concerned about money."

Birdie Tebbetts, Milwaukee Braves

"Power of conception—producing ideas; persuasive use of words. Appeals to player's hopes, wishes, desires. Has illusions—fantasies. Projects frequently discernment and discrimintation poor. Likes things complete—not one-sided. Reacts on common sense basis. No abstract ability. Interprets everything generally. Urge for action. Ambitious. Fatherly towards team. Good at fienting, that is, making one play seem like another. Does not utilize individual abilities of the players for concerted movements. Dislikes newness and improvisations. Old-fashioned, batchelor type at heart but good father. He needs sagacity and spiritual intensity. Tight cogent, organized strategy will succeed against this man. Move in hard when he is moody and drifting. That is when he seems inconsistent."

Gene Mauch, Philadelphia Phillies

"Conducts his team like an orchestra leader. Coordinates, harmonizes. Thinks quickly, reacts smartly with certainty of aim. Diagnoses situations like a doctor. Competent, matter-of-fact, helpfull. Always sets up objects and events for some spectacular play. Intimate understanding of each player. Prescribes ease and dexterity, practice body hygene. Good at personnel selection. Slave to timing and orderly proceedure. Does not take advantage of breaks. Self-esteem but no self-interest. Adapts himself too much. Poor in resistance not demanding. Appeals to the mechanical side of his player's neglects their personal and psychological motivations. Never secretive. Signals ovious. Very fair."

Danny Murtaugh, Pittsburgh Pirates

"A good and dangerous manager of baseball. Executive, direct, persistant and brilliant. Reliable sense of

Fred Hutchinson, Cincinnati Reds

"Considerable vanity and egocentricity. Too eager to win. Pretended amicability—calculated friendliness. Critical in a superfluous manner—wastes time on unessentials. Excellent rythm; good agility. Persevering, industrious and power of will, schemes up plays that are over complicated but confusing results not justifying the energy expended. Susceptible to flattery. Cannot see the forest for the trees. Judgement defective because he is too much obsessed by details. Introvert but talkative not effective because he emphasizes everything. Works uneconomically—takes too much time weighing and considering all sides of a problem. Does not adapt quickly to new circumstances. Defensive attitude."

Walter Alston, Los Angeles Dodgers

"Friendly obliging and good nature. Appeals to the players sportsmanship, fun, gamesmanship. Not critical or carping. Warm, genuine reassurance emphasizes courage and unselfishness. Good strategist. Plans far ahead, figures the whole season. Impulsive and instinctive, responds with intuition and repetition. Not very duty but not conventional. Explores the heights and depths of the game. Never satisfied. Likes change, imaginative variety. Touchy, precise, sarcastic. Pushes, drives misses nothing. Appeals to the abstract, the psycological values as well as the facts. Strong roots in the ground. Great scope and range but always practical. Has too many irons in the fire—scatters. Needs concentrated effort. Goes beyond his powers and limitations. Imparts nervousness to players. Slightly fussy and petty may have inferiority complex. A modest man of threatening intellectual force. Is no doubt going places. Curiosity is his weakness. Get him to go to far out, be extravagant. Will lose because he does not use the energies of his players economically."

Al Dark, San Francisco Giants

"He has initiative, daring and the imagination to deploy his forces in diverse ways. He, however, neglects details, does not take difficulties sufficiently into account —may fail because of his overconfident attitude. He likes pleasure and is not disciplinary enough to be a leader. Atheletes will like him for his great sportsmanlike manner, his tolerance, and his ingenuity. He will gamble and lose often, because he analyses the obvious and omitts in his calculations obscure but important factors. He is often aloof because he is easily influenced—thus players on the bench can distract him from his original intentions. In this case, someone else is the real manager of the game, the players or someone above. Remember he dislikes to make decisions—or they are made too quickly. He is a better friend than a boss."

Johnny Keane, St. Louis Cardinals

"Here is a leader—not a diplomat or strategist. He is demanding, exact, persistent, insistent and resistant. He compells others to adapt themselves to him. He trys to influence others but resists others influencing him. He is forceful and untiring. His weakness is his compulsion, obstinacy and one-sidedness. In new situations he will respond with stereotyped patterns. No illusions here, this matter-of-fact and systematic man will win where efficiency and organization is called for but not resourcefulness and strategy. Here is complete honesty but no pussyfooting. His ideal is beauty esthetic precision—his taste is Renaissance the unity of the Greek Gymnasium—mental and physical symmetry. He is relentless to himself and others. No weakness. When irritated he is clumsy and awkward. He does not finish with the same self-consciousness with which he begins."

Casey Stengel, New York Mets

"A pioneer, explorer, discoverer type. Goes into things with great verve and enthusiasm. Assumes responsibility in a paternal manner. Outspoken and unambiguous. Mentally objective, emotionally subjective. Rational, ethical, spiritually sincere. A real sales manager—wins through conviction not persuasion. He is modest in ego, noble and grand in conception, demanding more and expecting more from his men after he shows them how to do it, using his great originality which always appaers at the end of the game. His script shows that he has really studied the history of the game. He acts like a psychiatrist to his boys—open, receptive, giving standards that are capable of flexiblity only when necessary. He loves to excell, loves to surprise you at the finish, loves the new. His handwriting seems to prove that the pennant seems to hang on the personality of the manager—at least when all other things are equal."

Harry Craft, Houston Colt 45's

"Dignity, love of elegance, and craftmanship of the building variety is here shown. He will apply the tradional rules of the game and methods. He will waste time, effort and money. He will be self-assured but very cautious. He will be too slow in explaining or making decisions. A reserved, conservative individual but some artful showmanship and much color and ornament. pride is one weakness, slowness to adjust another, clinging to mothbitten ideas another. However, his boys will play as one team, undivided just as you were playing another country or blueblooded fraternaty club. If a club's success depend upon politics this man's influence with higher-ups must not be discounted. He appeals to teamwork, patriotism and to making a name for yourself. Only with good men can he succeed. This man is very productive, watch him always."

Final 1962 National League Standings
San Francisco
Los Angeles
Cincinnati
Pittsburgh
Milwaukee
St. Louis
Philadelphia
Houston
Chicago
New York

A Nice Little Career

A. D. Suehsdorf

Artie Schallock's mother, Alice, was a good friend of Lefty O'Doul's mother, so as Artie began making a name for himself pitching in the fast semipro leagues around San Francisco, Mrs. O'Doul urged Lefty to sign him for the Seals. "He's a nice young fellow, and Alice says he's doing very well." "Naah," said Lefty, "he's too small."

It's been forty years since Artie threw a baseball competitively, but he still enjoys telling the O'Doul story. In his seasons with the Hollywood Stars and Oakland Oaks, he beat the Seals every time he faced them—eight straight. Still, Lefty was correct. Artie *was* small: 5'8-1/2", 5'9", and 150-something pounds. As one reporter said, "You know they're little when they count those half-inches." He was bigger than Bobby Shantz, anyway, and, according to his Hollywood manager, Fred Haney, taller than the Clean Sox's Dickie Kerr.

In any event, he made the most of what he had. A natural athlete—and lefthanded—he won varsity letters in basketball, tennis, and golf as well as baseball at Tamalpais High School in Marin County, north of San Francisco, and was pitching semipro ball by the time he was fifteen. (Even today he is a four-handicap golfer and can shoot his age—73!)

As a youngster, he had a good curve and good control, and many more Ks than walks. He also practiced his pickoff move in front of a full-length mirror, eliminating everything that might give smart baserunners a

clue as to his intentions. A scrapbook compiled by his two daughters preserves accounts of a no-hitter against one team, a one-hitter against another, and 16 Ks in a seven-inning game against a third.

A letter from his San Mateo manager says: "All the scouts are sold on your ability, and Ted [McGrew, Brooklyn's chief scout] says he will have you up there with the Dodgers in a few years. Take good care of your arm, Art. Have you a couple of 100% wool undershirts? If not I will buy you a couple. After you have a work out, just rub your body off with a towel (no water) and change to a dry shirt. This is necessary as most sore arms are caused for that reason."

The Dodgers would have to wait. Two weeks after graduation, he was in the Navy, eventually becoming a radar operator on the USS *Anzio*, a small aircraft carrier with a complement of two dozen fighters and torpedo bombers. In several years of combat operations in the Western Pacific, he won eleven battle stars.

In 1946, now 22, Art enrolls at the College of Marin and resumes baseball. In four games he pitches 35 innings and has 62 strikeouts. He also plays semipro, now for the Moffatt-Manteca Packers, a powerhouse club which wins the Oakland *Tribune* State Baseball Championship. He has met Dona Bernard on a blind date; she sees the championship game and her heartfelt comments are preserved on her scorecard. "3rd [inning]: You just smiled at me. I love you. 5th: You were wonderful, but too many balls. No coives, O'Malley. 8th: Honey, they might have taken you out. I know it happens to the best pitchers, but I feel awful...I feel like crying...but you're such a damn good pitcher."

As Ted McGrew predicted, Art is considered big-

A.D. Suehsdorf *lives in the same Sonoma, CA, community as Art Schallock. Another neighbor played for a White Sox farm club. Still another neighbor's daughter married Cookie Lavagetto's nephew. And down the road a piece is an old gent whose godfather was Swede Risberg.*

league material. In September, with a signing bonus of $10,000, he becomes Brooklyn Dodger property. It is the most money he will ever make in baseball.

Spring training in 1947 is at the Dodger complex in Havana. These are the Durocher-led Dodgers of Pee Wee, Cookie, Dixie, Koiby, Stanky, and Reiser. Art is optioned to the Pueblo (Colorado) Dodgers of the Class A Western League, where Walter Alston is the first of his two favorite managers. Artie goes 13-8, appears in 31 games (11 complete), pitches 157 innings, allows 132 hits and 63 earned runs, has 117 Ks, 84 walks, and a 3.61 ERA. Pueblo has a fine season, becoming league champions by beating the Sioux City (Iowa) Soos for the Governor's Cup. Teammates Preston Ward, Turk Lown, and Sam Calderone will make the bigs with varying degrees of success.

Art and Dona are married, and he is recalled for spring training with Montreal at Cuidad Trujillo, Nicaragua, in 1948. Managed by Clay Hopper, the Royals are another powerful club. Don Newcombe and Jack Banta are a season away from the Dodgers. Jimmy Bloodworth at second, with seven major league seasons already under his belt, will be acquired by Cincinnati, and Chuck Conners at first will play briefly with Brooklyn and the Cubs before finding a career in TV and the movies. Sam Jethroe in center will make it with the Boston Braves next year. And Bud Podbielan is about to begin a nine-year career at Brooklyn, Cin-

Artie Schallock in happy retirement earlier this year.

A.D. Suehsdorf

cinnati, and Cleveland. The Royals not only win the International League pennant, but the Little World Series as well by sweeping the last four of seven games against Columbus of the American Association.

A Hollywood Star—Early in 1949, learning that the Dodgers have a working agreement with the Hollywood Stars, Art asks to be transferred. As a married man with a wife and infant daughter living on the Coast, it makes sense for him to be playing there. Baseball clubs' concern for their players' convenience is rather less prominent than a gnat's eyebrow, but—amazingly—the Dodgers consent. They sell his contract to Hollywood for $1, and Art goes to work for Fred Haney, his other favorite manager, and the Stars. Irv Noren, another Coaster, gets the same break from the Dodgers and joins him.

The Stars were a first-rate team. Irv, outfielder Jo Jo White, and pitchers Jack Salveson and Willie ("the Knuck") Ramsdell are probably best remembered, but almost everyone on the roster played a year or more in the majors. And one of their bat boys was a kid named George Anderson, not yet known as "Sparky," who'd have more years under the big top than any of them.

Artie pitches well, his best game coming in September against San Francisco. The Seals rap him for a single and a scoring double, and the Stars' bullpen goes into action. But Art settles down and retires 27 batters without allowing anyone as far as second. Eight strikeouts, no walks. In the top of the ninth the score is

1-1 and the Stars have the bases full with Artie at bat. The Seals' Con Dempsey cranks up to deliver his first pitch and Schallock backs out of the box. Dempsey, startled, halts his motion. The plate umpire calls a balk and the Twink on third scores. The Seals squawk, but briefly. It was Dempsey's lapse and a sure-fire balk. Artie sets down the Seals in the last of the ninth to win, 2-1. The Stars go on to win the Pacific Coast League pennant.

A Yankee—In 1951, Artie makes it to the show. At the top of his form, 11-5 for Hollywood in mid-July, he is sold to the New York Yankees for three players and "an undisclosed amount," which was, in fact, $50,000. The Yanks, who will win the third of Casey Stengel's five straight pennants and World Series, are in trouble. Their brilliant youngster, Whitey Ford, has been drafted and will spend the next two years in the Signal Corps at Fort Monmouth, New Jersey. Casey is desperate for another left hander. (All he has are Eddie Lopat, Bob Kuzava, and Joe Ostrowski!) Joe Devine, the Yanks' West Coast scout, has been watching Art and recommends him highly.

It takes a bit of front-office maneuvering. Under the terms of the old Brooklyn-Hollywood working agreement that enabled the Stars to get Artie for one buck, the Dodgers still can pick him up at season's end for $10,000. Money talks, however: Brooklyn keeps forty of the Yankees' fifty thou, Hollywood gets the other ten. Fred Haney has to be satisfied, too. "I'm not going to stop Schallock from going to the big leagues," he said. "But I'm not going to sacrifice the pennant chances of twenty-five other guys, either…I'm not going to let him go unless I get a good pitcher and someone else." The Yankees sweeten the deal with a pitcher from their Kansas City farm, a pitcher from San Francisco whose option is transferred to Hollywood, and a catcher they buy from Oakland at Haney's request. Fred says, "I think we are getting as much as we are losing." (Two of the three have a cup of coffee, but none of them ever reached the bigs again.)

Now George Weiss has to make room on the New York roster for Artie. He picks that rookie outfielder, Mantle. The kid's got promise, but he's not hitting a lick. But, George, he's leading the club with 45 RBIs. I know, but he's fanned 52 times in 69 games. Give him some time at KC to settle down.

So, that's how it happened.

Artie signs a Uniform Player's Contract—complete with reserve clause—paying him $6,000 for the balance of the season. Since ball players are an extraordinary fraternity whose careers mix and mingle at every level of the game, Artie immediately finds three friends in the Yankee locker room: Bobby Brown, whom he'd competed against in high school, and Jerry Coleman and Charley Silvera, who'd been teammates on the San Mateo Blues. The next day he starts against the Tigers at Detroit.

Art is nicked for three runs and seven hits in 2-2/3 innings. Spec Shea relieves. But the Yankees have their hitting shoes on. They hammer Bob Cain for six runs and stagger to an 8-6 win on late homers by Joe Collins and Yogi Berra. Stengel says he is "pleased" by Art's performance, but is not yet ready to work him into the regular starting rotation.

On the 17th he starts against the Browns at St. Louis, blanks them for three innings, but fills the bases in the fifth and Allie Reynolds relieves him. On August 3, the Tigers whack him for two quick runs. He does pretty well—only five hits in seven innings—but he takes the loss.

On August 16, success at last. He beats the Senators at Washington, 5-3, for his first win. He allows only three hits and one runner as far as second in four innings. In the seventh, DiMag, playing his final season, gets him out of the inning with a fine catch of Gil Coan's sinking liner, but it was obvious that Art was tiring rapidly and Joe Ostrowski relieved.

Five days later he goes the route against Detroit, allowing only seven hits. He fans Charley Keller for the final out. With 17 hits the Yanks win, 11-4. And five days after that he beats Billy Pierce and the White Sox, 8-6, allowing seven hits in 6-2/3 innings.

All told he pitches 46-1/3 innings in 11 games, six of them starts, has an ERA of 3.88.

What was it like, playing for the fabulous Yankees? Great! Casey didn't pay him much attention, but in the dugout he overheard the famous Stengel double-talk in pregame conversations with reporters and can confirm its impenetrability. On occasion, he also saw coaches nudge the napping manager awake.

DiMag was DiMag. "Hello and goodbye. Not much else." He still was a marvel to watch at bat or in the field. "That big stride. He covered ground so effortlessly. And let me tell you, any outfielder who wasted any time fielding a hit would find DiMag halfway to second base."

His best friends on the club were Gene Woodling, Ralph Houk, and Billy Martin. Jim Turner, "the Milkman," who had his big years with the Boston Braves and finished as spot reliever for the Yanks, was the pitching coach, but Art got most help from Steady Eddie Lopat, who was on his way to a 21-win season. Considered a "junk man" by many, Lopat knew all the ways to compensate for a lack of speed and supervised Artie's development of a slider and screw ball. "I guess I threw most like him," Artie says. "I had good control, but was only 'sneaky fast.' I threw both my fastball and my curve at varying speeds. The slider—well, I always say you throw it like a football, so the spin makes it move six inches or so laterally." Later, when he was with Kansas City, the *Star* described his pitching style thus: "Schallock doesn't have overpowering stuff, but he is a master at keeping hitters off stride."

His road roomie was Yogi. "He's supposed to be a dumb guy, but, boy, he had the book on every hitter in the league. He taught me a lot, but after every session with him I had to go down to the lobby and buy him some comic books."

In an interview with the San Francisco *Chronicle*, Art said, "Except for the twelve or fifteen really great hitters—the guys nobody can get out—the batters are about the same as I faced on the Coast. You learn to concede the great hitters their base knocks and work on the rest of the order." To me he said, "Of course, there always are exceptions. George Kell could hit anything I threw, but I was very lucky with Ted Williams. The several times I faced him he got grounders or pop-ups, but never a hit."

In July the Bowman Gum Co. signs him up for a picture card. He never sees the result, but doubts that it would bring the price of a 1951 Mantle. Offered $100 or two bicycles, he chooses the bikes. His little daughters could "grow into them."

Up and down—In the off-season, he takes Jim Turner's advice and tries to bulk up a bit by working for a construction gang. Dona picks him up after work, but a mile from the house he gets out of the car and sprints home.

It doesn't help. In 1952 he pitches briefly in two games and is optioned to the Kansas City Blues in May. Among his teammates there are Elston Howard, Moose Skowron, Andy Carey, Bill Virdon, and Vic Power. Under manager Harry Craft, KC wins the American Association pennant and the Little World Series. Artie contributes 12 victories before being recalled by the Yankees for work in seven no-decision games.

Although missing the Little World Series, he makes the big one in 1953, pitching the seventh and eighth innings against Brooklyn in the fourth game, one of two Yankee losses en route to the fifth consecutive Series triumph. The Dodgers have whacked Ford, Tom Gorman, and Johnny Sain for ten hits and are leading, 6-2, when Art goes to the mound. He gets Robinson on a liner to right and fans Hodges, but walks Campy, who scores on Snider's double. Furillo grounds out. In the eighth, Billy Cox singles, but Artie gets Loes, Gilliam, and Reese.

In mid-May, 1954, he is optioned again, this time to Oakland, where he is happy to be playing for, rather than against, manager Chuck Dressen. "He was the best signal stealer I ever saw," says Artie. "When I was with Hollywood, I had slightly different grips for my fast ball and curve, and since I was a lefthander, with my back to him, he could spot what I was going to

throw from his third base coaching box. One whistle was fast ball, two meant curve! When I finally caught on, of course, it was easy enough to show him one grip and shift to the other. Batters expecting a fast ball who got a curve soon stopped listening for Chuck's whistle."

Art is 12-4 in late July when the Yankees call him up for the fourth time. Dona, who is living in San Rafael with the two daughters, says, "He's such a nice boy. Some day I hope to get to know him."

Again, he is used very little, and after two relief appearances in 1955, the Yankees reduce the squad to 25 by selling Sain and Country Slaughter to the Athletics, and waiving Art—they are out of options—to Baltimore. The Orioles are the dregs of the American League. By a mighty, late-season effort they will move ahead of Washington to finish seventh. Manager Paul Richards is smart, taciturn, slow to praise, quick to criticize.

Art's first start is against the Yankees and is the best game of his major league career. The futile Orioles leave eight runners on base in the first six scoreless innings, but Artie has the Yankees eating out of his hand. A Baltimore game story says: "Using pinpoint control, an occasional fast ball, an excellent curve, and a tantalizing change of pace, Art had the Yankee sluggers talking to themselves for most of the afternoon." He allowed six hits, two of which scored a Yankee run in the ninth to win the game.

This was the day, incidentally, when a "good-looking, crewcut 18-year-old," who had been sought by eight other major league clubs, signed with the Orioles— Brooks Robinson.

Art pitches 30 games for Baltimore, mostly in relief. Dona comments wryly, "They must be saving him for the eighth game of the World Series." His season's record is three wins, five losses, and an ERA of 4.21.

In 1956, he gets a "slight raise" to $8,500, but sees no action before being sold to the Seattle Rainiers for $15,000. Luke Sewell is the not-very-well-regarded manager. The players include several familiar names on the downhill slide: Vern Stephens, Vic Lombardi, and Bud Podbielan. Art has a so-so season and in March, 1957, he retires.

He has a 33-year business career, most of them with a land title company. He begins as a gladhanding customer's man, is embarrassed by questions he can't answer, and tells his bosses, "Teach me." He departs a highly regarded vice president.

Lum Harris, his old coach at Baltimore, always said, "If you had nine players with the disposition and temperament of Schallock, you'd have a tough club to beat. He's all baseball. You never see him lose his head, or fail to cover first, or miss backing up a play. He's a great worker."

Hey, Blue!

Beth Martin

From the mid-1840s on, organized baseball games required the services of one or more umpires to enforce the rules of play. The umpire's formality of dress helped to establish his authority by distinguishing him from from players and spectators. A more active role in the game, changes in equipment and rules, and the visual demands of television necessitated occasional changes, but in any era the arbiter has been one of the more formally and conservatively dressed men at the ballpark.

When umpires were amateurs—As "the New York game" developed after 1845, written rules stipulated the presence of an umpire on the field to judge the fairness of play. The 1858 Knickerbocker Club's rules provided for an umpire to be both judge and scorekeeper. In the amateur National Association rules, adopted in December, 1865, the umpire was relieved of his recording duties. The selection of arbiters was made by the captains of the two contesting teams from among those in attendance, extending a tradition of asking social and business leaders to act as umpires.

None of the sets of rules mentioned the appearance of the umpire. As befits a gentleman spontaneously appointed to his position, he was allowed to wear what he chose, and could be distinguished from the players both by his position and demeanor. Players had begun to don identical clothing in 1849, and by 1869 the clas-sic knickerbocker style trousers and shirt appeared. The umpire was soon the only man on the field not wearing a distinctive uniform.

The earliest umpires were lawyers, merchants, and doctors. They dressed as gentlemen, in a "sober black suit, white linen, black scarf tie, [and] a tall silk hat." The informal sack suit was worn at first for leisure, not public appearances. With the democratization of fashion, a casual matched suit became acceptable at sporting events, then at the office. It also became the "good suit" of the working classes, worn for nonwork outings. By the time baseball emerged as the national pastime for the masses after the Civil War, a sack suit had become appropriate attire for all spectators, whether they were dressing up or dressing down.

By the Civil War the men of the country widely and enthusiastically played and watched baseball. However, in the late 1860s, the former gentlemen's game became a sport associated with rowdyism and gambling. Appearing shortly thereafter, baseball's early leagues tried a number of strategies to locate and eventually to hire qualified arbiters. By the time the American Association was established late in 1881, its rules referred to a staff of four men who traveled to the various cities where games were played. These umpires were attired in blue suits.

A professional staff of umpires—By the middle of the 1870s, the popularity of the game of baseball, an increase in the number of games played and in the number of cities where professional matches took place, and innovations in communication and transportation necessitated changes in the way umpires were

Beth Martin *is the daughter of SABR stalwart Jack Kavanagh. This article is excerpted from her master's thesis at the University of Rhode Island. She also has a Certificate of Museum Studies and works in nonprofit fundraising in New York City. Married, she is the mother of five.*

Red Stockings v. Atlantics. In this early professional era umpires were usually professional men who were agreed on by both teams. They wore the clothes appropriate to their station, and no protective equipment at all.

chosen and compensated. In 1871 the new National Association of Professional Base Ball Players allowed the home team to choose an arbiter from a list of five men submitted by the visiting club. In 1878, the two-year-old National League instructed its teams to pay umpires $5 per game. The following year the league compiled an approved list of twenty men from which teams chose umpires. The process of actually engaging an arbiter remained unwieldy, especially when intercity play was involved. There were frequent accusations that umpires' decisions favored the home team.

When the major league American Association was formed for the 1882 playing season, it created "an umpiring staff that was hired, paid, and assigned to games by the league itself. Paid $140 a month and $3 per diem for expenses while on the road, American Association umpires were required to wear blue flannel coats and caps while working games." The Association remained the only baseball organization to write dress regulations for umpires into its Constitution and Playing Rules, although the National League adopted a staff of uniformed umpires in 1883. The American League followed the established practice regarding umpires when it was founded in 1901.

By 1884, AA umpires were directed to purchase navy blue sack suits to wear while officiating. They were also subject to behavioral regulations. Rule 56 stipulated that "No Umpire shall while in uniform enter any Pool Room or Saloon, under penalty of removal."

When the National League followed the example of its junior rival in 1883, the Playing Rules merely provided for the election of a staff of four umpires to be paid in a certain manner, and to be under the control of the league secretary, who was empowered to ensure "…that he shall appear in proper dress when acting as umpire." That was evidently sufficient description for the senior circuit since the same wording was followed in subsequent years.

Blue suits—Although their role underwent major changes, the appearance of umpires remained very much the same for almost ninety years. From the early 1880s until the late 1960s, umpires were almost indistinguishable from one another. Minor alterations in suit styling, and shirt and necktie design followed contemporary men's fashion trends until the early 1960s. Few men wore suits to ball games by that time, substituting casual slacks, sport shirts, sweaters, and windbreakers, but umpires continued to sport what they described as the "blue embalmer's suit."

To a great extent umpires' appearance, like other aspects of their lives, depended on the preferences of their league president and other powerful figures. William G. "Billy" Evans (AL, 1906-27) and William Harridge, American League president, 1931-58, both exerted major influence on their circuit's umpires. Evans, as both umpire and league executive, was known as a fastidious dresser who insisted that his peers follow his example. Harridge wore a detachable hard collar long after the fashion had passed. As late as 1950, he insisted that his staff sport button-on soft collars and neck-band style shirts. These could still be procured from the Sears, Roebuck & Co. catalog, among other sources.

Larger crowds in an era before public address systems inspired senior umpire Bill Klem of the National League to devise a system, adopted in 1906, of semaphore signals to indicate fair and foul balls. The adoption of the "clean ball rule" in 1920 obliged the umpires to carry a supply of new balls in their jacket pockets when they were working home plate. As the use of inside chest protectors became common, jackets needed to be worn two sizes larger than usual to present a neatly tailored appearance.

All of this required a more relaxed fit, so umpires often wore informal suits. The Norfolk jacket, an

(AL 1905-09) always wore street suits of blue serge. He needed to change only his hat as he strode onto the field. When Jim Honochick (AL 1949-73) began his career with the American League in the late 1940s, wartime clothing shortages resulted in his purchase of a blue Brooks Brothers suit. He also needed to borrow his protective equipment from other arbiters. Hank Soar (AL 1950-73) remembers ordering lightweight wool suits from a New York menswear manufacturer with whom he was friendly.

Protection, accessories, and other appendages—

Umpires themselves, as well as their chroniclers, appear much more interested in the development of protective equipment than in the style of suits, collars, and ties. Masks and protectors, of course, have saved lives and preserved health on many occasions. Also, the adoption of protective gear influenced the history and rules of the game by making it feasible for the catcher and umpire to stand closer behind the batter without fear of being hurt by a foul ball.

The fascination with umpires' equipment really stems from the fact that for many years American and National

The "man in blue" image of umpires changed almost imperceptibly from the early twentieth century into the 1960s. That's a Norfolk jacket, second from right, on Bill Klem.

informal style with two vertical pleats in back and a full self-belt, was developed for rowers and golfers. It also suited the needs of arbiters. As the popularity of baseball grew, the business of clothing and equipping the participants grew more specialized as well as more lucrative. A number of companies such as A.G. Spalding, Wright & Ditson, and Sears, Roebuck & Co. vied for a share of the player uniform market. The smaller number of professional umpires made them a less desirable target audience, but a number of uniform manufacturers advertised and sold the blue suit.

Not all umpires, however, appeared on the field in suits procured from uniform manufacturers. Tim Hurst

League arbiters wore different types of body shields which influenced their working style. American League umpires, wearing the external protector, stood behind the catcher and looked over his head. They called more "high strikes." Their National League counterparts, wearing the compact inside protector, were able to view the play from just over the catcher's shoulder nearest the batter. These arbiters were known for calling more "low strikes."

The origin of the protector is shrouded in mystery. Historians accept that catchers wore outside chest protectors by the 1890s. These were merely a canvas shield with cotton batting inside. Since the catcher also relied on his glove held out in front of him to stop the ball, these shields were just barely sufficient. Umpires needed more help.

An early arbiter, Jack Sheridan (AL 1901-1914), is credited with the development of the inside protector. Bill Klem (NL 1905-41) stated that Sheridan, after many injuries, improvised a shield from an old fashioned hotel ledger. The heavy cardboard and leather book measured ten by twenty inches when closed. Sheridan purchased one and put it inside his buttoned coat, holding the edges with his fingertips. A foul tip bounced off the book without causing pain, so the improvised protector served for the season. During the winter, he developed a finished chest protector with straps from the prototype.

Klem himself was a strong proponent of the inside protector. Throughout his long career, he served as a role model for younger men and repeatedly advised them that an inside protector and mastery of the art of "weaving" would preserve them from injury. Unfortunately, Klem suffered a broken collarbone, smashed wrist, and numerous shoulder injuries despite wearing an inside protector. He reportedly had a hole under his collarbone that, "...you could put your finger in."

The A.J. Reach Co., Spring/Summer Sports Catalog of 1906 mentions the inflatable outside protector. Their device was patented in 1903, and two versions were offered for $12 each. One was shield shaped and covered the umpire's shoulders and arms. The other, narrower across the chest, allowed more freedom of movement. It had a strap to go around the neck and one that crossed behind the lower back. Catalog copy warned against the purchase of lower quality inflated body pro-

The air-filled outside protector, the bar mask, protective shoes, and—peeking out below the cuff—shinguards, combine with the miniature whisk, the short-billed cap and the dark suit and tie to complete the ensemble of the well-equipped, properly turned-out AL home plate umpire.

tectors.

Similar buffers appeared in an illustration of several arbiters demonstrating semaphore signals. A special umpire's protector was advertised for only $4 on page 871 of the 1918 Sears, Roebuck & Co. catalog. It had two arm straps and inflated with a patent valve.

Jocko Conlan (NL 1941-64) developed another style of outside protector, the mattress, and had it made by the Wilson Sporting Goods Company in 1950. Conlan covered the inflatable protector with black canvas and squared off the corners. This style, which was held high to protect the throat, appealed to Conlan after damage to his collarbone, larynx, and elbow. It offered better coverage than either the inside or standard inflatable protector, but was bulky and awkward to use.

Sometime in the 1930s or 1940s, minor league umpires became aware that their choice of protection could influence their selection by one or another of the major leagues. After World War II, baseball's umpires generally trained at one of two umpire schools, one of which used National League equipment and techniques while the other used American League standards. In 1964 the Umpire Development Program was created to control the passage of umpires from training to league work. Most of its direction came from former National League staff members who urged young arbiters to adopt the inside protector.

In the mid-1960s the American League also informally encouraged its arbiters to "go inside." Sportswriters speculated that this was for a better appearance before television cameras, while the league denied that this was the motivation. Jerry Neudecker, who retired in 1985, wore the mattress until the end of his career with the American League.

Adoption of the mask was far less controversial. Fred W. Thayer, Harvard team captain and third baseman, invented the protective face guard for catchers in 1876. An improved commercial model came out in 1877. Umpires adopted it in the early 1880s to the derision of sports reporters who suggested that the first umpire to don the mask was so ugly that his face alone would deflect oncoming baseballs. By the turn of the century, Sears, Roebuck & Co., A.G. Spalding & Bros., and other sources sold a variety of masks. In 1918, the Sears, Roebuck & Co. Catalog offered a catchers' and umpires' neck-protecting mask for $3.

Shinguards, possibly because they were worn inconspicuously beneath the trousers, or because other protective garb had already been widely accepted, were in common use among umpires by 1911. In that year, Hank O'Day (NL, scattered years, 1888-27) described them as part of his wardrobe saying, "The average citizen does not know how our manly forms are protected."

The quality of protection offered by these early devices varied. Shinguards in the 1907 edition of the Sears, Roebuck & Co. catalog for 58 cents were made of canvas and leather and stiffened with reeds. Jocko Conlan recollects padding the knees of his guards with a square of rubber sold for women to kneel on while washing floors. Many umpires suffered cuts when a direct hit by a foul ball punched in their masks. Hank O'Day is reported to have had his face stitched with red thread in the same pattern as the stitching on a baseball.

Other protective clothing included special shoes. Initially, spiked plates were sold to be attached with screws to a player's (or umpire's) regular footwear. By 1906, the Wright & Ditson Catalog of Spring and Summer Sports offered a variety of shoe styles. The spikes on base umpires' shoes helped a participant not to slip while running to make or observe a play in the field. By the middle third of the twentieth century, umpires working home plate wore shoes reinforced with a steel plate over the instep. At $22.50, they cost almost half of what a uniform suit did, but they were well worth it to an arbiter hit on the foot.

Likewise, blue caps differed according to whether an umpire was working the bases or home plate. The base arbiters wore long billed caps to shield their eyes from the sun. In the Wright & Ditson catalog, the style was identified as "university." At home plate, umpires needed shorter bills to fit the cap underneath a mask. This hat, the classic headgear of an umpire, was referred to as "Boston style."

A white shirt and tie completed the umpires' costume. Extant images suggest that most umpires preferred to wear four-in-hand neckties, but a significant number sported bow ties. Apparently, either style was acceptable. Ties were either black (Felker1944, 3) or merely "dark." Photographs at the National Baseball Library show neckties that are definitely black, as well as some that are somewhat lighter in color.

Two pieces of equipment completed the arbiter's outfit. A handheld indicator, used to record balls and strikes, cost 50 cents at A.G. Spalding. In 1885, Spalding claimed that the indicator was in general use among National League and American Association umpires. Last, what arbiter would be completely equipped without his whisk broom? Originally, the broom was a full-sized, four-foot-long model, which was used to sweep off home plate, then thrown aside. In the interests of safety around the plate, the broom became pocket-sized in 1910. It is used with the umpire facing the crowd to deny them the frequent pleasure of seeing corpulent umpires split their trouser seams.

Clothing and equipment expenses and care—Umpires had the responsibility of buying and maintaining their uniforms and equipment for nearly a hundred years. During that time a number of writers investigated their equipment needs and expenses.

An undated clipping from *The Sporting News* can be traced, from its text references to Bill Klem's career, to the late 1930s. Under the byline of J.G. Taylor Spink, the editor and columnist whose family published the newspaper, were ruminations on the salary and clothing of baseball's arbiters. At that time, the starting salary was $4,000 and the highest paid umpires received $10,000. Every five years each umpire had a chance to work in the World Series, for an extra $2,500 earned in a maximum of seven games. In addition to uniforms and equipment, umpires paid for hotel rooms and meals on the road. They were reimbursed only for railroad fares and berths, meals on trains, and taxicabs.

Umpires' expenses in the Depression-era 1930s included a blue suit for $65, a dozen white shirts at $1.50 each, four caps at $2.50 each, eight ties for $1 apiece, two sets of underwear at $3 a set. They also needed four supporters and one aluminum cup at a total cost of $8. Protective gear included a $7 mask, a $12.50 chest protector, a pair of shinguards for $6, and two pairs of shoes ($7 base shoes and $17 plate shoes). Indicators and whisk brooms, as well as rosin for the pitchers' bags, added about $3 to the total. All of this, as well as clothing for off-the-field use, had to be carried from town to town for six months away from home. A $10 suitcase served the purpose.

The fact that they required only one suit indicates that there must have been some way to get uniforms cleaned quickly. Hank Soar remembers that the clubhouse attendants, who cared for the home and visiting team members' woolen uniforms, also cleaned and pressed for the arbiters. Sending shirts out to a laundry took more time and was done only when an umpire expected to spend longer than usual in one city. Presumably, neckties had a higher mortality rate than hats, which would not be as exposed to accidents with ballpark food. Underwear was rinsed out in the washbowl whenever possible instead of being sent to the laundry since unmentionables needed no starching and pressing.

A decade or so later, in 1944, little had changed when *The Sporting News* surveyed arbiters from each league to determine their sartorial spending habits. National League umpires bought two uniforms a year(one with large pockets for use when working the plate, one normally styled), at $50 each, as well as a windbreaker for spring games ($7.50), and two $2.50 hats. Only four shirts and two ties were considered necessary, at $1.50 for each item. Five pairs of wool socks made the list, as well as two pairs of light wool underwear. Two supporters and one cup added $5.50 to the $15 underclothing total. Equipment included an inside protector ($20), mask ($10), shinguards ($7.50), base shoes ($14), plate shoes ($22.50), and a $1 indicator.

American League umpires spent a similar amount, except that the outside protector cost only $18, because of its simpler construction. One of the umpires mentioned that he had his suits custom made at a cost of $75 each. Surprisingly, the article made no mention of clothes rationing, coupons, or clothing shortages occasioned by World War II.

Clothing generally needed replacement each year, as did base shoes. However, a pair of plate shoes might last for five years, as did a set of shinguards. Masks lasted two years. Chest protectors needed replacement every year and a half. A good suitcase could withstand three to five years of hard wear.

By 1936 the National League had begun to issue an annual list of instructions to the umpire. They give no description of the uniform, but, in a section called "Good of the Game," instruct the men to keep it in good condition. They were also told to compare their watches to make sure the time agreed with that of the other umpires.

The completely revised 1958 edition of the *Manual for Umpires* gave much more attention to the arbiters' appearance. The men were told to wear a regulation, dark navy blue uniform with large pockets to carry spare baseballs. They were to make sure that the suits were clean and well pressed. Caps were to be the same shade as the uniform and should be discarded when soiled or greasy. A "sharp-looking" one was said to be very important for afternoon and Sunday games. Plate and base shoes must be black and shined regularly, and the belt must be "dark," not brown or tan. Rules stipulated wearing white shirts with dark ties . Even dress off the field appeared to be controlled by the league. It needed to be kept neat and a jacket and tie

were to be worn whenever an umpire ate in a restaurant or a hotel dining room.

By far the most specific source for advice on umpiring dress was a manual written for his students by George Barr (NL 1932-49), who founded the first umpire school in 1935. A school manual written in the early '50s provided explicit advice to men who still needed to buy their own clothing and equipment.

Twelve- or fourteen-ounce navy blue serge was favored for its ability to withstand hard wear and hang well. Mr. Barr advised purchasing two suits, one for use at the base and another, with a roomier cut in the shoulder, chest, and armhole, for plate umpiring. He assumed that many of his graduates would adopt the inside protector. The favored style incorporated a free swing or semi-swing back and had no vent. This permitted free play of the arms at the shoulders without pulling on other parts of the jacket. The closed vent helped the jacket skirt to lie smoothly over a pocketed whisk broom. The only permissible style was a three-button sack coat with a half belt in back and notched lapels.

Three patch pockets, buttoned and with inverted pleats, were on the jacket front. The two lower pockets unbuttoned and expanded to carry extra balls. Barr recommended reinforcing the inside of the pocket next to the jacket with duck or twill. This would prevent wear on the body of the coat while still permitting the pleats to release in order to accommodate the balls without distorting the lines of the jacket. The breast pocket provided a place for a handkerchief, line-up cards and pencil, and the ball and strike indicator. These items could also be carried in an inside pocket.

Cuffed, full-cut trousers with wide knees were needed to fit over the leg protectors. The trousers had to have two hip pockets, one open for holding the whisk broom, the other closed to store a handkerchief and safety pin. Pants for the base suit could be cut a little slimmer than those of the plate suit. Barr advised his students to avoid embarrassing accidents by wearing both belt and suspenders.

Barr mentioned three sources for the eight-piece crowned umpire's cap which was made full and loose, unlike the player's cap. The Partridge cap was a little fuller in the crown than the Covington or Spalding cap. All three caps were to be held in a straight-front, high-peaked style by "insertion of a paste-board strip, two by sixteen inches, between the sweatband and the front of the crown." Shirt cardboard was the recommended source for pasteboard.

Heavy woolen underwear was recommended to avoid sweat stains on the uniform, but Barr admitted that most arbiters preferred one-piece cotton undergarments. The men in blue could wear either white or navy sweat socks held up by garters.

A white shirt with detachable collar and a black four-in-hand or bow tie completed the arbiters' attire. Working behind the plate, an inside protector could substitute for both shirt and tie, since they would be covered up completely.

Barr told the arbiters how to do their own upkeep. The cap needed washing at least five times each season, using a dental plate brush and lots of suds. Because the bill was lined with paste-board, it had to be kept dry while the crown was washed, wrung out, stuffed and hung to dry, bill up. He had some rather unusual advice for keeping the uniform clean. He suggested that it be brushed daily and cleaned and pressed at least weekly. In sultry weather he insisted on daily brushing and pressing. If this was not possible, he warned his men to get out all the sweaty grime before it set—by throwing the whole uniform into the shower. Shoes had to be polished before each game, even if the field was wet or dusty. Barr equated good grooming with an umpire's self-respect, an essential element in deserving respect from others.

Arbiters were enthusiastic about easy-care clothing and regularly used synthetic-fiber clothes as soon as these became available. A set of instructions to umpires in the minor International League in 1960 allowed the arbiters to be reimbursed for the purchase of two "drip-dry" white shirts. Hank Soar recalls that baseball-loving manufacturers often sent samples of their nylon or Dacron clothing to the umpires.

Umpires sometimes adapted clothing to their physical needs. Although American League arbiters had to wear the full suit and tie no matter what the weather, the National League staff was given more leeway. National League President Ford Frick responded to an intense heat wave in July, 1936, by allowing his men to work—temporarily—in shirtsleeves. Much later, in the

early 1950s, the National League provided its umpires with blue tropical worsted blouses for the hot months of July and August. Thermal underwear was likely to be worn at the ends of the season during early games in April and when umpiring the World Series play. The type of undergarment remained an arbiter's individual choice.

Alternative Uniforms—Even in the long period of the blue suit use, arbiters had an occasional change of costume. On April 24, 1913, President Ban Johnson of the American League announced that for the upcoming season his umpires would follow popular fashion by appearing in white flannels on special days. Umpires wore "full dress" on holidays and when the president of the United States attended a game. On May 3 Johnson further decreed that arbiters would wear on their coat sleeves one row of braid per year of service. After each five-year period the braid was to be replaced by a gold star. Photographs in that year depict umpires dressed in white or light-colored suits, but none appear with braid on their sleeves.

Although the white uniforms were quickly retired, in 1926 the American League was ready to try again. That year umpires were attired in light brown khaki suits for summer games, in addition to the traditional blue. On gala days they again donned "peachy ice-cream outfits," most likely an offshoot of the white suit popular at the time. The following year a blue blazer and gray flannel slacks were the gala suit of choice. Umpires accepted this outfit enthusiastically, even to the point of tucking carnations in their buttonholes on Mother's Day, the first day the new garb was worn. Hoots and catcalls greeted the arbiters when they took the field, and the American League settled down to the blue suit for the next forty years.

Just a few years later the National League decided to experiment with blue blazers and white duck trousers for their own special games. Predictably, the players made a sport of kicking dirt on their referees. Speaking of a similar uniform from his years in the International League, Joe Rue (AL 1938-47) recollected, "One year they had us wear white pants on Sundays. Now we looked like zebras. The players called us a bunch of sissies. They'd sneak up behind you and spit tobacco juice on your pants legs. Every time we'd see one of them walking by we'd say, 'Get the hell away from me.' I had to have those trousers cleaned every Monday morning."

The 1952 *Baseball Guide* mentions that umpires in that year were outfitted in jumpsuits, and a photograph in the collection of the Hall of Fame shows a group of arbiters dressed like garage mechanics. Needless to say, such an unauthoritative uniform didn't last long. True change would have to wait for

NBL

the upheavals of the 1960s.

The umpires' sporty new clothes, 1968-80—By the late 1960s umpires' dress was badly out of style compared to the clothes of nonplayers at the ballpark. Except for the umpires, men at the ball park were likely to wear sports shirts with khaki pants or jeans in pleasant weather. When cold, they put on a windbreaker or sweater, and on hot days they donned shorts.

The average man would not wear a suit or even a sport coat to a game unless he had gone to the ballpark straight from work. Even then, his tie would be loosened or removed for comfort.

In this relaxed atmosphere the arbiter appeared to project a "formal, stiff 'undertaker' image of the dark blue suit and tie. Television coverage of baseball games undoubtedly influenced changes in arbiters' attire. Not only did an overly formal umpire look out of place, white shirts photographed badly. In June,1970, the National League outfitted its arbiters with blue short-sleeved shirts instead of the white ones

Over the years, there were a few attempts to break out of the formal blue mold. On the opposite page, an ump calls a play at the plate, probably in the khaki suit of 1926. Above, a natty Beans Reardon discusses a philosophical point with Casey Stengel in the late '30s. Right, Leo Durocher among a crew of "garage mechanics" in the early '50s.

previously worn. "...the league office decided the blue shirts would 'look a little better.' It was denied that the blue shirts are for the benefit of television."

The alterations in arbiters' appearance raised an old problem of visually establishing the umpires' authority on the field. How was the arbiter of play to be recognized without "...the uniform and mark of me trade?" After dispensing with the suit, umpires adopted a variety of combinations of blazer, shirts, and slacks in different colors and styles to project a contemporary appearance while maintaining superior status. "Problem is, they [league officials] had no idea what image was to be created—hence the frequent changes."

On March 20, 1968, the American League announced the first change in their umpires' attire in over thirty years. The boys in blue became the boys in blue and gray as a blue blazer-style jacket and "Madison Avenue" gray slacks replaced the navy suit. A white shirt usually accented the jacket, but in hot weather the ensemble could be replaced by a blue shirt with the league's symbol on the breast pocket. Arbiters wore the blue shirt with gray slacks.

The National League retained the blue suit and in 1970 adopted white identification numbers for its arbiters, placing them on the right sleeve. For summer wear, the suit jacket was replaced by a blue short-sleeved shirt like that of the American League but

with white numbers on the right sleeve. At this point, the leagues supplied two new uniforms every other year, made of wash and wear, drip-dry material (Archive of the National Baseball Hall of Fame and Museum).

Sometime in the early '70s, the National League permitted umpires to wear black turtlenecks under their blue suit jackets.

In 1975 the American League again proved its willingness to break with tradition. It attired its umpires in maroon jackets, seen in both a blazer and semi-Norfolk style. This was the first complete deviation from the blue uniform since the 1920s "ice cream suit." Umpires wore the blazer with very dark gray or black slacks, a white shirt, black tie, and a hat with a white shield. Turtleneck sweaters were added to the choices in 1978. No numbers were on the jacket sleeves; this was still reserved for senior circuit arbiters. Sticking stubbornly to the blue suit, the National League continued to allow its umpires to sport dark tee shirts under their summer uniform shirts for a popular layered look as well as wear black turtlenecks beneath the jacket.

Uniform uniforms, 1980-96—National and American League leaders appeared ready to move toward accepting the same umpiring standards by the late 1970s. In part this was due to the almost universal adoption of the inside chest protector. More important was the rise of the Umpire Development Program. Staffed by National League officials, it was created in 1964 to control the two major umpiring schools and ensure an orderly progression of the best graduates through the minor leagues and into the majors.

At the 1978 winter meetings in Orlando, Florida, officials made a number of changes to ensure interleague uniformity in procedure, position, hand signals, rules interpretation, and dress. The 1979 umpires' strike delayed implementation for a year.

Both leagues adopted the blue blazer and gray trouser combination with a white AL or NL on the dark blue cap. League emblems settled onto the left jacket pocket but would continue to vary in shape and size. Turtlenecks and short-sleeved shirts continued to enhance umpires' looks by keeping them up-to-date in sportswear style. American League umpires adopted the practice of layering a black tee shirt under their summer shirts. When suit jackets came off for summer play, umpires lost the use of their commodious pockets. Another means of holding extra baseballs needed to be devised. After a number of attempts, arbiters settled for suspending a ball bag from the belt. Amateur umpires had been using such bags for years, if not decades.

The Sporting News began to publish descriptions of umpires' uniforms in 1988, as part of its *American League Red Book* and *National League Green Book* se-

ries, which appears each spring to inform fans of rules changes, team rosters, stadium statistics, and the like. The first issue stated that all arbiters would wear gray slacks, navy jackets, light blue shirts and turtlenecks, navy windbreakers, black belts, and navy caps. American League umpires would receive navy V-neck sweaters. The caps would have "AL" or "NL" in white letters on the front, and the sleeves of shirts, sweaters, and windbreakers would have identification numbers on the right sleeves. League insignia would be on the shirt, sweater, jacket, and windbreaker.

American League innovations appeared again in 1996. Umpires working important games such as playoff series, World Series, and All Star contests wore turtlenecks and tee shirts in red. They continued to wear navy for regular games, as National League arbiters did at all times.

Amid the many changes to the umpires' uniforms and the frequent alterations to sartorial styles the umpire, no matter how he dressed, remained the most formal man on the field or in the stands. The authoritative uniform established that the man behind the catcher or at the bases was the person empowered to enforce the rules of play.

LITERATURE CITED

American Association of Base Ball Clubs. 1884. Playing rules of the American Association of Base Ball Clubs. In *Reach's Official American Association Base Ball Guide*. Philadelphia: A.J. Reach & Co..

American League of Professional Baseball Clubs. 1989-1996. *American League Red Book*. St. Louis: The Sporting News Publishing Co..

Barr, George. n.d. *Baseball Umpiring*. Tulsa: Key Printers.

Conlan, Jocko and Robert Creamer. 1967. *Jocko*. Philadelphia: J.B. Lippincott Co.

Felker, Carl T. 1944. IT'S $200 OR HIGHER FOR AN UMPIRE'S ATTIRE; BOYS BUY OWN, FROM BONNET TO BROOM. *Sporting News*, April 13.

Frick, Ford. 1936. *1936 Instructions to Umpires*. New York: National League of Professional Base Ball Clubs.

Gallico, Paul. 1979. "The Umpire's Revenge" in *Fielder's Choice*. New York: Harcourt, Brace, Jovanovitch.

Gerlach, Larry R.. 1989. "Umpires." In *Total Baseball*, eds. John Thorn and Pete Palmer, 465-73. New York: Warner Books.

_____. 1993. Letter to Henry Brophy, February 23. Special Collections, Baseball Hall of Fame and Museum Library, Cooperstown, NY.

_____. 1994. *The Men in Blue: Conversations with Umpires*. 2d ed. Lincoln: University of Nebraska Press.

_____. 1997. Letter to author, August 16.

Gorsline, Douglas. 1980. *What People Wore*. New York: Dover Publications.

Hollander, Anne. 1994. *Sex and Suits*. New York: Kodansha International.

Kahn, James. 1953. *The Umpire Story*. New York: G.P. Putnam's Sons.

Kavanagh, Jack. 1989. "Uniformly Fine." In *Diversion*, April, 285-93.

Lang, Jack. 1970. N.L. UMPIRES OUTFITTED WITH NEW BLUE SHIRTS (July 11).

Mann, Dene Hofheinz. 1965. *You Be the Judge*. Houston: Premier Printing.

Marguiles, Allan S. 1989. "Eyes of America's Game." In *Sports History* (September) 34-40.

Michelson, Court. 1985. *Michelson's Book of World Baseball Records*. Chicago: Adams Press.

National Baseball Hall of Fame and Museum Video Archive.

National League of Professional Baseball Clubs. 1989-1996. *National League Green Book*. St. Louis: The Sporting News Publishing Co..

Nemec, David. 1994. *The Rules of Baseball*. New York: Lyons & Burford.

New York *Times*. 1968, March 21 [Archive of the National Baseball Hall of Fame and Museum, umpire file].

Padden, Pat, Jim Tobin, and Hal Weafer, comp. 1958. *Manual for Umpires: Advice and Instructions for Umpires in the National Association of Professional Baseball Leagues*. Special Collections, National Baseball Hall of Fame and Museum Library, Cooperstown, NY.

Schrier, Barbara A. 1989. "Sporting Wear." In *Men and Women: Dressing the Part*, eds. C.B. Kidwell and Valarie Steele, 91-126. Washington: Smithsonian Institution Press.

1918. Sears, Roebuck & Co. Catalog. Chicago: Sears, Roebuck & Co..

1951. Sears, Roebuck & Co. Catalog, Spring/Summer. Philadelphia: Sears, Roebuck & Co..

Spalding's Official Baseball Guide. 1909. Chicago: A.G. Spalding.

Spalding's Official Baseball Guide. 1987. Chicago: A.G. Spalding & Bros, 1885. Reprint, n.p. Horton Books (page references are to the reprint edition).

Spink, J. G. Taylor. n.d. SOME THINGS I NEVER KNEW BEFORE ABOUT UMPIRES. *Sporting News* [Archive of the National Baseball Hall of Fame and Museum, umpire file].

Sporting News. 1980. 8 March Umpire File. National Baseball Hall of Fame and Museum Library Special Collections, Cooperstown, NY.

1906. Spring/Summer Sports. Philadelphia: A.J. Reach Co..

Soar, Albert "Hank," retired umpire. 1997. Interview by author, August 11, North Kingstown, RI. Telephone.

Steele, Valerie. 1989. "Dressing for work." In *Men and Women: Dressing the Part*. eds. Claudia Brush Kidwell and Valerie Steele. Washington: Smithsonian Institution Press.

Sullivan, Dean A., ed. 1995. *Early Innings: A Documentary History of Baseball, 1825-1908*. Lincoln: University of Nebraska Press.

Zimmerman, Hy. 1980. PANTS RIP, GALLANT UMP CARRIES ON (May 3).

"My Best Efforts"... The Baseball Life of René Gonzales

Karl Lindholm

In the spring of 1984—it doesn't seem that long ago—my friend Jon found himself in Florida with time on his hands. Recently divorced, he was taking the baseball cure and visiting spring training camps. Jon is an extrovert. He has always been able to engage people easily. Before a Dodger game at Vero Beach, he struck up conversations with two young players hoping to stick with their big clubs. He pulled out his newspaper from that day and asked them both to sign it, and he sent the paper with those autographs along to me, his friend, the high school baseball coach and fan.

Both of those players did make it to the majors, the pitcher that year with the Dodgers, and the infielder with his club, the Expos. Both have had remarkable careers in the majors, spanning the last decade or so. The pitcher is Orel Hershiser. He signed his name in a precise script and added the common Biblical citation "John 3:16." The infielder is René Gonzales, whose autograph is more elaborate and robust. Above his signature, he wrote "To Karl, My Best Efforts."

Recently I was going through some baseball stuff and came across the *Miami Herald* sports section from March 4, 1984, with the Hershiser and Gonzales autographs over a story titled "The Boys of Spring." I am moved now to consider the career of René Gonzales. In baseball's troubled post-strike era, I am struck by his pledge of "my best efforts" to me and Jon and other fans like us.

It strikes me also that he has been true to his pledge.

Karl Lindholm *is the dean of advising and an assistant professor of American literature and civilization at Middlebury College in Vermont. He teaches a course called "Baseball, Literature, and American Culture."*

Just who *is* René Gonzales?—He is hardly a household name, yet he has spent all or part of the last *fourteen* years (with the exception of 1985) in major league baseball. In 1996, he was a reserve infielder for the Texas Rangers. Last summer, he spent most of the season with the Colorado Sky Sox, the Rockies' AAA team, before being called up by the big club for a cup of coffee in September. At this writing, he is the starting left fielder and fifth batter in the lineup of the Calgary Cannons, the Chicago White Sox's top minor league affiliate. He earned this spot with a sterling spring training performance, batting .367 in sixteen games (11 hits in 30 at-bats with 10 RBIs.)

Perhaps the most shining moment on the national stage for René Gonzales came on October 2, 1995, in the AL West playoff game in Seattle before 52,000 Mariner diehards and millions of fans across the country (like me) watching on TV. Seattle's unhittable Randy Johnson was mowing down Gonzales' California Angels en route to a 9-1 win. In the eighth, Angel Manager Marcel Lacheman sent up a parade of pinch hitters to flail at Johnson's swift offerings, Gonzales among them.

TV announcer Bob Costas identified Gonzales as a "utility infielder" for the Angels and then he added, "In fact, he is the *most* utility infielder in history. He spent two years as Cal Ripken's backup in Baltimore."

Gonzales then lined a Johnson slider into the gap in left-center for a double.

From a distance here in New England, I have casually followed Gonzales' career over the years. As a consequence of my Rotisserie baseball interest, I know all American League rosters. René had never been drafted in my league (except once, a mistake: Tony thought he was getting Juan). I had consigned him to an ethnic stereotype: Hispanic utility infielder, the sons of Luis Aparicio, small in stature, quick, Eddie Romero, Alvaro Espinosa, a pepperpot sub.

I finally saw Gonzales in person in a Red Sox-Orioles game in 1989 at the Shrine in Boston during one of my annual pilgrimages with my father. We got there early for infield practice and I saw a man at third taking ground balls whom I didn't recognize. He was lithe and tall, athletic, scooping up grounders with grace and agility, firing hard accurate throws to first. He ran off the field with Ripken, chatting and smiling, and he was nearly the same size as big Cal.

I checked my program—this was Gonzales, this knight, this ideal ballplayer, 6'3", 210 pounds, straight from central casting. That was the last I saw of him that day. Cal, of course, played the entire game.

A career "utility infielder"—How does one sustain a major league career of over a decade as a "utility infielder"? Often an extra infielder is a former starter on the downside of his career, or one who has demonstrated as a regular that he can't hit enough to stay in the starting lineup: Dick Schofield, Spike Owen, Tim Foli come to mind. Occasionally, he's a player waiting his turn: the American League's talented young shortstops, Alex Rodriguez (Seattle) and Alex Gonzalez (Toronto) both served brief apprenticeships in backup roles.

However, I suspect Gonzales' career has no precedent and he really is "the *most* utility infielder in baseball history."

He has spent sixteen years in organized baseball. His major league career encompasses 705 games (1,539 at bats, 368 hits for a .239 batting average). In the minors, he has played 839 games (2,731 at bats, 701 hits, .257 average). He has played for seven big league clubs: Montreal, Baltimore, Toronto, California, Cleveland, Texas, and Colorado. The "official" major league baseball website describes him as a "career journeyman."

From 1988 to 1993 he played exclusively in the majors, never being sent down, for the Orioles, Blue Jays, and Angels. Primarily a shortstop and third baseman, he has played every infield position and the outfield—and in a 1993 blowout he pitched a hitless, scoreless inning for the Angels. He played short and third, and pinch-ran, but didn't bat in two games for Toronto in the ALCS in 1991.

In the seasons in which he played most in the majors, he played well. For California in 1992 and 1993, he played in over 100 games each season, mostly at third base, and had over 300 at bats. He batted .277 in '92 and .251 in '93, with 17 doubles each year. As expected, he played solid defense with just 21 errors in over 800 chances in that two-year period.

He was the Angels' regular third sacker in 1992 until he went on the disabled list in early August, and he started at third on Opening Day in 1993. Despite these best efforts for the Angels, he opened 1994 with Charlotte, the Indians' top minor league team.

Gonzales was born in Austin, Texas, and prepared for his career at Rosemead (CA) High School, Glendale (CA) College and Cal State Los Angeles. Two years after being selected by Montreal in the fifth round of the free-agent draft in 1982, he was in the majors, appearing in 29 games for Montreal in 1984. In 1986 he was traded from Montreal to Baltimore, the "player to be named later" in the Dennis Martinez deal.

In the winter of 1996, he was signed as a free agent with the Rangers, but failed to make the big club despite a good spring training and was sent to Oklahoma City, their AAA farm club. He was batting .266 in late May (with three doubles in one game) when he was called up. He stuck with the Rangers for the rest of the summer, batting only .216, alas.

In 1997 he started out with the Las Vegas Stars, the Padres' affiliate in the PCL. After batting .186 in 13 games, he was released. Nine days after he was cut, he was picked up by the Colorado Rockies and assigned to their AAA affiliate in Colorado Springs. Here he remained for the rest of their season, playing all the infield positions (22 games at first, 34 at second, 9 at third, and 10 at shortstop), batting .283, and leading the Sky Sox into the playoffs, emerging as a team leader when injuries on the Rockies claimed the Sky Sox's best prospects. In his brief stint with the Rockies in September, he got up twice and had one hit, knocking in a run.

A valuable man—Why hasn't René Gonzales been a starter, the regular at third or short over a sustained period for some team? The short answer is probably he doesn't hit, run, or field well enough. He's good at all three important skills, but spectacular in none. He doesn't hit homers in bunches like third baseman Matt Williams. He's not peerless with the glove like shortstop Ozzie Smith (nor again does he clout like Ripken). He can't create havoc on the bases like second baseman Robbie Alomar.

Gonzales is steady and dependable. His gift is his versatility. His role is to play many roles. A manager can send him up there to pinch hit in the ninth, or insert him as a defensive replacement, and know he will get Gonzales' best effort, a competent major league performance. He can give a star (other than Ripken) a day off when he's tired or hurt. Gonzales is a roster saver—he can do the jobs of two or three specialists. A manager with Gonzales can add a pitcher to the roster during the dog days of summer and not sacrifice strategic opportunities.

Skills don't tell the whole story. I figure he also must

be a good fella. You don't spend a dozen years, off and on, in the majors if you're a pain in the neck, a whiner, a clubhouse lawyer. Teams seem to like to have René Gonzales in their dugout.

Gonzales was 36 in September. Surely his days as a player are numbered. It will be interesting to see where he ends up. Clearly, the White Sox have signed him as "insurance:" their middle infielders are young and relatively untested. If one of them goes down with an injury during the pennant race, or even in the postseason, they could then call on Rene Gonzales, professional infielder, and not some jittery kid.

In his professional career spanning the past sixteen years and well over a dozen teams, I suspect he has been richly rewarded in experience and friendship. I bet he has some stories of places seen and people met. He has made a good living too, though not on the lav-ish scale of the game's stars. (In 1993, the New York *Times* reported his salary as $600,000. The Padres reportedly signed him for $225,000 in the spring of 1997.

I have seen him in person only that one time at Fenway, but I enjoy following his career in baseball publications or the occasional item in the newspaper. Last year I looked up the Colorado Springs Sky Sox box scores on the Web. Now he is back in Canada, and I will check his progress through the '98 season on the Calgary Cannons site.

Like Cal Ripken, his more gifted and famous former teammate, Gonzales has shown up every day at the job site for a long time, and given his "best efforts." By doing so, he inspires me. He inspires me to persevere out of the limelight, to love my work, to be a good teammate, to give the "games" I play every day my best efforts as well.

From the Sporting Weeklies

The color line has been drawn very tight in Organized Baseball, but there is no denying the fact that there were and are many many colored players who, if they had the opportunity, would be stars in the National or American Leagues. (The Sporting News, *January 4, 1917.*)

...the time is not far distant when the Boston club of the National League will be shifted to some other city.... (The Sporting News, *July 3, 1919.*)

In the long ago, when Gleason, McGraw, Jennings and others were on that famous old Baltimore Oriole team, they finished the season, played their final exhibition game, and each man was handed his check and his transportation home.

The gang had dinner together, and during it a big argument cam up regarding a certain kind of play. They scrapped and argued for some time. Then, although all had their tickets in their pockets, they stayed over till the next day so they could try out the disputed play on the ballfield.

It's hard to imagine a group of players doing such a thing in this day and age. (The Sporting News, *November 22, 1923.*)

Napoleon Lajoie made five errors in one game [4/22/15], but how many 40-year old men could get near five chances?—James C. Isaminger, Philadelphia beat writer (Sporting Life, *May 15, 1915.*)

—Kerry Keene

A Yankee Fan— The Second Time Around

Lyle Spatz

In mid-1993 I began writing a history of the New York Yankees. The book, recently published, looks at the team from the perspective of their Opening Days, beginning in 1903, when they moved to New York from Baltimore, through the 1996 opener.

When I told friends and relatives what I was doing, they expressed approval; all agreed that it was "about time you wrote a book." That being said, almost every one followed with variations on the same question: "Why the Yankees? Why not the Dodgers, or even the Orioles?" It was a logical question. I grew up in Brooklyn and from 1946, the time I began to take baseball seriously, rooted zealously for the Dodgers. Despite my outrage at their 1958 defection to California, I continued to root for them, although not quite so zealously.

Finally, in the early 1970s, my loyalty to the Dodgers, which had been waning for several years, ended. Sandy Koufax and Don Drysdale, the last links to Brooklyn, were gone, and I had absolutely no attachment to any of the team's newer players. By this time I had been living in Maryland for ten years and had two young sons who were starting to get interested in baseball. I can't recall if I encouraged them to do so or if it just came naturally, but both became Orioles fans. Knowing how painful it is to youngsters when their team loses, I began rooting for the Orioles to do well to spare them that pain. In retrospect, I doubt that they, or any other young fans experienced the highs and lows of team devotion that my generation did. But, of course, my generation is not the first to make that observation.

Lyle Spatz *is the author of* New York Yankee Openers *(McFarland, 1997) and the chair of SABR's Baseball Records Committee.*

Gradually my attachment to the Orioles became less related to fatherly instincts and began to stand on its own. The attachment was not nearly as all-encompassing as it had been in my Dodger days, but it was comfortable. An added bonus in rooting for the Orioles was their success against the Yankees, something that I was not familiar with, More familiar to me was the way their fans hated the Yankees. That's the way I had grown up.

So the question remained, "why the Yankees?" It was important to me that my book deal with not only baseball, but also with life in America throughout the Twentieth Century. That eliminated the Orioles, who did not re-enter the American League until fifty years after the Yankees replaced their original team—part of the reason for Baltimore's antipathy to New York. But an even stronger reason for choosing the Yankees existed. While I would be taking a "slice of life" look at events around the world for each Opening Day, there would be a natural emphasis on life in the city of the team I chose. I wanted that city to be New York, the one whose history meant most to me. To write about the Dodgers meant setting half the book in Los Angeles, a city I have little knowledge of and no affinity for.

Some friends said, half-seriously, that by the time the book was finished I'd probably be a Yankee fan. Not likely, I thought. While it had been years since I'd "hated" this team, I still bore the emotional scars of 1947, '49, '52, '53, and '56. I had often read about biographers who began their projects feeling great admiration for their subjects only to end up hating them. It worked the other way, too, with contempt and disdain turning to respect and adoration. I was also fa-

---

miliar with what psychologists call "the Stockholm syndrome," a condition where victims sometimes identify with their tormentors. All these potential pitfalls I found interesting, but irrelevant.

As the book progressed through the winter of 1993 and spring of 1994, I gave no further thought to the possibility of such an emotionally wrenching transformation. Then, in early summer '94, I began work on the 1945 season and something very strange happened. Like Saul on the road to Damascus, I, on the information highway, had a kind of epiphany.

In reading and talking about players like Nick Etten, Johnny Lindell, George Stirnweiss, Russ Derry, Atley Donald, and Bud Metheny, I felt that somehow I had done this before. Of course, as both a baseball fan and a baseball researcher, I read and speak about losts of players, from all eras, but this was different. An eerie feeling persisted that I had read and talked about these men while they were *active* players. No problem with Etten, Lindell, and Stirnweiss. All continued their careers after World War II—that is, into 1946, the beginning (I thought) of my baseball awareness. However, Derry and Metheny were strictly wartime players, and Donald, while a legitimate major leaguer, never pitched after 1945.

The name that had the biggest impact on me was Hank Borowy. I knew as an historical fact the details of the Yankees' seemingly inexplicable July, 1945 waiver sale of Borowy to the Chicago Cubs. But now, suddenly, I remembered with great clarity hearing about the sale when it happened—it was the same day a bomber crashed into the Empire State Building. At eight years old I had no idea what waivers were, but I knew that

Nick Etten

Atley Donald

Borowy was the Yankees' best pitcher and that his loss was bad for "my team." Oddly, I saw Borowy pitch against Brooklyn in person and on television through the 1950 season without ever having this memory surface. Nor did I remember it while I wrote my chapter on 1944, when he was the Yankees' Opening Day pitcher.

I tried to recall what my day-to-day life was like in the spring and summer of 1945, a time when momentous events were happening almost daily. Within a period of five months I listened to radio accounts of President Roosevelt's death, V-E Day, the liberation of the concentration camps, the atomic bombs on Hiroshima and Nagasaki, and finally, the end of World War II. Heated and passionate discussions among the adults in my little world accompanied all these events, and I hung on every word.

The more I thought about this time, half a century ago, the more I recalled an older boy who lived in my apartment building. He was probably twelve or thirteen and often took the time to talk with me, serving as a kind of mentor. Yet as I think back, we discussed only two subjects: the war and baseball. For the past fifty years I had always thought it was an uncle who had initiated me into the world of baseball, but now I remembered it was actually this older boy who had done so. I was a willing pupil and learned fast, and because he was a Yankee fan, most of the baseball talk revolved around the Yankees. And as young boys often do, I adopted the team of my mentor.

So there it was, the shocking knowledge that I had begun my baseball life as a Yankee fan. In my mind, I has always dated my baseball beginnings to the first week of the 1946 season, more specifically to April 23, the day Brooklyn's Ed Head no-hit the Braves, 5-0. Some other older boys were talking about what had happened and the conversation captivated me. The next day I tuned in the Dodger game to hear about this fascinating game first-hand. To my disappointment, the Dodgers were rained out. However, the station broadcast a game between the Pirates and the Cardinals with Red Barber, in the studio, doing a recreation. The next day I was back and listened as the Dodgers, led by the hitting of Dixie Walker, beat the Giants. I was hooked. I pestered my uncle and the older boys for information while trying to listen to at least part of every afternoon's Dodger broadcast—there weren't many night games back then. By the time my uncle took me to see my first game, I believed I knew everything there was to know about Ebbets Field. it was July 5, 1947. We sat in the bleachers and saw the Dodgers lose to Boston, 3-1. Bill Voiselle beat Vic Lombardi, and the Braves' Danny Litwhiler hit a home run that landed not too far from where we were sitting.

I can still remember with great clarity many details of that day,. A short walk followed the subway ride to Franklin Avenue, during which my uncle pointed out the Ebbets Field light towers in the distance. Then, after turning a corner, I got my first look at this absolutely magnificent structure. Since then I have read many nostalgic accounts of young boys getting their first glimpse of the incredibly green grass of a major league park. Each time I do it brings back to me my own first game. I had never seen anything as awe-inspiring as that field and those gods in white uniforms going through their pregame practice. I imagine that kids still get that thrill, despite growing up with color television, but I am sure that it can be neither as strong nor as memorable as it was to boys of the pre-television age.

My task now was to uncover something that happened between the end of the 1945 season and the beginning of the 1946 season that led me to abandon the Yankees for the Dodgers. Eventually I pieced together what seemed a reasonable explanation. For one, the older boy in my building moved. He and his mother had been living with his grandmother, but with the end of the war his father had returned from the Army to put the family back together. His departure meant that I

Johnny Lindell

had no one to guide me through the off-season. With all the players returning from the war, that off-season between 1945 and 1946 must have been among the most interesting ever. Yet, without my mentor, I had no ready access to it. You had to seek out information back then, and I was not knowledgeable enough to do so. I don't think I really knew what an off-season was, although I probably was vaguely aware that come next spring the Yankees would be playing again, I also must have know that this time they would have Joe DiMaggio with them (I can't remember ever not knowing who Joe DiMaggio was), but I had not yet fallen into the rhythm of season, off-season, and new season that is the essence of being a fan.

It's likely that when I heard those older boys talking about Ed Head and the Dodgers it rekindled my interest. Obviously my attachment to the Yankees had been a tenuous one, making it easy for me to forget. I became a Dodger fan, just like my uncle and these older boys were.

The question remains, however, of why it took me almost half a century to remember this early flirtation with the Yankees. Why had I repressed it and completely blocked it out of my memory? In working on subsequent years, after 1945, I began to view the Yankees differently that I would have had I not made my discovery. That is not to say that I rooted for them retroactively. I didn't. Nevertheless, I no longer feel a twinge of guilt for having liked and admired players like Tommy Henrich, Vic Raschi, and Mickey Mantle.

Earlier I compared my conversion to the one on the road to Damascus. Of course, I did it facetiously. After all, Saul changed not only his name but his religion. However, that is not to say that changing the team one roots for is a trifle. Kids growing up in New York in the days when the city had three teams had their characters judged and their compatibility measured more by their baseball allegiance than their religion.

The realization that I had started my baseball life as a Yankee fan occurred just about the time of the 1994 players strike. When the season closed down, the Yanks were in first place with a good chance of winning their division title. I wondered whether I would have been rooting for them to do so had the season continued. By the time the 1995 season began I knew that I would have. I knew also that it would not have been the first time.

On the Silver Screen

Rob Edelman

Across the decades, major leaguers have played roles both small and significant in baseball and non-baseball films. They have been extras, made cameo appearances, had featured and starring roles, and worked off-screen as technical advisors. They have played themselves (or variations of themselves) as well as fictional characters in big-screen Westerns, melodramas, biographies, comedies. On occasion, a major leaguer, upon closing out his career, even has gone on to win success as a professional actor.

Whatever their on- or off-screen function, the involvement of real ballplayers in motion picture productions not only lends a certain fascination and authenticity but makes for valuable visual and historical records. And more often than not, the dialogue they speak once the cameras roll is funny, knowing, ironic, and revealing.

Some ballplayers get to poke friendly jibes at their fellow jocks. *The Kid from Cleveland* may not be the best baseball movie ever made, but it is jam-packed with major leaguers. Quite a few—including Lou Boudreau, Tris Speaker, Satchel Paige, Hank Greenberg, Bob Feller, and Bob Lemon—are Hall of Famers. At one point in the movie, the troubled youngster of the title, played by Russ (billed as Rusty) Tamblyn, is on the ballfield during spring training, warming up beside Paige and Feller. Tamblyn's character, Johnny Barrows, asks Satchel, "Is this the right

windup for your hesitation pitch?" The legend responds, "Now Johnny, watch old Satch," as he shows him how with Feller looking on. Then Johnny tries, and fails miserably. "Don't worry about that, Johnny," Paige tells him. "It took me twenty years to get that pitch." At which point Feller breaks in, "Satch, some folks say it took you thirty years."

In baseball movies, ballplayers are allowed to comment on their real-life on-field adversaries. "I wish all my problems were that easy," declares Indians player-manager Lou Boudreau in response to a minor plot development in *The Kid from Cleveland*, "Like getting rid of Ted Williams without the Boston Red Sox putting me in jail for it." And early on, Boudreau asks Hank Greenberg if he ever came to bat against a ghost. "I sure did," Greenberg responds. "His name was Dizzy Dean. I never even saw the ball."

Occasionally, fictional characters offer statements about real players. In *Slide, Kelly, Slide*, an egocentric ballplayer named Jim Kelly (William Haines) arrives in Delano, Florida, "spring training camp of the New York Yankees." Soon he is on the field, warming up in the company of Bob Meusel and Tony Lazzeri. "Not a bad bunch, Mac…," he tells his manager (who is *not* Miller Huggins). "Looks like I'll get some good support."

Another Yankee to appear on-screen is Lou Gehrig, who starred as himself in a B-Western, *Rawhide*. At the outset, the Iron Horse announces to reporters that he is hanging up his spikes, replacing his Yankee cap with a ten-gallon hat, and settling out west. But Gehrig finds no peace there, as he takes on a gang of bad guys and gets to employ his athletic prowess by tossing billiard balls at the villains in a barroom scuffle and batting a

Rob Edelman *is the author of* Great Baseball Films *(Citadel Press) and* Baseball on the WEB *(MIS: Press), and co-author (with his wife, Audrey Kupferberg) of* Angela Lansbury: A Life on Stage and Screen *(Birch Lane Press),* The John Travolta Scrapbook *(Citadel Press), and the forthcoming* Meet the Mertzes *(Renaissance Books).*

ball through a window to halt a contract signing.

One of the bits of dialogue in *Rawhide* is sadly ironic. As Gehrig explains to reporters that he is quitting the Yankees, he notes, "...I'm gonna wallow in peace and quiet for the rest of my life. I'm gonna hang up my spikes for a swell old pair of carpet slippers." Of course, no one—least of all Gehrig—knew that he would pass away a scant three years after the film's 1938 premiere. Nonetheless, the ballplayer gives an affable performance in *Rawhide*. Had his life not been so tragically short, Gehrig might have gone on to fashion a career as a B-Western star.

Another ballplayer who could have enjoyed a stellar silver screen career is Babe Ruth. He did, in fact, appear in the features *Headin' Home*, *The Babe Comes Home*, *Speedy*, and *The Pride of the Yankees*, as well as in various short subjects. Among the latter is *Home Run on the Keys*, a Vitaphone one-reeler from 1937, two years after the Babe played in his final major league game. Ruth impersonates himself, taking on the role of a retired gentleman of leisure. At the outset, one of his pals is attempting to conjure up an idea for a radio broadcast. Those present soon are comparing a songwriter's past hits to Babe's base hits, with the Bambino adding, "Ah, don't mind about my old hits. The copyright is out on those."

In both sound and silent films, the Bambino's robust personality registers well on screen. While he did not have the looks to become a leading man, he might easily have been a successful farceur and second banana. One can imagine the Bambino comically cavorting as a Fourth Stooge, or in a revamped act known as Abbott, Costello and The Babe.

Even though it is about soccer and not baseball, Tommy Lasorda, one of the newest members of the Baseball Hall of Fame, has a dream role in *Ladybugs*, a Rodney Dangerfield comedy. He plays a character named Coach Cannoli.

Lasorda also has the stage presence and personality—and show business connections—to have cultivated an acting career. One can see him cast as Manager Dutch Schnell or Coach Joe Jaros in *Bang the Drum Slowly*, or as Skip in *Bull Durham*.

Perhaps the most famous ballplayer-turned-actor is Chuck Connors, who played in one game for the Dodgers in 1949 and 66 more for the Cubs in 1951. Connors would earn his greatest fame, and become a staple of Baby Boomer childhoods, as television's *The Rifleman*.

Connors has a supporting role in *Three Stripes in the Sun*, cast as an American GI stationed in post-war Japan. In one sequence, he and his fellow soldiers play ball in an exhibition against some Japanese. Prior to the game, both teams line up across home plate. The Japanese remove their caps, and ceremonially bow to their opponents and then to the umpires. Connors looks disconcerted, as if he has just been served a plate of sushi when he would rather be chomping on an onion-smothered hamburger. The jock-turned-thespian most probably ad libs a comment that reveals his Dodger roots, as he exclaims to a teammate, "What would Durocher say if he saw this?"

Given his flair for theatrics, and the fact that between 1947 and 1960 he was wed to screen star Laraine Day, it is surprising that Leo the Lip did not become an on-screen regular. He did make a memorable appearance in *Whistling in Brooklyn*, a Red Skelton comedy.

The scenario has Skelton's character a murder suspect who is attempting to elude the authorities. In one sequence, he finds himself in Ebbets Field, masquerading as a pitcher for the Battling Beavers, a House of David team playing the Bums in an exhibition. Durocher is on the field, jawing first with Skelton and then with an umpire. Meanwhile, Skelton gets to comically pitch to (and clown with) Billy Herman, Arky Vaughan, Ducky Medwick, and Dolph Camilli.

Dizzy and Daffy Dean, billed as "Jerome and Paul Dean," are the stars of *Dizzy & Daffy*, a Vitaphone two-reeler in which they clown around with Shemp Howard, of Three Stooges fame, cast as "Lefty Howard," a blind-as-a-bat pitcher. The joke of it all is that Diz, then in his prime, gets to ask Shemp how to throw a curve. When Shemp is told that the player is named Dean, the Stooge quips, "Dean...Dean...the only Dean I ever heard of is Gunga."

In some films, ballplayers have no dialogue, but their mere presence adds to the viewing pleasure. *Pastime* is a *Bull Durham* variation about an aging career minor leaguer who mentors a fireballing young black hurler. Ten minutes into the film, just at the onset of the initial game sequence, you can spot Duke Snider sitting in the stands, munching a hot dog. Blink and you will miss Don Newcombe raising the flag during the playing of the National Anthem, and Ernie Banks singing along with the crowd. Bob Feller, Bill Mazeroski, and Harmon Killebrew also have bit parts in the film.

Ballplayers have found themselves unwitting participants as minor characters in thrillers, with their mere presence adding a jarring sense of reality. In *Experiment in Terror*, Glenn Ford plays a San Francisco cop on the trail of a psycho. The finale unfolds during a Giants-Dodgers night game at Candlestick Park. As damsel-in-distress Lee Remick enters the ballyard, San Francisco rightfielder Harvey Kuenn arrives at home plate. As she is seated, Kuenn bashes a hit. Next, Felipe Alou is announced. There is a closeup of Don Drysdale as he gets his sign from his catcher.

Then the Dodgers come to bat. A closeup of Wally Moon at the plate is followed by one of pitcher Mike McCormick—and then there is the unmistakable voice of Vin Scully calling the subsequent play. All the while, there is behind-the-scenes commotion as the authorities prepare to capture the villain, with the on-field clips blending seamlessly into the film's action.

Occasionally, baseball films attempt to offer historical perspective on the game. *Dizzy & Daffy* purports to reveal how the Deans acquired their nicknames. In one sequence, Diz is firing fastballs to home plate. Soon his catcher's glove begins to smoke, then a pitch deflates the umpire's chest protector. "That fastball has got 'em dizzy," Shemp quips. Adds Paul, sitting beside him on the bench, "Yeah, when I get through with 'em, it'll be daffy."

"That gives me an idea," declares Shemp. "Dizzy and Daffy Dean. He's gonna be Dizzy Dean, and you're gonna be Daffy Dean. What a name! What a moniker!"

Obviously, Shemp is clowning here. But in other instances, incidents which may or may not have happened are presented as pure, unadulterated fact.

The Kid from Cleveland was released in 1949, the year after the Indians won their last World Series—and three years after Larry Doby became the first black to play in the American League. This milestone is paid homage in a monologue spoken near the finale by Indians' owner Bill Veeck:

When Larry first joined the club, he was kind of in a spot, something like Jackie Robinson of the Brooklyn Dodgers...His first time up, he was nervous. Very nervous. Much more nervous than the average rookie. Because, you see, he had the additional load of some 15 million people riding on his back. And that's quite a load. Larry wasn't just batting for himself. He was batting for some 15 million people—15 million people who really believed in him.

And so when he struck out, he felt he let all those people down.... And after Larry struck out, he made that long trip to the dugout, and he went down the dugout steps and walked the entire length and sat down at the extreme corner. He was the picture of absolute dejection. And the next hitter was Joe Gordon, one of baseball's really great hitters. (Gordon is depicted on screen taking two strikes.) Joe took a terrific cut at the ball. He missed it by at least six inches more than Larry had. I don't say that he did it intentionally. But I know he's never missed a pitch by that much before. Joe too made that long trip back to the dugout. He didn't stop, but walked the entire length to sit next to [Doby]. He too sat in exactly the same position, to prove to this boy that, here at least, he was just another ballplayer.

In *Home Run on the Keys*, Babe Ruth gets to offer, for the record, what he must have hoped would be the final word on one of his most famous and controversial home runs. Upon his being asked to recall his greatest baseball thrill, Ruth immediately cites his "called shot" in the 1932 World Series:

The papers said it was the longest and most dramatic home run hit at the Cubs' park.... Well, this one particular time when I went to bat, Charlie Root was pitching. And the first pitched ball was a called strike. Well, I thought it was outside and didn't like it very much. So the boys over there [in the Cubs' dugout] would give me this [razzing]—you know what I mean.

Well, the second pitched ball was another called strike. Well, I didn't like that one either, so I let it go by. And by that time [the Cubs' dugout was] going crazy. Well, I stepped out of the box, and I looked over to the bench, and then I looked out at centerfield, and I pointed. I said, "I'm gonna hit the next pitched ball right past the flagpole."

Well, the good lord and good luck must have been with me because I did exactly what I said I was gonna do. And I'll tell you one thing. That was the best home run I ever hit in my life.

In the classic John Ford western *The Man Who Shot Liberty Valance*, a reporter observes (regarding the creation of Western mythology), "When the legend becomes the fact, print the legend!" The same may be said for baseball lore. Veeck's recollection makes for a nice anecdote regarding race relations, while the Babe's explanation adds to his larger-than-life persona. But as we are learning more and more often (see this issue's lead article), even first-person accounts can be inaccurate. So historians who are attempting to separate fact from fantasy certainly can't accept celluloid commentary as gospel.

There is one bit of celluloid commentary, from Carl Hubbell (playing himself in *Big Leaguer*), which cannot be faulted by anyone who truly knows and loves baseball. Edward G. Robinson stars as Hans Lobert, ex-major leaguer who runs a New York Giants' tryout camp. The finale is a game between the Giants and Brooklyn Dodger wannabes. Managing the latter is Al Campanis, who even gets to share some repartee with Robinson.

King Carl is in the stands, scouting the game for the Giants. It's the bottom of the ninth. The Giants are four runs behind, and come up to bat. They get a few baserunners, and score a run—with the promise of more to follow.

It is just the right moment for Hubbell to casually but knowingly observe, "The game's just now getting interesting."

Jean Dubuc

Cappy Gagnon

Jean Dubuc's life and athletic career are not easy to summarize in a short essay. He was a versatile baseball player as well as a star college basketball player. He also played a significant role in professional hockey. He had a distinguished career as a minor league baseball manager and big league scout, signing one of baseball's all-time greats. Sadly, although universally considered to be a fine gentleman, he was also a footnote in the biggest scandal in baseball history.

The Jean Dubuc story began in St. Johnsbury, Vermont, where he was born September 29, 1887. His family owned a construction company that specialized in building churches, so Jean traveled throughout New England during his youth, playing ball in every state except Maine. In 1899 he entered the Seminary of St. Theresa in Montreal. He enrolled at Holy Cross in 1904, spending a year and a half there. He was not permitted to pitch for the Crusaders because he was considered too young at fifteen (he was in their prep program). In the Spring of 1906 he moved to St. Michaels (Winooski, Vermont), pitching for the college team.

In the fall Dubuc enrolled at the University of Notre Dame where his first athletic experience was as a starting forward on the varsity basketball team. The following spring, Dubuc contributed a 5-1 pitching record to ND's 21-2 baseball season. His only loss was 2-1, to Minnesota. Dubuc could hardly be blamed for the defeat as he gave up only one hit and one walk,

Cappy Gagnon, *president of SABR in 1984 and 1985, is a native of Gloucester, Massachusetts. He apologizes for the excessive mentions of athletes named Gagnon. Cappy's grandfather grew up in Fall River, Massachusetts, and knew Dubuc as a youth.*

while striking out 16 and getting three hits of his own! After the college season, Dubuc played semipro ball for the Independents and the Benedict and Burnham team in Waterbury, Connecticut.

The following year the Irish posted a 20-1 mark, with Dubuc upping his record to 9-1. His only loss came to the University of Vermont, 6-3, on May 19. Vermont was led by third baseman Larry Gardner and pitcher Ray Collins. Notre Dame has had very few varsity athletes from Vermont, so it was ironic that one of its greatest athletes would be from the Green Mountain state and he would absorb the only loss the best team in its history would receive, in his home state. This intersectional travel preceded by five years Notre Dame's football team going east to play the Cadets of West Point. Until that famous, Knute Rockne-led upset, the Notre Dame baseball team was far more prominent than the gridiron squad.

To the bigs—Dubuc intended to return to Notre Dame for the 1909 season, but a Chicago episode changed those plans. For the first two decades of this century, Chicago semipro baseball was the best in the country. Notre Dame baseball players were often brought in as "ringers." Dubuc adopted the alias of "Williams" to pitch for the White Rocks after the conclusion of his 1908 season.

Unfortunately, the ruse became widely known, and Notre Dame ruled its best pitcher ineligible for further athletic competition. Dubuc's two-year 14-2 college record included seven shutouts. Seven major league teams offered contracts. He accepted the offer of the Cincinnati Reds. The Reds were so pleased with Dubuc that the following year they sent scout Louis Heilbroner to Notre Dame with instructions to "find another Dubuc."

Jean spent two years with the Reds, winning 7 and losing 11. He lost a three-hitter and a four-hitter in September of 1908. He beat Iron Man McGinnity on September 25, as the Giants moved toward the pennant. His final game was a loss to Ed Reulbach. Reulbach had also attended Notre Dame, had played semipro under aliases, and had a Vermont connection, finishing his college career with the University of Vermont in 1905.

Dubuc accompanied the Cincinnati team to Cuba in the off-season, winning three of four games. For the year, he won more than 20 games as a collegian, semipro, and big leaguer. Dubuc caught malaria and missed most of the 1909 season. He was sent to Buffalo for the 1910 season, where he pitched poorly at first, earning his release and a transfer to Montreal. Clark Griffith later admitted that dropping Dubuc was a "big blunder."

Montreal was a perfect location for the French-speaking Dubuc. He went 21-11 in 1911 and opened a successful business, the Palace Bowling Alley and Pool Room. He had friends on the Montreal club. His catcher was Harry Curtis and the second best pitcher on the 1911 Montreal team was Billy Burke (16-17). Like Dubuc, both of these men were from New England and had attended Notre Dame. Curtis caught for ND in 1907 and coached the team in 1908 and 1909. Burke was the star pitcher of the 1909 team.

To the American League—In the off-season the Detroit Tigers purchased Dubuc's contract. On January 20, 1912, Dubuc wrote Frank Navin a letter declining his contract offer. Dubuc pointed out that the Tigers were offering him only $2,250 for seven months when he had made $2,196.68 for five months. He also pointed out that his business was doing well and he would have to "hire a good man at a substantial salary" to take his place if he left Montreal. Dubuc countered Navin with a choice of increasing his offer to $2,800 or permitting him to buy out his own contract for $1,500. The salary outcome is unknown, but Jean began a five-year stay in Detroit in the spring of 1912.

He was an instant star for the 1912 Tigers, winning 17 while losing only 10, with an 11-game winning streak. On July 6, he pitched a one-hitter against the White Sox, with Buck Weaver getting the only hit. A month later he two-hit the Yankees. His eleventh consecutive win was against Connie Mack's Athletics. He went 16-14 in 1913, losing a two-hitter in July and winning a two-hitter in September. On September 22, A's Hall of Famers Eddie Plank and Herb Pennock combined to defeat Dubuc, 1-0, to cinch the pennant on their way to a World Championship.

After the 1912 season, Dubuc had another bargaining ploy up his sleeve for Navin. He reported in November that the Paris Club of the French Union Base Ball League had offered him a $3,000 increase to be player-coach for a term of five years. The Philadelphia *North American* reported that Dubuc was one of the few diamond stars who could say "work the corners...in the language of the frog absorber."

On January 20, 1913, the Detroit papers reported that Dubuc had spurned Navin's offer of $4,000. The article also reported that Dubuc was playing hockey in Montreal and intended to coach the Notre Dame baseball team in the spring. Navin said: "The Detroit club is not a mint...the salaries our stars are trying to get from us are entirely out of the question."

Many stories were written about Dubuc's marvelous pitching that year. F. C. Lane, editor of *Baseball Magazine* called him "the Slow Ball Wizard" for his mastery of the off-speed pitch. "He is without question the greatest master of this difficult art since Mathewson discovered the secret of his fadeaway." The November 1913 issue of *Baseball Magazine* featured a picture of Dubuc, posed in a tee shirt in his pitching motion. The photo revealed the "tremendous muscular development" of his pitching arm. Ty Cobb also spoke about Dubuc's pitching specialty in his 1914 book, *Busting 'Em*: "Home Run Baker has great trouble in hitting Dubuc...because he is a slow ball pitcher."

Dubuc was frequently used as a pinch hitter in the majors. He was mediocre (16-93) in that role. His batting figures while pitching were impressive (134-559, .240). Manager Ty Cobb used Dubuc in the outfield on five occasions in 1912 and 1913. He hit four homers in the majors. On July 23, 1912, Dubuc was leadoff batter in right field. Ty Cobb was third batter in center, and Sam Crawford batted cleanup and played left.

Dubuc dropped to 13 wins in 1914, but garnered 17, with five shutouts, in 1915. After a 10-10 mark in 1916, he was released to Salt Lake City in January, 1917. He won 22 games, batting .279. The following year he was 10-10 with a .303 batting average. The Red Sox picked him up in July, 1918, when the Pacific Coast League suspended operations because of World War I. He pitched in only two late-season games. He had one World Series appearance as a pinch hitter.

John McGraw acquired Dubuc for the 1919 New York Giants. Dubuc pitched in 36 games for the Giants, 31 in relief, which led the league. He won six, lost four and saved three games (a high total for that era). His ERA was 2.66. He allowed only 119 hits in 132 innings.

On October 10 the Giants went to St. Johnsbury, Vermont to take on a team of local players. Dubuc got the 10-4 win for the Giants against his birth city, defeating Dana Fillingim of the Boston Braves who was loaned to the locals for the game.

Dubuc signed with the American Association Toldeo

Mud Hens for 1920, as a third baseman, outfielder, pitcher, and first baseman. He hit .292, won nine games, had a 2.72 ERA, and served as team captain and assistant manager. Roger Bresnahan elevated him to manager at midseason.

In those pre-Marvin Miller days, it was very common for major league team owners to schedule revenue-producing exhibition games on off days. On September 15, 1920 the Yankees played an exhibition in Toledo. Babe Ruth hit two homers for six RBIs, but Dubuc came in to pitch a scoreless 10th and then singled in the winning run, much to the pleasure of nearly 12,000 fans.

Tarred with the Black Sox brush—Eight days later Rube Benton testified before the Chicago Grand Jury investigating the 1919 World Series. He was asked if he had seen a telegram indicating that the Series was fixed. "Yes, I did,"was his answer. "I don't know who sent it, but it came to Jean Dubuc, who was barnstorming with us. It simply said: 'Bet on the Cincinnati team today.' I suppose it came from Bill Burns who had been close to Dubuc a few weeks before the series when both were living at the Ansonia Hotel in New York City. Chase was getting telegrams, lots of them, just before and during the World Series…I am sure Hal was betting heavily on Cincinnati. I couldn't go on the witness stand and swear to it, but it is my belief he won as much as $20,000 on the Series."

On November 11, 1920, *The Sporting News* published an article entitled "Why Dubuc was Dropped." In the

Transcendental Graphics

article John McGraw was quoted as saying that he dropped Dubuc from the Giants after the 1919 season because Dubuc "constantly associated" with Bill Burns. According to McGraw, Burns and Hal Chase had something to do with the Giants' failure to beat the Reds in 1919. Some sources indicate that Dubuc was banned from baseball for this "guilty knowledge." This was clearly not true as his later career in the minor leagues and services as a major league coach and scout would attest.

Back to the bushes—In 1921 Dubuc played in two semipro leagues in Montreal, the Atwater Park Twi-Light League and the Montreal City Baseball League. League totals were not recorded, but Dubuc hit .386 and posted a 17-8 pitching ledger in 47 games for which box scores could be located. On July 29, 1921, he hit two home runs off pitcher Green of the New York (Colored) Red Sox. There were several former big leaguers in this League including Chick Gagnon, Ivy Wingo, Del Bissonette, and Stuffy McInnis, of Gloucester, Massachusetts.

A February 16, 1922, "Caught on the Fly" column in *The Sporting News* reported: "There is astounding news from Syracuse that Landgraf plans to take on Jean Dubuc, former major leaguer, and later with Toledo, from which club he drew his walking papers because he was supposed to know too much about throwing of 1919 World Series."

Dubuc won only eight of his 17 decisions, but hit .351, playing all over the field. The following year he won five of seven decisions while hitting .237, playing mostly in the outfield.

Dubuc returned to Canada for 1924, serving as manager, outfielder, and pitcher for the Ottawa team of the Quebec-Ontario-Vermont League and also serving as a special assistant to the league president. The *Spalding Guide* reported that Dubuc was responsible for securing "many players...who have perfected their play by gaining the experience of his career in the states." His pitching mark was 2-2 and he hit .286, playing in 43 games.

For 1925, Dubuc was playing manager with the Manchester Blue Sox of the Boston Twilight League. The first half-season featured 13 teams, with the Nashua Millionaires posting the best record. They were managed by Tom Whelan, their third baseman. (When facing Whelan, Dubuc was once again around a fellow New Englander who had played in the majors after attending Notre Dame.) The second half-season featured ten teams. Dubuc led the Queen City to the second-half title, playing right field when not pitching. Nashua won the championship series. There were many big leaguers in the Bos-Twi including Gagnon, Jocko Conlan, Jeff Tesreau, Leon Cadore, and Otto Miller.

Dubuc's last year as a player was 1926, when he served as playing manager of Manchester of the New England League. In limited action he hit .311 and won two of four decisions. Clyde Sukeforth caught Dubuc. Fifty-six years later Sukeforth remembered Dubuc as being the team's best pitcher at age 37. "It was a pleasure to catch him. Marvelous control, constantly changing speeds. As a kid, I read about his 'slow ball' and on occasions it was very slow but it was thrown for effect, not to be hit. To a great extent he was responsible for present-day pitching, changing speeds. Previously it was pretty much power, everything thrown hard."

Coaching and scouting—Following the 1926 season, Dubuc was hired by Brown University as baseball coach. He also coached the Brown hockey team in both 1928 and 1929. Dubuc was again hired by Frank Navin, in January of 1928, to serve as the Tigers' eastern representative, scouting players, primarily among the eastern colleges. He was paid $1,200 and expenses for the season with the understanding that he would receive a "suitable bonus" if he "picked up someone that

was promising and of any use to us."

Dubuc succeeded magnificently in that mission, as attested by a September 11, 1929, letter from Navin enclosing a check for $6,000 "payable to you as agent...in the Greenberg matter." Navin had earlier written Dubuc on August 29, "You have told me so much about Greenburg [sic], I am quite enthused about him and hope you will be able to get him."

Greenberg's signing was said to have caused great angst for Paul Krichell, superscout of the Yankees. Krichell wanted the hometown Greenberg for his attraction as a Jewish idol in New York as much as for his powerful slugging. There was a story that Krichell spent more than a year visiting the Greenbergs and eating "Yiddish food." He later was quoted as saying, "in stepped Jean Dubuc...who called at the Greenberg house, bringing along his own ham sandwich, and signed up Hank right under the very shadow of Yankee Stadium."

Dubuc had an advantage, because Greenberg did not want to sign with a team that already had Lou Gehrig at the initial sack. Fifty-three years later, Hall of Famer Greenberg remembered Dubuc as "a perfect gentleman, well-educated, and married to a lovely lady."

Dubuc also signed Birdie Tebbetts and Gene Desautels among others. Dubuc and Roger Bresnahan were hired as Detroit Tigers coaches for the 1931 season, reuniting the duo who led the 1920 Mud Hens. They were released prior to the 1932 season.

Dubuc introduced professional hockey to Rhode Island in 1932. He managed the Rhode Island Reds of the Canadian American Hockey League for the next thirteen years, winning five League titles. Among his talented players was the legendary Johnny "Black Cat" Gagnon, who went on to fame with the Montreal Canadiens. Gagnon recalled Dubuc as "a soft-spoken man and fine gentleman."

In 1934 Dubuc became owner and manager of the New Bedford team of the Northeastern (formerly New England) League. He received a lifetime pass from National League President Ford Frick in 1935 with a personal note: "It is gratifying to see that your fine sportsmanship in baseball has carried along into your later career."

Dubuc coached Burlington (Vermont) of the outlaw Northern League in 1936. He worked twenty years as a printer's ink salesman before retiring to Florida. He passed away on August 28, 1958, in Fort Myers.

The First Charley Horse

Peter Morris

The origins of the term "charley horse" have baffled and fascinated word lovers for generations, and while many theories have been advanced, no one has ever been able to establish where it came from. The Oxford English Dictionary simply lists it as "origin unknown," while Paul Dickson's *Baseball Dictionary* cites a wide variety of contradictory theories, but reaches no conclusion. More recently, Gerald Cohen has attempted to sort through the maze of legends surrounding the term. Building upon the work of Dickson and Cohen, I believe I can shed some light on the term's origins.

Of the many theories about "charley horse," the most credible ones associate it with either the Chicago White Stockings baseball team of the 1880s or the Baltimore team of the 1890s. Since there are at least a couple of citations of it in the late 1880s, the Baltimore theory can safely be eliminated. This leaves the Chicago team as the originator of the term, but at least four disparate accounts offer considerable differences in the details.

The notes of etymologist Peter Tamony indicate, "When George Gore hit what should have been an inside-the-park homer and strained a thigh muscle rounding second, so that he had to limp into third, Billy [Sunday] cried, 'Here comes the Charley horse.'" Unfortunately, neither the date nor the source of this version are extant.

The earliest known account dates from June, 1889 and, as baseball-related notes frequently did in those days, it seems to have appeared in several newspapers. Here is the version that appeared in the Grand Rapids (Michigan) *Daily Democrat* on June 28, 1889:

> A Newcastleman gives the origin of Charley horse. "Years ago Joe Quest was employed as an apprentice in the machine shop of Quest & Shaw in Newcastle [Pennsylvania], his father, who was one of the proprietors of the firm, had an old white horse by the name of Charley. Doing usage in pulling heavy loads had stiffened the animal's legs so that he walked as if troubled with strained tendons. Afterwards, when Quest became a member of the Chicago club, he was troubled, with others, with a peculiar stiffness of the legs, which brought to his mind the ailment of the old white horse Charley. Joe said that the ball players troubled with the ailment hobbled exactly as did the old horse, and as no one seemed to know exactly what the trouble was, Quest dubbed it 'Charley horse.' The name has spread until today it has become part of the language of the national game."

A virtually identical account appeared in the Cincinnati *Enquirer* two days later.

The third account comes from the July 10, 1898, issue of the Bay City (Michigan) *Tribune*, and is credited to Mike Joyce, who had recently succeeded Adrian "Pop" Anson as New York manager. According to Joyce's account:

> "Mike Kelly was the author of the expression "Charley horse." In the 80s, when Kel was

Peter Morris *has been a baseball fan since he was four. Before that he just loafed.*

with the Chicago Whites, he had a friend who owned a string of race horses. In the stable was an old bread winner named Charley. White was the name of the owner. He entered Charley in a selling race one day and tipped Kel to play the animal. Charley went to the post as long as 20 to 1, and he was hammered down to even money. He led into the stretch, stumbled and fell, and his fall cremated a hundred of Kel's money. For a year after Charley took that twister in the stretch that cremated Kel's coin White told Kel of Charley's hind leg. "If that Charley horse of mine hadn't taken a crimp in his leg the bookies wouldn't have taken that crimp in your roll, eh Kel?" was White's lament. Kel applied the word Charley horse as the name for a strained muscle in a ball player's shaft.

In 1906 the first account attributed to someone who claimed to have witnessed the events appeared. According to the September 9, 1906, issue of the *World*, a New York City newspaper, Hugh Nicol stated, "It was coined by Joe Quest back in the summer of '82, when I was playing with the Chicago team." He goes on to recount how most of the members of the Chicago team took advantage of an off-day to travel to a southside Chicago race track, and all but Quest bet on a horse named Charley which ran to an early lead but then pulled up lame. Quest had been mercilessly kidded for not backing the horse and now got even with the rest, yelling "Look at your old Charley horse now." Then, according to Nicol:

It was during the progress of the game the next day that the term came to be applied to ball players. We were hooked up with New York on the old lake front grounds. Corcoran and Kelly were working. Captain Anson was on first. Quest, Burns and Williamson were playing the infield, and Flint, Gore and myself were in the outfield. We had the Giants 3-1 and were at bat. Quest was down the left coach line and was a good coacher. Gore had rapped out a single and Williamson was up. He was a pretty sure hitter, but Gore was a good sprinter and Quest figured he could do the trip to second and he sent him away. About half way down Gore stepped into a pocket and sprung a strain, just the way the racing pony had the day before, and Quest sang out "There's your old Charley horse—he'd have made it all right if it hadn't been for that old Charley horse." Gore was nailed, but the term stuck. He had the "Charley horse" for a couple of weeks afterward and it's been called by that name ever

since.

It should be noted that Nicol's version is incorrect in at least one detail: there was no New York team in the league in either 1881 or 1882, the only years Nicol played for Chicago, so he was obviously mistaken about the team Chicago was playing.

Which version is true?—This superabundance of accounts poses quite a conundrum. Was Charley a racehorse or a workhorse from Joe Quest's father's shop? Was the term coined at the ballpark or at the racetrack? Who coined it—Quest, Kelly, or Sunday? There seems little reason to credit one account over the others. The 1889 version is the earliest but gives no source. The 1897 version has a source but it's a secondhand one. And the 1906 version does have a first-hand source but is at a sufficient remove that details may have been misremembered, as is suggested by the mistake about the opposition.

The obvious path to enlightenment lay in discovering the ballgame that coincided with the one described by Nicol. I believe that the game in question took place on August 23, 1881. In the Chicago-Detroit game on that date, pitcher Fred Goldsmith pitched the first two innings but then, while running from first to second, twisted his ankle and had to leave the game. (Larry Corcoran, who had been taking tickets that day, came in to relieve Goldsmith.) The Chicago *Times* wrote the next day that Goldsmith "'pulled up lame,' to use a turf expression."

Joe Quest missed that game as well, presumably due to an illness reported in the Chicago papers a couple of days earlier, and was coaching at third when Goldsmith's injury occurred, which corresponds to Nicol's account. Nicol was playing second base that day in Quest's absence. At the same time, George Gore was suffering from a similar injury. In the game the day before Goldsmith's injury, Gore had hit what should have been a triple but was only able to make first on it.

Two days later, the *Times* wrote that Gore "has been hobbling considerably of late" and was "dead lame." Another Chicago paper wrote on the same day that Gore, "who occupied his customary position in center field, was not in any sort of condition to play." Consequently, he "grossly misjudged and then helplessly limped after" what should have been a routine fly ball. Notes for several days after this refer to his continued lameness.

The confluence of the leg injuries to Goldsmith and Gore satisfies the description of the 1889 account that "when Quest became a member of the Chicago club, he was troubled, with others, with a peculiar stiffness of the legs." Quest was also out at the same time, although the only explanation of his injury that I can find attributes his absence to illness. I have searched in vain for an account of how and when Gore suffered his injury. If Gore did injure himself running the bases, no account of the event appears to have made any extant newspaper.

While this pinpointing of the date of the game answers some questions, it does not offer a definitive answer to the question of which story of the origin of charley horse we should credit. It does, however, allow some informed speculation. In the absence of a description of Gore suffering an on-the-field injury, it seems most likely that Nicol's account conflates the Goldsmith injury with the similar one to Gore which left him limping for over a week. Nicol's account contains far too many specifics for so belated an account. It's hard to see how or why he would remember what the score was or who was pitching that day. Since he had been wrong about the opponent, it seems reasonable to think he was also wrong about who the baserunner was.

More difficult to reconcile are the differing versions of who Charley was. But it seems possible that there is at least some grain of truth in apparently contradictory ones. The Kelly/Nicol version that Charley was a race-horse seems unlikely, but it seems reasonable to assume that there was a racehorse, whose name has been lost to time, who had that calamity befall him while the Chicago players were watching. If Quest compared the racehorse to "Charley the horse," it is easy to see how Charley replaced the horse's original name in the memories of Kelly and Nicol.

But another possibility exists. At least three sources suggest that "Charley horse" may have existed as a slang term prior to 1881, meaning a broken down old horse. If so, Quest's reference to his father's work-horse was probably as "our old Charley horse," not to Charley the horse. And, presumably some of the other players understood the reference, while others thought he was simply referring to the name of the horse. This confusion no doubt added to the murkiness which has for so long enveloped the origins of the term.

So the next time you hear someone complain of a "charley horse," you can tell them about the Chicago ballplayers' fateful trip to the racetrack, the injuries to Goldsmith and Gore, and the old workhorse in Samuel Quest's shop, all of which played their roles in the birth of this term.

Motivation and perspective

Bison Slugger Rapp, Pinned By German Fire,
Vowed He'd Learn To Hit Lefties If Spared
(The Sporting News, *August 28, 1948.*)

Game Aims At Total Take Of $100,000,000 In 1948
Based on the 1947 attendance, when the turnstile take was 60,810,645, roughly divided 20,000,000 in the majors and 40,000,000 in the minors, the total gate receipts will approximate $65,000,000—$33,000,000 in the majors and $32,000,000 in the minors. An added $32,500,000 from concessions will boost the amount for the season to $97,500,000, while the sale of radio, television and other privileges, amounting to some $2,500,000, will bring the grand total to approximately $100,000,000. (The Sporting News, *April 21, 1948.*)

Indians' Home-Road Draw Topped Five Million In 1948
...Numerous oddities are revealed by the breakdown of Cleveland attendance figures. Chief among these is that the Browns played to 367,763 paid in Cleveland, while the club's entire season draw in St. Louis was only 335,564. (The Sporting News, *November 17, 1948.*)

—Andy Moursund

Babe's Banyan Tree Grows in Hawaii

Frank Ardolino

Everything about Babe Ruth was big: his home runs, his statistics, his appetites, his paunch as he got older, his zest for life, and his ability to generate enthusiasm in his many fans. As a result, Ruth has gained a mythic, almost spiritual dimension, which has been compared to Elvis Presley's posthumous presence as the "King." Both of these figures were so much larger-than-life that they still seem alive.

As part of his continuing legacy, the places Ruth is associated with have been endowed with memorial importance. His birthplace in Baltimore has become a popular museum, and the modern house on the site of his home in Sudbury, Massachusetts, "Home Plate Farm," where he lived with his first wife Helen in 1916, has a plaque commemorating his residence there. Three of the Babe's earliest and most prodigious homers are memorialized by plaques in Fayetteville, North Carolina (March 7, 1914); Toronto, Canada (September 5, 1914), and Tampa, Florida (April 4, 1919). Finally, Yankee Stadium is known as the "House that Ruth Built," and behind the left field wall is Monument Park, which contains a Ruth monument among the surrounding tributes to other Yankee immortals.

But all of these memorials are man-made and have been created by other people, not the Babe. In Hilo, Hawaii, there is a living monument that he began himself when he planted a young banyan sapling during a two-week barnstorming tour of the islands of Oahu and Hawaii in 1933. (Which I wrote about in "Sluggers in Paradise," *National Pastime* 12, 1992).

On October 19, 1933, Babe Ruth, accompanied by wife Claire and daughter Julia, arrived in Honolulu to play two exhibition games and to engage in a series of lectures, dinners, golf exhibitions, and autograph sessions. Herb Hunter, the baseball impresario who organized the trip, also planned to take him to Japan to play exhibition games after the completion of his stay in Hawaii. But this deal fell through and only Hunter and his wife subsequently travelled to Tokyo for three days on a "secret mission" known to himself alone.

Babe was guaranteed $10,000 for his two Oahu games, but Hunter claimed that he made only $4,000 in gate receipts, and had lost money. He asked Babe to go to Hilo on the island of Hawaii for another exhibition game on which they would split the gate, and the Babe agreed. The people of Hilo were overjoyed to welcome the Babe as the first major leaguer to visit their town, although some expressed incredulity at his fee for the two games in Honolulu, believing that as a high-salaried professional he did not need the money.

Ruth sailed with his family and the sports editors of the two local papers on the evening of Friday, October 27, and arrived in Hilo the next morning. He was greeted by 3,000 adoring fans at the Kuhio Wharf, and thousands more lined the path of his motorcade up King Kamehameha Avenue to Mooheau Park. Dressed resplendently in golf knickers and a blue serge sport coat, Ruth, as in Honolulu, was treated like visiting roy-

Frank Ardolino *is a professor of English at the University of Hawaii who has written articles on the history of baseball in Hawaii.*

alty by the people of Hilo. Babe and his family were decked with pansy leis, and he received a large silver key to the city, inscribed, "Aloha from the Hilo baseball league," and a special koa bat. After the ceremony at the park, he visited Volcano House, golfed at the Hilo Country Club, and enjoyed a gala banquet at the Seaside Club. In his after-dinner speech, he called Hawaii "God's Paradise on Earth," and declared that "It doesn't matter whether we're Hawaiians, Japanese, Americans or what not. We enter this world as persons, as individuals, and we are all brothers under the skin."

On Sunday October 29, "one of the outstanding events in the history of the Big Island" culminated in the game at Hoolulu Park with Ruth playing on an all-star contingent composed of twenty-two players from three teams against Nobuo Maruyama's champion Waiakea Pirates. The Pirates' pitcher was eighteen-year-old Futoshi "Taffy" Okamura, who has toured Hawaii bookstores regaling audiences with his recollections of pitching against the great Bambino. Admission prices were $1.50 for reserved seats, $1.10 general admission, 55 cents for children 15 or older, and 25 cents for those under 15. Babe gave hitting tips during batting practice, and any balls he hit over the heads of the outfielders, who were stationed about 275 to 300 feet out, were fought over by crowds of kids lining the outfield. During the game, Babe hit two mighty clouts, one of which sailed beyond the line of cars parked some 400 feet from home plate. Overall, he went 3-5, played right field, first base, pitched, and made some great plays, all of which was thoroughly enjoyed by the crowd of around 2,000 people. However, despite his heroics, the Babe's team lost, 7-6.

After the game, Babe participated in a banyan tree planting ceremony on Banyan Drive, a graceful three-quarter-mile stretch of land next to Hilo Bay. In 1933, famous people were enlisted to plant banyan saplings, and the first trees had been planted on October 14 and 24 by Cecil B. DeMille, his wife Mary Bland, Leo Carillo, William Gargan, Herbert Marshall, and Edna Best Marshall, who were in Hilo filming *Four Frightened People* (1934). A total of 53 trees were planted (47 survive) between 1933 and 1972 by such celebrities as Franklin Roosevelt, Amelia Earhart, James Farley, Fannie Hurst, and Richard Nixon and his wife Pat.

The Babe planted a Chinese banyan tree (*ficus retusa*), which develops small, thick, deep-green leaves that form a dense umbrella-like spread. The outstanding characteristic of the banyan tree is that its roots grow down from the branches into the ground eventually forming new trunks which thus provide further support. Despite their density and size, banyans can also look delicate. Today, Babe's bountiful banyan stands proudly in front of the Hilo Hawaiian Hotel surrounded by red ginger and marked with the name plaque of George Herman "Babe" Ruth.

University of Hawaii, Hilo

Baseball and Fidel Castro

Peter C. Bjarkman

Don Hoak didn't exactly create the myth of Fidel Castro the baseball pitcher. Nonetheless the light-hitting infielder did contribute mightily to the spread of one of balldom's most elaborate historical hoaxes. In June, 1964 (only weeks after his final release by the Phillies) he conspired with writer Myron Cope and the editors of *Sport* magazine to spin a fictionalized tale about facing the future Cuban revolutionary dictator in a highly improbable batter-hurler confrontation dripping with romance and patriotic fervor. The fabricated story became part of the "record" establishing Fidel Castro's impressive baseball credentials.

As Hoak tells the story, his unlikely and unscheduled at-bat against young Castro came during his own single season of Cuban winter league play, which the ex-big leaguer conveniently misremembers as the off-season of 1950-51. Hoak's account involves a Cuban League game between his own Cienfuegos ballclub and the Marianao team of legendary outfielder Pedro Formental. During the fifth inning and with Hoak occupying the batter's box, a spontaneous anti-Batista student demonstration suddenly broke out (Hoak reported such uprisings as all-too-regular occurrences during that 1951 season) with horns blaring, firecrackers exploding, and anti-Batista forces streaming directly onto the field of play.

Hoak's account continues with the student leader,

Peter C. Bjarkman *has traveled widely in Cuba to research baseball and is author of two forthcoming books on the subject. His earlier book,* Baseball with a Latin Beat: A History of the Latin American Game, *won a 1994 Macmillan-SABR Baseball Research Award. This article is a truncated version of a chapter for his forthcoming* Baseball and Castro's Revolution *for McFarland Publishers.*

Castro, marching to the mound, seizing the ball from an unresisting Marianao pitcher, and tossing several warm-up heaves to catcher Mike Guerra (a Washington big league veteran). Castro then barks orders for Hoak to assume his batting stance, the famed Cuban umpire Amado Maestri shrugs agreement, the American fouls off several wild but hard fastballs, the batter and umpire suddenly tire of the charade, and the bold Maestri finally orders the military police ("who were lazily enjoying the fun from the grandstand") to brandish their riot clubs and drive the student rabble from the field. Castro left the scene "like an impudent boy who has been cuffed by the teacher and sent to stand in the corner."

Hoak's details are charming, but they are suspicious from the opening sentence. Amateur baseball historian and Cuban native Everardo Santamarina pointed out in *The National Pastime*, No. 14 the implausibility of the Hoak account by stressing the inconsistencies related to Hoak's own winter league career, the errors in players' names, the confusion of both baseball and political details, and irreconcilable dates. Santamarina is on target especially in emphasizing that Umpire Maestri (not Cope's spelling of Miastri) was the island's best arbiter, a man of gigantic respectability and courage, who had once ejected Mexican League mogul Jorge Pasquel from the grounds in Mexico City. He would assuredly never have yielded control of the field for even an instant to troublemaking grandstand refugees of any ilk.

In short, the details of Hoak's story are so scrambled and outrageously inaccurate as to suggest that Hoak had indeed related his tale with tongue firmly planted in cheek. Nonetheless, his tale entered the baseball canon as fact. Santamarina astutely notes that "not even Babe Ruth's 'Called Shot' ever got such a free ride."

The gullible—What is most remarkable about Hoak's clearly apocryphal tale is the degree to which its easy acceptance over the years parallels dozens of other accounts concerning Fidel as a serious moundsman—even a talented pitching prospect of big league proportions. Most fans have run across the Fidel Castro baseball legend in one or another of its many familiar forms.

The story usually paints Fidel as a promising pitching talent who was scouted in the late '40s or early '50 and nearly signed by a number of big league clubs. The widely circulated version is the one that involves famed Clark Griffith "bird-dog" Joe Cambria and the Washington Senators, but the New York Giants and New York Yankees are often mentioned, too. It is a grand story, and has been swallowed hook, line and fastball. If only scouts had been more persistent—or if only Fidel's fastball had a wee more pop—the history of the Western Hemisphere would likely have been reshaped. Kevin Kerrane quotes Phillies Latin America scouting supervisor Ruben Amaro as observing that "Cambria could have changed history if he remembered that some pitchers mature late."

Even reputable baseball scholars, sports historians, and broadcasters have been taken in by the charming tale. Kerrane reports the Castro story in his landmark book on scouting (*Dollar Sign on the Muscle*, 1984) by noting (accurately if incompletely) that "at tryout camps Cambria twice rejected a young pitcher named Fidel Castro." Others have done the same and often with considerably less restraint. Oleksak and Oleksak (*Béisbol: Latin Americans and the Grand Old Game*, 1991) quote both Clark Griffith and Ruben Amaro on the legend of Fidel and Papa Joe, without much helpful detail but with implication that it is more fact than fiction.

The most egregious elaboration of the myth is found in a *Harper's* article (May 1989) penned by David Truby. Truby repeats the well-worn saw that a Castro signing might have truly changed history. He also reports that Horace Stoneham had his New York Giants hot on the trail of young Castro, who was "a star pitcher for the University of Havana baseball team," and quotes scouting reports from Pittsburgh's Howie Haak ("a good prospect because he could throw and think at the same time"), Giants Caribbean scout Alex Pompez ("throws a good ball, not always hard, but smart...he has good control and should be considered seriously"), and Cambria ("his fastball is not great but passable...he uses good curve variety...he also uses his head and can win that way for us, too"). No other known source reports such available scouting reports.

All additional commentary (especially that coming from Castro's biographers and from Cuba itself) indicates that as a schoolboy pitcher Castro threw hard but wildly (the exact opposite of these reports). And Castro never made the University of Havana team. His schoolboy baseball playing was restricted to 1945, as a high school senior. Truby caps his account with a report (supposedly from Stoneham's lips) that Pompez was authorized to offer a $5,000 bonus for signing, which Castro stunned Giants officials by rejecting. In fact, no Latin prospects were offered that kind of cash in 1950, and it's doubtful that a player who was 22 or 23 at the time would even have been considered.

To their credit, SABR's John Thorn and John Holway (*The Pitcher*, 1987) quote Tampa-based Cuban baseball historian Jorge Figueredo's rebuttal that "there is no truth to the oft-repeated story" of Castro's desirability to major league teams.

With the recent explosion in Latin American ball-playing talent (and thus interest in the history of the game played in Caribbean nations), the Castro ballplaying legend has taken on a commercial tone as well. One producer of replica Latin league hats recounts the glories of Fidel the pitcher and turns him into a regular in the Cuban winter leagues. The Blue Marlin Corporation website reports that their catalogue image of Castro shows him pitching for his famed military team ("The Barbudos") in the Cuban League, whereas the outing shown was in reality a staged onetime affair preceding a Sugar Kings International League game. ESPN recently produced a handsome promotional flyer that used Fidel's baseball "history" as part of the hook to sell their own televised games. A 1994 ESPN poster promoting Sunday night and Wednesday night telecasts features the same famed 1959 photo of Fidel delivering a pitch in his Barbudos uniform, with the bold-print headline "The All-American Game That Once Recruited Fidel Castro."

One of the more interesting promotions of the Fidel ballplayer myth comes with a Eugene McCarthy essay in *Elysian Fields Quarterly* (reprinted from an editorial in *USA Today*, March 14, 1994). The ex-senator and former presidential candidate stumps for Fidel as the much-needed big league baseball commissioner ("what baseball most needs—an experienced dictator"). While McCarthy's proposal was tongue-in-cheek, he nonetheless buys into the myth of Fidel's ballplaying background ("Another prospect eyed by the Senators was a pitcher named Fidel Castro, who was rejected because scouts reported he didn't have a major-league fastball.") The journal's editors commissioned Andy Nelson to create a cover fantasy 1953 Topps baseball card of a bearded Castro in a Washington uniform.

A 1953 Topps card neatly fits the artist's purpose, since in that year Topps used just such painted portraits (mostly head portraits only). But of course

Castro in early-season 1953 was still an unbearded student about to launch his revolutionary career (not his ballplaying one) with an attack on the Moncada barracks in Santiago.

It ain't so—Despite all of this, the whole Castro pitching career is myth. Fidel was never a serious pitching prospect. He was never pursued by big league scouts or by Joe Cambria. (Cambria's modus operandi was to sign up every kid in Cuba with even passing promise and let the Washington spring training camp sort them out later—if Castro had any legitimate big league talent Cambria could hardly have missed him.) Baseball did not nearly turn aside the history of the Cuban Revolution and its global ramifications.

What are the facts surrounding Castro and baseball? The young Fidel, from his earliest years in Cuba's eastern province of Oriente, did have a passion for the game. Robert Quirk (*Fidel Castro*, 1993) reports on the youngster's apparent fascination with baseball, and especially his attraction to its central position of pitcher (the man in control). Widely available biographical accounts make it clear that young Fidel loved the chance to dominate in sports (as in all other schoolboy arenas) more than he loved the game itself. He organized an informal team as a youngster in his hometown of Birán when his wealthy father supplied equipment (Tad Szulc, *Fidel: A Critical Portrait*, 1986). When he and his team didn't win he simply packed up his father's equipment and went home. Fidel was never a team player or a true sportsman.

Fidel's baseball fantasies (like those of so many of us) were never matched by his talent. As a high school student Fidel played on the basketball team at Belén, the exclusive, private Havana Catholic school he attended during the years 1942-1945. He also pitched on the baseball squad as a senior, and he ran middle distances and high-jumped for the track team. He was also Ping Pong champion.

Biographer Quirk, whose exhaustive study is the most recent and one of the most scholarly in a long list of Fidel biographies published in both Spanish and English, reports on hearing numerous accounts that Fidel was selected Havana's schoolboy athlete of the year in 1945. Tirelessly pouring over every single daily issue of the Havana sports pages for that year, however, Quirk found not a single mention of Castro's name. (The outstanding schoolboy star of that season was Conrado Marrero, a pitcher who became legendary on Cuban diamonds of the late '40s and early '50s and actually played for the Washington Senators. Connie Marrero, ironically, appears on a real 1953 Topps card.)

Another substantial biographer, Peter G. Bourne (*Fidel*, 1988), acknowledges Castro's status as a top basketball player at Belén, and pinpoints his recognition as Havana's top schoolboy sportsman in his *junior* year. So Fidel wasn't a bad athlete. But Bourne emphasizes Fidel's penchant for using sports—as he used academics, the debate society, and student politics—as a method for proving he could excel in any endeavor imaginable. Fidel was so driven in this way that he once wagered a school chum he could ride his bicycle full speed into a brick wall. He did, and landed in the school infirmary for several weeks.

It is the Belén athletic successes that contain the hidden key to the legend of Fidel the baseball prospect. Joe Cambria was running his Washington Senators scouting activities from a Havana hotel (his part-time residence) in the mid-'40s, beating the bushes to seek out cheap Cuban talent and holding regular open try-out camps.

Fidel is reported by Bourne to have showed up at two of these camps between his junior and senior years. (Castro, in other words, sought out Cambria and the pro scouts and not vice versa.) No contract was ever offered, and as Bourne stresses, any offer would almost certainly have been rejected. Fidel was a privileged youth from a wealthy family and had prospects far more promising than playing professional baseball. There were no big bonus deals in the '40s. Cambria's mission for the penny-pinching Griffith was to find dirt-cheap talent among lower-class athletes desperate to sign for next to nothing. Fidel's own future was already set in law and politics. His interest in baseball was a diversion, not a dream of escape into big league glories and big-time money.

Fidel did play freshman basketball at the University of Havana, and he tried out—unsuccessfully—for the baseball team. It was evident to Fidel by college that he had little serious baseball talent. And his political activities from 1948 on left him almost no available time for any serious practice on the ballfield. While his numerous biographers cover every aspect of his life in painstaking detail, none mention any further tryouts for baseball scouts, any serious playing on organized teams—indeed any baseball activity at all until his renewed passion for the game as a dedicated fan after his successful rise to political power in January 1959. Quirk and Bourne alone among Castro biographers emphasize Fidel's ballplaying, and then only to report that baseball never quite measured up to basketball or track and field as an arena for him to display his athletic skill or his obsessive drive for success and power.

Szulc reports an interview in which Fidel expounded on the important symbolic values of his favorite schoolboy sport, basketball. Basketball, Fidel observed, could provide valued indirect training for revolutionary activity. It was a game that required strategic and tactical planning and overall cunning, plus speed and agility, the true elements of guerrilla warfare. Baseball, Fidel noted, held no value for a future revolutionary.

Most significantly, Szulc points out that Fidel's comments on this occasion came in a candid response in which he "emphatically denied" that he once envisioned a career for himself as a major league pitcher.

Perhaps the most balanced view of Fidel's ballplaying comes in a sixties-era book by American photojournalist Lee Lockwood (*Castro's Cuba, Cuba's Fidel*, 1967). The one reference to baseball in the 300-page tome is a two-page spread featuring photos of brother Raul batting ("a competent second baseman, he is the better hitter") and Fidel pitching ("Fidel has good control but not much stuff"). Both are dressed in ballcaps and informal gear. In an interview segment that follows, Fidel comments on his lifelong love for sports, emphasizing basketball, chess, deep-sea diving, and soccer as his lasting favorites. He stresses his high school prowess in basketball and track and field ("I never became a champion…but I didn't practice much."). But there is nary a mention of baseball.

Castro in flannel—The impetus for stories of Castro as serious ballplayer seem to flow as much from his later fascination with the game as they do from phony stories about a schoolboy prospect. There are reports of exhibition appearances at stadiums in Havana and elsewhere across Cuba during the first decade following the initial successes of the Cuban Revolution. The most renowned event was Fidel's single appearance on the mound in El Cerro Stadium wearing the uniform of his own pickup team, aptly named "Los Barbudos" ("The Bearded Ones"). Rarely, however, have the North American press or stateside baseball historians ever gotten the story quite straight.

The famed but little-understood Barbudos game took place in Havana on July 24, 1959, before a crowd of 25,000 "fanaticos," as a preliminary to an International League contest between the Rochester Red Wings and Havana Sugar Kings. A newspaper account in the Rochester *Democrat and Chronicle* is the source for the details of the evening's events and for the familiar Castro pitching photo found in the above-mentioned ESPN poster. Fidel is reported to have practiced all day in his hotel room for his two-inning stint for the Cuban Army team which faced a squad of military police. (He is also reported in this account to have been a onetime high-school pitcher and to have tried out for the college team, but no mention is made of any college competition or of interest among scouts in his moderate talents.) Castro pitched both innings and was captured on the mound in the several photos which would later become the only widely seen images of

The ace of the Barbudos in Havana's El Cerro Stadium, July 24, 1959.

Cuba's Maximum Leader turned baseball pitcher. The entire public impression of Fidel as moundsman is built upon these photographic images.

Fidel struck out two batters, one with the aid of the umpire on a call which had him dashing to the batter's box to shake hands with the cooperative ump. He is reported to have "needlessly but admirably" covered first on an infield grounder, to have bounced to short in his only turn at bat, and to have demonstrated surprisingly good mound style—"wild but fast, and with good motions." But the most memorable exercise of skill that evening was displayed by Major Camilo Cienfuegos, who originally was scheduled to hurl for the opposing squad. "I never oppose Fidel in anything, including baseball," quipped the astute Cienfuegos, who then donned catcher's gear and went behind the plate to become his leader's batterymate.

Castro's appearance with the Barbudos team was strictly a onetime event. "El Jefe" did not pitch regularly with any such team in the Cuban League, as reported by Blue Marlin in their published catalogues. But Fidel did continue over the next decade and more to play informally in pickup games within his inner circle of revolutionary colleagues. Quirk reports that

Camilo Cienfuegos was able to maintain favor with Fidel for a time largely because of his ballplaying skills. (The ever-popular Major Cienfuegos became a liability, however, within a year of the revolutionary takeover, and soon disappeared under mysterious circumstances on a solo flight from Camaguey to Havana in late 1959.) Even Che Guevara (an Argentine, who preferred soccer) and brother Raul (who showed little athletic skill or interest to match Fidel's) were occasionally photographed in military fatigues taking their enthusiastic cuts during exhibitions before Cuban League games of the early '60s. Fidel himself made exhibition appearances in Havana, Matanzas, and elsewhere around the island.

Camilo Cienfuegos, right, consults with his batterymate. There was never any doubt who called the game.

Baseball, Fidel, and Cuba—Fidel might not have been a crack player, but his influence on Cuban baseball was enormous. The decision to strip Cuba of its International League franchise in July, 1960, as much as anything else in the early stages of the Cuban Revolutionary regime, may have soured Castro on the United States. Fidel reinstituted baseball in 1962 as a strictly amateur affair, and under his revolutionary government a new "anti-professional" baseball spirit came to dominate.

The Cuban regime found in baseball its one proven arena for international triumphs. For thirty-five years Cuban teams have dominated world amateur competitions, and few other achievements of the Revolution have been as great a source of national identity and pride. In the astute words of historian Louis Pérez, under Castro's regime, baseball—the quintessential American game—has most fully served the Cuban Revolution—the quintessential anti-American embodiment.

It is clear from the historical record that Fidel was an accomplished and enthusiastic athlete as a youngster. His biographers underscore his repeated use of schoolboy athletics to excel among fellow students. His strong identification with baseball after the 1959 Revolution was more than anything else an acknowledgment of his nation's national sport. It was also a calculated step toward using baseball as a means of besting the hated imperialists at their own game. And the Maximum Leader also saw baseball early on as an instrument of revolutionary politics—a means to build revolutionary spirit at home and to construct ongoing (and headline grabbing) international propaganda triumphs abroad.

Fidel and baseball have remained linked for the forty years of Castro's rule in Revolutionary Cuba. But it was only as dictator and Maximum Leader—not as legitimate ballplayer—that Fidel Castro emerged as one of the most remarkable figures of all Cuban baseball history. He was never Cuba's Walter Johnson or even its latter-day Dolf Luque; he was instead a cross between the mythic hero Abner Doubleday and the marketing genius A.G. Spalding. Without ever launching a serious fastball or swinging a potent bat, Castro—like Judge Landis north of the border a generation earlier—had a far greater impact on his nation's pastime than generations of leather-pounding, lumber-toting players.

See?

NEW YORK—Joe DiMaggio's fame doesn't stop at the U.S. border. Even Fidel Castro, the former baseball prospect turned Cuban dictator, is a big fan of the Yankee Clipper.

According to the New York Daily News, Castro recently revealed to a group of visiting Americans that he had always dreamed of owning DiMaggio's autograph.

When word made its way back to DiMaggio, the Hall of Famer was initially reluctant. But he relented and sent Castro a signed ball, which Castro received two weeks ago.

"He doesn't approve of Castro's politics," a friend of DiMaggio told the paper. "But he figured, if it helps relations between Cuba and the U.S., then OK." (Associated Press, April 1, 1998.)

Baseball's Intriguing Couple

Larry Bowman

In 1888, after only one year of marriage, the union between noted New York actress, Helen Dauvray, and John Montgomery Ward, the star shortstop of the New York Giants, began to deteriorate. Baseball fans knew Ward and Miss Dauvray well. He, of course, was one of the superstars of his era, and Miss Dauvray, who married Ward in October of 1887, earned baseball fans' admiration when she donated a silver cup estimated to be worth $500 as the trophy for the winner of the annual playoffs between the National League and the American Association.[1] Dauvray and Ward each enjoyed celebrity, and when they married their activities drew ample attention. The saga of their romance and the publicity it generated recalls another ill-fated marriage between an actress and a New York ballplayer in the 1950s.

John Montgomery Ward was one of the titans of baseball's early history. He came to the National League in 1878 as a pitcher for the Providence Grays and won 164 games before switching to the infield on a full-time basis. When he came to the New York Giants in 1884, Ward's arm was about finished, but he easily made the transition to shortstop and extended his career by another decade.[2] Ward was a unique player for his era. Ballplayers in the 1880s and 1890s were normally a rough and tumble lot; Ward was different. He graduated from Columbia University, earned a degree in law, allegedly spoke several languages, and reflected a more genteel manner than was common among his contemporaries. He organized the Brotherhood of Professional Ball Players in 1885, and served as its leader

during the great players' revolt in 1889 and 1890. He was a full-fledged celebrity in every respect.[3]

Helen, on the other hand, was largely unknown to the average baseball crank prior to her appearance in Ward's life. She had been born Helen Gibson in San Francisco, California, on February 14, 1859, and spent her earliest years in Virginia City, Nevada.[4] Her family eventually returned to San Francisco, where Helen embarked upon a career on the stage. She first appeared as Eva in "Uncle Tom's Cabin," and drew favorable attention from local critics. In 1870, after playing a series of child's roles in productions in San Francisco, the eleven-year old actress arrived in New York City with her family, and pursued her stage career. Billed as "Little Nell the California Diamond," Helen appeared in several productions.[5] Little Nell joined a touring company that traveled about the western United States and on to Australia. After reaching her early twenties, Helen moved to France, studied acting in Paris, became fluent in French, took on the stage name Dauvray, and appeared on the stage in Paris. Finally, in 1885 she returned to the United States to conquer the New York stage.

Upon her return to New York City, Helen won a role in the comedy "One of Our Girls" which proved to be her greatest triumph. She also became a producer, took a lease on the Lyceum Theatre, and briefly worked on and off the stage to promote her career,[6] earning herself in the process some notoriety in New York acting circles. She soon gave up on the business side and refocused her efforts on acting. She took a brief vacation to Europe in the summer of 1886, and returned to New York City reinvigorated and ready to

---

Larry Bowman *is a professor of history at the University of North Texas.*

resume her quest for fame and fortune as an actress.[7]

Ward and Helen—When Helen returned to the United States in 1886, the New York Giants were completing the club's third year in the National League. Even though they had usually been mired in the middle of the league standings, local baseball fans had quickly adopted them, and equally as quickly, the New York press (some things never change) heavily criticized them for failing to win the pennant.

As the team became more competitive it became stylish for members of the New York stage community to be seen at the Polo Grounds. James D. Hardy, Jr., in his *The New York Giants Base Ball Club* amply documents the growing affinity between the professional ballplayers and the actors and actresses of the city's theater society. Actors and actresses spent the afternoons at the ballpark, and players spent evenings in the theaters. Ward and Helen met sometime in 1886.

During the 1887 season Helen rarely missed a New York Giants' home game. She was always seated in the balcony of the grandstand next to the reporters' box, and she was usually accompanied by one of her several sisters and a brother.[8] Reporters further noticed that Miss Dauvray kept score during the game, and if she missed a play, she asked one of the reporters how he had scored the play. She clearly was a dedicated "crank." What reporters did not know was that, sometime in 1887, she and the Giants' shortstop had secretly become engaged to be married, although, according to her brother, Adolph Gibson, they believed that their respective careers and commitments demanded that they wait until 1888 to wed.[9]

Helen had a busy and not altogether pleasant year. In March, she returned to New York from appearances in the Midwest, and was followed by a stalker named Joe Golding. Golding, carrying a six-inch knife, was eventually arrested at 2:30 AM outside Helen's home at 49 Park Avenue. He was detained, questioned, and sent home to Chicago and never again troubled Dauvray, but the incident left Helen understandably unnerved.[10]

Soon after this unsettling event, Helen's name became associated with a minor scandal involving her first husband, Leonard Tracy, whom she had married in 1881 and divorced less than two years later. When Tracy was sued by an actress named Etellka Wardell, Helen's name arose in the legal proceedings. Wardell claimed she had lent Tracy $5,000 in 1880, when she believed she and Tracy would soon wed. Instead, Tracy married Dauvray, and Wardell claimed that she had been victimized. Even though Tracy had been out of Dauvray's life for several years, she was embarrassed by the sordid episode, and she wrote a letter to the New York *Times* disassociating herself from the quarrel.[11] Tracy eventually settled his dispute with Wardell, but it added to the stress Dauvray was feeling from the Golding situation.

These events contributed to a collapse of Helen's health, and in the spring of 1887, she canceled her professional engagements and retired to her home to recuperate. Although her health faltered, her interest in baseball and John Ward did not. She donated the Dauvray Cup, to be awarded each year to the victor in the championship playoffs between the pennant winners of the National League and the American Association. She continued to attend Giants' games at the Polo Grounds, and early in October of 1887 rumors of an impending wedding of Dauvray and Ward circulated among members of the New York press.

On the evening of October 11, a reporter for the *Times* called upon Miss Dauvray at her home and pointedly asked her to confirm or deny the rumor she was soon to wed John Montgomery Ward.[12] She denied the story, but the next morning she, her mother, a sister, and Ward left New York and traveled to Philadelphia where the party was joined by another of Miss Dauvray's sisters. Later that day, Dauvray and Ward were married. Why the pair was so coy remains unclear, and neither revealed why they chose a private ceremony in Philadelphia. Perhaps, like modern celebrities, they just wanted to avoid a circus atmosphere.

A few days after their wedding, Dauvary and Ward attended a World's Series game between the Detroit Wolverines and the St. Louis Browns, which was played in Philadelphia. They then departed for the West Coast on a wedding trip, certainly hoping to live happily ever after. It was not to be.

Strains—When the Dauvray-Ward marriage publicly faltered is apparent. What created their differences is not. In October of 1888, Ward and his New York Giants clinched the title of World's Championship of professional baseball in St. Louis against the American Association's Browns in a hard-fought and exciting series. Helen accompanied her husband to St. Louis to witness the final games of the series, and ostensibly to join him for the winter on a trip to Australia. Ward was scheduled to join Albert Goodwill Spalding's traveling baseball promotional show. Spalding, who was obsessed by the idea of sponsoring an exhibition tour of professional baseball in areas outside the United States, used his Chicago White Stockings and an all-star team of National League players headed by Ward to travel originally to Hawaii, Australia, and eventually on to Asia, Africa, and Europe, to play exhibition games to popularize the game around the world. It was an ambitious undertaking, and one that offered a good deal of excitement to all who participated. Ward was anxious to go, and Helen was originally expected to join him, but she abruptly left St. Louis and returned to New York City. She and John were separated until the following April when the teams returned home.

One factor that may have hastened the beginning of the end of the Wards' marriage was Helen's desire to renew her acting career. At the time of their wedding and on John's request, Helen announced her retirement from the stage, and for the next year she remained inactive as an actress.[13] Not long after arriving back in New York City, however, Helen resumed her life as an actress. (She remained intermittently active well past the turn of the century.) On Ward's return in April of 1889, Helen again announced she was leaving the stage to return to domestic life with her husband.[14] It didn't last. On May 1, 1890, Dauvray and Ward again separated.

Jessie McDermott—This time the catalyst seems to have been a woman named Jessie Dermot, who undoubtedly was a prime reason for most of the tension in the marriage. Jessie Dermot was born in Rockland, Maine, on February 5, 1868, where she lived until she moved to New York City in 1884 to live in the home of Laurence and Eliza Kiernan, who were friends of Jessie's family.[15] The Kiernans' house quartered several bachelor boarders, and Jessie, a beautiful young aspiring actress, attracted a good deal of attention. Among the gentlemen she met while living with the Kiernans was George McDermott, Mrs. Kiernan's brother. On December 1, 1884, Jessie, not quite seventeen, married him back in Rockland.[16]

McDermott, an attorney and a petty Tammany politician, made a good $2,500 salary as the City Marshall in charge of issuing licenses, collecting fees, and inspecting vendors' sites. He was a good deal older than Jessie, but he offered her a fairly comfortable lifestyle and entry into a society she at first found intriguing. McDermott's contacts with all manner of New York City enterprises led him to open a potentially lucrative law office in 1885. He and Jessie lived at 155 East 46th Street in what appeared to be marital concord. In fact, they regularly quarreled, McDermott became abusive, and Jessie barred him from her room.

At this point in late 1885 and early 1886, before Ward and Dauvray became attached to one another, Ward became an escort to Mrs. McDermott during her separation from her husband, who now followed her about the city. This led to an incident on a public street. Jessie's account of the episode declared that she was "walking on Broadway with a lady friend one day when I accidentally met Mr. John M. Ward who boarded at one time in the same house where I was, and I stopped to talk to him. My husband was following me, and while I was speaking with Mr. Ward he came up and attempted to strike Mr. Ward, whereupon Mr. Ward struck him in return. I got into a cab and drove home leaving my husband engaged in a scuffle with Mr. Ward on the sidewalk."[17] Shortly thereafter McDermott appeared, confronted her and struck her.

Jessie fled the city. Ward accompanied her back to Rockland where she wanted to spend some time with her family, avoid her husband, and gather her thoughts. I have found no conclusive evidence that the two were intimately involved, but the relationship caused a sensation among those who took notice of Ward's activities. Jessie returned briefly to New York, and then moved on to California late in 1886.[18]

The whole Ward and George McDermott story is a bizarre and mysterious one. They clashed on the street in 1886, but Ward's address in the autumn of 1887 just prior to the time he hastily departed with Helen to get married in Philadelphia, was 155 East 46th Street— McDermott's residence.[19] McDermott was quoted in the *Times* on October 13, 1887, the day after Ward and Dauvray were married, as saying:

> "I know Ward and I am not friendly to him. While living at my house he did something that led me to drive him from it. I was justified in what I did, but I do not care to reveal the cause. It was concerning a friend of mine, someone close to me, and when I meet with Mr. Ward, I shall settle with him. But this matter is wholly between him and me. I have not been seeking him to kill him as has been reported. I have no such purpose. If I had I should have achieved it before this. My grievance will keep, but there is no danger of bloodshed resulting from it."[20]

The *Times* added to the account that McDermott's words were calmer than his manner, and that his "... eyes flashed, his lips quivered, and he seemed to be laboring under suppressed excitement."[21]

Jessie McDermott returned to New York, probably in mid-1888, and from that point forward the relationship between Ward and Dauvray rapidly disintegrated.

On May 1, 1890, Jessie, who was in rehearsal for a play on the New York stage, petitioned for a divorce from George McDermott. The local press reported that she declared his gambling addiction had brought near ruin to her finances and that she sought no alimony, only her independence.[22] A reporter solicited a reaction to Jessie's suit from Dauvray at her suite in the Hotel Vendome. Helen became tearful and distracted, and later the same day, she and Ward signed an agreement to live apart.[23] After she and Ward reached an accord on another separation, Helen immediately went to Brooklyn and took a room in the Clarendon Hotel where she steadfastly refused to talk to anyone outside her family.

None of the contemporary accounts speculated why Helen became so upset. None mentioned or alluded to an untoward relationship between Ward and Jessie McDermott. But the message between the lines seems clear. To get away from all the tension she felt in New York City, Helen joined a company of actors engaged to make several appearances in England and departed the country later in 1890.

Ramifications—One can only speculate how the Wards' marital difficulties affected John. In 1890, as their ongoing quarrel reached a new level of intensity, Ward was in the midst of leading the players' revolt against the owners, and playing some of the best baseball of his career while managing the Brooklyn team in the Players' League. Mark Alvarez asserts that Ward proved, "a great organizer and an inspirational leader" at a time the major league players made a daring challenge to attempt to face down their greedy and dictatorial owners.[24] But it is tempting to speculate on the effect his private life had on his public role as the leader of the Brotherhood Rebellion. At the eleventh hour, with victory within the players' grasp, Ward seemed to lose focus, and Al Spalding stole victory from jaws of defeat for the National League.

After the heartbeaking defeat of the Players' League, Ward traveled to Great Britain, met with Helen in February and proposed another reconciliation. She thought it over for several days, agreed to accept his proposal, canceled her engagements, and returned with him to the United States.[25] But the couple soon separated again. On November 29, 1893, they were officially divorced.[26]

Afterwards—Ward continued his career as a player and a manager, remarried, established a successful law practice, lived out his life after baseball on Long Island, and died in 1925.[27] Dauvray pursued her career as an actress and also married again. Her third husband was Albert Gustavus Winterhalter, an officer in the United States Navy, who rose to the rank of admiral and commanded the American fleet in the Pacific during World War I. Helen made her permanent home in Washington, D.C., after she wed Winterhalter, and lived there until her death in 1923.[28]

Jessie McDermott changed her name to Maxine Elliott, and went on to considerable fame and fortune as an actress and owner of the Maxine Elliott Theatre in New York City. At the time of her death in 1940, her obituaries usually remarked on her stunning good looks as a young woman, and *Newsweek* observed that, "...she became the toast of America and Europe—for her beauty more than her acting."[29]

After she retired from the stage, Jessie Dermot/ McDermott/Maxine Elliott lived in her villa, Chateau de l'Horizon, in the south of France.[30] She maintained an opulent lifestyle in old age. Guests at her villa included such notables as the Duke and Duchess of Windsor, Winston Churchill, David Lloyd George, Charlie Chaplin, and assorted notables from the stage and the British aristocracy. After her death, the Aga Kahn purchased the villa. Aly Khan and his new bride, Rita Hayworth, lived there for a time.[31]

Notes

1. N. E. Young, President, National League to Helen Dauvray, June 1, 1887, in *The Sporting Life*, June 22, 1887, 1.

2. Mark Alvarez, "John Montgomery Ward," in Frederick Ivor- Campbell, Robert L. Tiemann, and Mark Rucker, eds., *Baseball First Stars*, (Cleveland: The Society for American Baseball Research, 1996), 167. Cited hereafter as Alvarez, "John Montgomery Ward."

3. James D. Hardy, Jr., *The New York Giants Base Ball Club: The Growth of a Team and A Sport, 1870 to 1900* (Jefferson, North Carolina: McFarland & Company, Inc., Publishers, 1996), 15-16. Cited hereafter as Hardy, *The New York Giants*.

4. James Grant Wilson and John Fiske, eds., *Appleton's Cyclopedia of American Biography* (New York: D. Appleton and Company, 1900), II, 80-81.

5. New York *Times*, January 4, 1885, 3.

6. Oral Cloud Sumner and Edwin M. Mims, Jr., *The American Stage* (New Haven: Yale University Press, 1929), 272. *The New York Clipper Annual for 1887* (New York: The Franklin Queens Publishing Company, 1887), 49.

7. *The Sporting News*, June 21, 1886, 4.

8. New York *Daily Tribune*, October 16, 1887, II.

9. New York *Times*, October 12, 1887, 4. *The Sporting Life*, October 19, 1887, 4.

10. New York *Times*, March 9, 1887, 8.

11. Helen Dauvray to the Editors of the New York *Times*, ibid. May 20, 1887, 8.

12. Ibid., October 12, 1887, 1.

13. *The Sporting Life*, October 19, 1887, 1.

14. New York *Times*, April 10, 1889, 8.

15. Diana Forbes-Robertson, *My Aunt Maxine: The Story of Maxine Elliott* (New York: The Viking Press, 1964), 47. Cited hereafter as Forbes-Robertson, *My Aunt Maxine*.

16. *The Sporting News*, May 10, 1890, 4.

17. *The Sporting News*, May 10, 1890, 4. Forbes-Robertson, *My Aunt Maxine*, 54-55. Robertson account has Ward exiting a shop on Broadway with Mrs. McDermott and makes no mention of a "lady friend."

18. Ibid.

19. New York *Times*, October 13, 1887, 5.

20. Ibid.

21. Ibid.

22. New York *Times*, May 1, 1890, 8.

23. *The Sporting News*, May 5, 1890, 5.

24. Alvarez, "John Montgomery Ward," 168.

25. Ibid. February 14, 1891, 4.

26. New York *Times*, November 30, 1893, 9. *The Sporting News*, December 2, 1893, 1.

27. New York *Times*, March 5, 1925, 17.

28. Washington *Post*, December 6, 1923, 5.

29. *Newsweek*, March 18, 1940, 15:8.

30. New York *Times*, March 7, 1940, 23. "Maxine Elliott," *Current Biography*, 1940, 277-79.

31. Forbes-Robertson, *My Aunt Maxine*, 8.

Nick Altrock

Jim Blenko

What would you get if you mixed the clowning of Max Patkin, the crafty southpaw pitching of Jimmy Key, and the organizational loyalty of Jimmie Reese with the endurance of ageless Minnie Minoso? The result of this unlikely baseball recipe might be something like Nick Altrock, a man who pitched, coached, clowned, and yes, drank his way through the major leagues for almost sixty years.

Like many players, Altrock followed an uncertain path to the majors. Born in 1876 in Cincinnati, he was trained in the shoemaking trade of his father. When it became obvious that the boy had a strong and unusually accurate left arm, he began to pursue a career as a professional pitcher. His first minor league appearances were in the Inter-State League before the turn of the century. In 1898, he pitched a few games for the National League team in Louisville, where his teammates included Tommy Leach and a young first baseman named Honus Wagner.

Altrock pitched rarely and ineffectively for Louisville and could not stay in the bigs. He spent the next four seasons pursuing wins and steady paychecks in the minors. This was the least secure period of Altrock's life. Years later, after his fortune had been secured, he recalled finishing the season with one Ohio team only to be told that no money remained in the team treasury for player salaries. Altrock bragged that he took the team uniforms and bats hostage until he was paid in full.

The young southpaw's quick-wittedness and talent became increasingly obvious. Pitching for the Los Angeles team of the Pacific Coast League, Altrock began one game by walking the leadoff man and promptly picking him off first. Lacking his usually excellent control, Altrock reportedly walked seven more batters during the game and picked off six of them. His move, described as a "near balk," would prove devastating through his career, and as late as 1965, a baseball writer would argue that Altrock had the best pickoff ever.[1] Altrock had more than just guile, however. After minor league stints in Grand Rapids, Binghamton, Los Angeles, and elsewhere, he won a whopping 28 games for Milwaukee in 1902 and was bought by the new Boston team in the American League.

The Hitless Wonders—Unable to crack a pitching staff that featured Cy Young and Big Bill Dinneen, Altrock was lucky enough to be traded to the Chicago White Sox in 1903. His greatest pitching triumphs would come pitching for the Sox and their owner Charles Comiskey. The year after the trade, Altrock suddenly emerged as an effective starting pitcher, going 62-39 while averaging more than 300 innings pitched per season, 1904-1906.

During his peak, Altrock displayed outstanding control. He did an excellent job of keeping runners off base, even for a pitcher in the Dead Ball Era. He also helped himself with both the great pickoff and a skillful glove. Although ninety seasons have passed, Altrock's number of chances fielded per game is still among the highest in major league history, suggesting that he induced a lot of ground balls and knew what to

Jim Blenko *has clowned but never coached at a baseball game. He is writing a dissertation on baseball fiction and will begin law school at the University of Chicago in the fall.*

do with the ball when it reached him.

Altrock's sudden effectiveness could not have been better timed. He was part of an excellent White Sox staff that also featured the underrated Doc White and a rising young pitcher named Ed Walsh. Riding largely on the shoulders of these three pitchers, the "Hitless Wonders" won the American League pennant in 1906 despite batting .230 as a team.

The Sox faced stiff opposition in what was then called the World's Series. The cross-town Cubs, proud possessors of a 116-36 regular season record, were one of the greatest teams ever assembled. Sox manager Fielder Jones assigned Altrock a difficult task that no one else wanted: facing Cubs ace Mordecai "Three Finger" Brown in the opening game of the Series. Cold weather and snow flurries helped create a pitchers' duel, won 2-1 by Altrock and the Sox. Years later, Altrock claimed that he had screamed at his center fielder to make the game's final catch because he could no longer move his frozen fingers.[2] After the win, ebullient White Sox fans swept onto the Cubs' field and carried Altrock and hitting hero George Rohe off on their shoulders.[3] Altrock had allowed only four hits.

He was brilliant again three days later, when he allowed seven hits and only one run in a complete game, only to lose to future Hall of Famer Brown. With the series deadlocked at two games each, Altrock and Brown seemed destined to pitch a conclusive seventh game, but the Hitless Wonders rallied to sweep the fifth and sixth games and bring the championship to the South Side. While the Sox managed only to split his

Nick Altrock with a characteristic prop.

starts, Altrock's two complete games, ERA of 1.00, and dramatic series-opening win were a significant contribution to one of the greatest upsets in Series history.

Decline—Sweet as it must have been, Altrock's moment in the sun was short. In 1907, he pitched reasonably well but his record dipped to 7 and 13 and he was not able to throw the number of innings that he had been accustomed to. Although it now appears that he may simply have thrown his arm out after almost a decade of complete games and little rest between starts, his contemporaries had less flattering theories. One 1908 newspaper cartoon shows a grinning Altrock happily preparing to down some booze. The caption blames the decline of the Sox on Altrock's drinking habits and notes that the team had inserted a temperance clause in the pitcher's new contract.[4]

This was not the only allusion to Altrock's questionable lifestyle. Even in an era of hard-drinking players, his tippling seems to have attracted attention. Whatever the cause, his athletic decline was quick and significant. He was out of the American League by 1909 (even the Senators wouldn't have him!) and after several years in the minors was dropped by Kansas City in 1912.

Although prospects must initially have seemed bleak for a thirty-five-year-old pitcher with a tired arm, Altrock managed to shape a profitable and long-lasting second career for himself. Now that he could no longer compete athletically, Altrock had two remaining assets: his face and his utter lack of inhibitions. He was an extraordinary-looking man. He had protruding jughandle ears and a prominent and bulbous nose. By all accounts, he also had a face of rubber—flexible, pleasantly homely, and always funny. Altrock had, in short, a face made for clowning and a personality to match. He made a comic breakthrough one day in Cleveland after seeing a boxing clip at the movies the night before. Before hundreds of puzzled, then increasingly delighted fans, Altrock proceeded to stage a fight against himself. He shadowboxed furiously before proceeding to pummel himself with a wild punch. A box-office sensation was born.

Clown—By this time Altrock had already been hired as a coach for the hapless Senators. He was one of baseball's very first fulltime coaches, so there were few models for him to follow and no obvious contradiction in clowning for the fans while advising pitchers.[5] His gags became increasingly numerous and popular. He often imitated the stances of opposing batters or mimicked umpires behind their backs. He lugged a huge glove several feet across onto the field as a massive sight gag. Altrock would also contort himself into a pretzel and try to outwrestle himself. As Bill James has noted, before games Altrock "would pretend to help the umpire sweep off the plate, all the while piling more dirt on top of it. At first base in the pregame drills he would take throws behind his back, between his legs; sometimes he would juggle the throw as if it were a hot potato."[6] He could also throw three balls simultaneously—one each to catcher, first, and third. Nobody had seen anything like Altrock before. Even Ban Johnson, a man not noted for his sense of humor, laughed at Nick's antics before banning them during the course of play.

Altrock continued his solo shtick but also began working with partners on the Senators' roster. In the 1910s he teamed with teammate Germany Schaefer before forming his longest-lived and most successful partnership in 1920 with a slender young pitcher named Al Schacht. Altrock and Schacht performed countless silent on-field pantomimes, figuring that comedy based on sound would not do well in large, noisy stadiums. Among their most famous routines were an extended reenactment of the famous "long count" heavyweight fight between Gene Tunney and Jack Dempsey. The two clowns also recreated a tennis match between Suzanne Lenglen and Helen Wills and a recent swim across the English Channel. The performances were wildly popular and drew more fans to the park than anything on the Senators except Walter Johnson himself. From 1921 until the early 1930s, the antics of Altrock and Schacht were part of every World Series. Their popularity soon extended into the off-season as well. They became regulars on the vaudeville circuit and toured across America and Europe. The newspapers of the day reported that the duo were offered some film roles but could not come to an agreement with the studios.

Unfortunately, Altrock and Schacht hated each other. It was lucky that their comedy relied on sight and not sound, because they reportedly did not speak to each other for much of the time they worked together. Schacht was once quoted as saying that the two worked together but "took separate cabs to get to the theater and separate cabs to get home."[7] No one has been able to explain this breach, which was a great disappointment to Clark Griffith, among many others. It has been suggested that the two men fought over Altrock's refusal to enter the film business or over a boxing skit in which fake punches became real ones. Another theory suggested that Altrock had angered Schacht with a fake telegram from Ban Johnson forbidding all clowning.[8] As James has noted, constantly living and working together can only have worsened things between the two performers.[9] Years after Altrock's death, Schacht told his side of the story in an interview: "I worked with Altrock for eight years and never spoke to him because of a nasty remark he once made about my Jewish heritage".[10]

It is obviously impossible to know whether Altrock was prejudiced or not. His story was buried with him. Schacht's story does point to what may have been a pervasive prejudice among some members of the early baseball community. A 1930 newspaper piece blithely entitled "Kidding on the Square," explained the Altrock-Schacht rift by saying that Schacht had hit Altrock with a real blow during one of their staged "fights." The unsigned piece closes with the following "punchline": "I'll teach that Jew," Nick said, as he walked away mumbling, "to pull his punches after this."[11] To this reader at least, it is unclear whether this quote speaks worse of Altrock or the writer and editorial policy that jokingly repeated his comment. Whatever the source of Schacht's dissatisfaction may have been, he left the Senators with Joe Cronin in 1935 to join the Red Sox.

Coach—Despite (or because of) Altrock's on-field antics, he became a respected and valuable coach for the Senators. When a promising young prospect named Cliff Bolton appeared during the Senators' great season of 1933, it was Altrock who was assigned to hit fly balls and teach the rookie how to field.[12] As the Senators' pennant hopes grew that year, manager Cronin and owner Griffith sent Altrock as part of a delegation to scout the powerful New York Giants, the Senators' eventual World Series opponent.[13] Altrock influenced less important games as well. No less a baseball authority than Christy Mathewson argued that Altrock "won many a game by his work on the [coaching] lines in pinches."[14] As Mathewson (or his ghostwriter) described things, Altrock had a gift for inciting the crowd into distracting, repetitive cheers just as opposing pitchers most needed to concentrate. From our now-distant vantage point, Altrock's cheerleading might seem to resemble the distracting clowning that Ban Johnson had forbidden during games, but none of Altrock's contemporaries seem to have objected. Mathewson, for example, appears to have admired, not condemned, Altrock's tactics. The often woeful Senators stood only to gain from their coach's unusual skills.

More surprisingly, the team continued to call on Altrock as a hitter and pitcher long after his career appeared to have ended. In an era when major league rosters lacked the formality they have today, Altrock was used as a pinch hitter and gate attraction in the last game of several seasons. By pitching in a game at the ripe old age of 57 and getting a hit (a triple at that!) at a sprightly 48, he set major league records that lasted for decades.[15] Impressively, he pitched and won a complete game in Detroit in 1918, with little to fall back on but spit, guile, and a "shine ball." Altrock also led the American League in hitting (in theory, at least) for the seasons of 1925 and 1929, when he managed hits in his only at bats for the season. In 1931, his clowning tied Red Sox pitcher Jack Russell up in knots of laughter. Altrock drew a walk when Russell could not compose himself enough to throw a strike. Never one to pass up a chance to entertain, the fifty-five-year old Altrock

later ended the game (and the Senators' season) by being caught stealing.[16] Two years later, in his final professional at bat he grounded out weakly but tried to elude the tag by taking an elaborate basepath from home to the dugout to first.

With his striking features, unusual gags, and shrewd, well, nose for the spotlight, Altrock appears to have been a genuine baseball celebrity until his retirement from coaching in 1953. In addition to his many performances at major league games, he also served as a popular ambassador for baseball at numerous galas and local benefits, including a fundraiser in 1919 to pay for repairs at Babe Ruth's fire-damaged St. Mary's.[17] Columns ghost-written by Altrock appeared across the country. The Hall of Fame has a check to him from the Christy Walsh syndicate that funded and produced baseball columns by Ruth and others. Altrock's popular stature may be best gauged by an appearance at the 1931 World Series. Sharing pens and signing autographs were three of baseball's most distinctive personalities: John J. McGraw, Babe Ruth, and Nick Altrock.[18] Although Altrock's successes on the field paled beside those of his companions, he appears not to have felt threatened by their famously strong personalities or their considerable fame.

Altrock died on January 20, 1965, in the capital city where most of his professional career had taken place. His tenure as a professional baseball employee and entertainer spanned nearly six decades and ranged

---

The Wit and Wisdom of Nick Altrock

"I mastered the shoe cobbling profession so well I could pitch a peg through leather for a strike every time."

After watching his first pitch of the 1908 season soar off Ty Cobb's bat over the right field fence: "I always was unlucky early in the year."

"Hey, Nick," shouted a fan, "how is it you don't play anymore?"
When Altrock noticed that his heckler was a fat, bald man, he responded "For the same reason, you poor bozo, that you don't part your hair anymore."

Upon entering a swanky New York night club, Altrock asked the waitress, "Any raids tonight so far?"
"Why no, Nick,"
"All right," said Nick. "I'll wait."

"There is nothing certain in baseball except waivers. That gets 'em all. A waiver means that your arm is in the ragbag and the old clothesman is singing his twilight song to the little birdies in the trees."

Upon being released from the minors in 1912: "Oh, don't mind me…I'll find another job. Why, with my face I might break into movies—you never can tell."

from World Series glory to some truly bad Senators teams. He received Hall of Fame votes seven different times and in one season narrowly outpolled eventual Hall of Famers Pie Traynor, Joe Sewell, Sam Rice, and Harry Hooper, among others. Perhaps there is room in the Hall for this pioneering pitcher, coach, and clown? Unlike Altrock, I'm only half-kidding.

Notes:

1. Frances Stann, "Best Pickoff Ever," *Baseball Digest*, March 1965, 59-61.

2. Gene Kessler, "Nick Altrock, the Ed Wynn of Game, Just Wiggles Ears and Goes Ahead Drawing Big Pay for His Clowning," October 5, 1933, newspaper unknown. Altrock file, Baseball Hall of Fame, Cooperstown, NY.

3. Unsigned article. New York *Times*, October 10, 1906.

4. Unsigned newspaper clipping, February 6, 1908, newspaper unknown. Altrock file, Baseball Hall of Fame.

5. Fred Stein, "Managers and Coaches," in *Total Baseball*, ed. John Thorn and Pete Palmer. Third edition. New York: Harper, 1993, 2179.

6. Bill James, *The Baseball Book*. New York: Villard, 1990, 233-234.

7. Unsigned Associated Press obituary, January 21, 1965. Altrock file, Hall of Fame.

8. Kessler, *op. cit.*

9. James, *op. cit.*, 234.

10. Rich Marazzi, "Al Schacht, 'The Clown Prince of Baseball,'" *Baseball History* Winter 1986 1(no. 4), 44.

11. Unsigned newspaper article, November 27, 1930. Newspaper unknown. Altrock file, Hall of Fame.

12. Morris A Bealle, *The Washington Senators*. Washington, D. C.: Columbia Publishing Co, 1947, 144.

13. *Ibid*, 147.

14. Christy Mathewson, *Pitching in a Pinch: Baseball from the Inside*. New York: Putnam, 1912. Rept. Lincoln: U. of Nebraska P., 1994, 123.

15. Peter C. Bjarkman, "Washington Senators-Minnesota Twins: Expansion Era Baseball Comes to the American League." *Encyclopedia of Major League Baseball Team Histories: American League*. Westport, CT: Meckler, 1991, 497-98.

16. Frank H. Young, Untitled article. Washington *Post*, Monday September 28,1931, 13.

17. Marshall Smelser, *The Life that Ruth Built*. New York: Quadrangle, 1975,161.

18. *Ibid*, 435.

Nick Altrock and Harry Geisel

It's Time to Open the Door

Ted Williams

*Shoeless Joe Jackson, universally considered one of baseball's best hitters and finest players, was banned from baseball for life by Commissioner Kenesaw Mountain Landis in 1920 for his involvement in the Black Sox scandal of 1919, in which members of the Chicago White Sox threw the World Series to the Cincinnati Reds. Jackson's degree of culpability and the propriety of Landis' act have been debated ever since. Two of the game's all-time greats made headlines earlier this year by urging Jackson's election to the Baseball Hall of Fame. Bob Feller and Ted Williams, so often opponents on the field, have joined to express their belief that Jackson deserves his place in Cooperstown. Williams puts his case in this piece.*Copyright © 1998 Total Sports.

I want Baseball to right an injustice.

It's not to me. It's to the memory of one of the greatest hitters, greatest players, who ever played this game.

I'm talking about Shoeless Joe Jackson. And it's about time we say he's paid the price, served his sentence—served his sentence for a crime no court of law ever found him guilty of.

Right now, the Baseball Hall of Fame has most—I say most—of the greatest players who ever lived. But when you look at all the measurements of greatness, all the statistics, you can't help but notice that one of the very, very, very best isn't in Cooperstown.

And that's wrong. Damn wrong. And Baseball

Hall of Famer **Ted Williams** *is a SABR member.*

shouldn't tolerate injustice. It's too good for that.

Back in 1966 when I was fortunate enough to stand at the podium at the Hall of Fame and give my induction speech, I made a pitch for Satchel Paige's induction. It was wrong that he wasn't in the Hall of Fame, and it was just as big a wrong that his fellow Negro league greats were ignored.

We've undone part of that unfairness—although some qualified Negro leaguers still remain out of Cooperstown. I know that Buck O'Neill and Monte Irvin will continue to counsel the Veterans Committee on that.

As to Joe Jackson's nomination and qualifications...I think I know a little about hitting. And Joe Jackson was one of the finest hitters of all time. Look at the numbers: a .356 lifetime average, third best ever. He hit .408 in his first full year in the majors. And he hit with power. Cobb spread his hands apart and punched out those hits. Jackson lashed away and pushed out a ton of doubles and triples, the real power hits of his day.

I'm not going to bore you with numbers. You can look them up as well as I can, maybe better. But I can tell you that anyone I talked to who saw Jackson play was just amazed at what he could do. Eddie Collins—a great guy, a great friend—was with Jackson on the White Sox. Collins told me, "Ted, you're the closest thing I ever saw to Joe Jackson. All I could think about when I saw Ted Williams was Joe Jackson."

When Babe Ruth wanted to model his swing after the perfect swing, it was Jackson he imitated—Jackson, with his big Black Betsy, wailing the tar out of the ball. Hitting for the third highest average in history. Hitting with power, triples all over the place. The greatest natural hitter of all time is what some say. I think they may be right.

And he could field too. His glove was where triples went to die. His arm may have been better than Clemente's. When he started out in the semipros he was a pitcher, you know. Or at least he was until he broke his catcher's arm with a pitch.

Well, yes, you'll concede all that. You have to. Hell, how could anyone argue against Joe Jackson as a great hitter, great player. You can't. Don't even try.

Of course, there is that matter of the World Series. Let me tell you about Jackson and the Black Sox. I know all about them. Now, Joe shouldn't have accepted money from a teammate, and he realized his error. He tried to give the money back. He tried to tell Comiskey, the White Sox owner about the fix. But they wouldn't listen. Comiskey covered it up as much as Jackson did—maybe more. And there's Charles Albert Comiskey down the aisle from me in Cooperstown—and Shoeless Joe still waits outside.

How dishonest could Jackson have been in that 1919 Series? How much a fixer? He hit .375, slugged .563, got 12 hits—that was a record—and even homered, homered into the right field bleachers in Cincinnati. Homers didn't come easy then. It was a dead ball. Hell, it was the only homer of the Series—by either team. And to top it off he led the Sox in RBI and runs scored.

The White Sox made twelve errors in that Series. So did the Reds. How many did Jackson make? Zero.

Of course, no jury ever convicted Jackson. Consider that. He was acquitted, walked out of the courthouse a free man. That is until Judge Landis threw him out of baseball, threw him out for life. They say Landis was a vindictive man—but Joe served his sentence and paid his debt to baseball. Baseball can't impose a sentence longer than Judge Landis did.

Joe Jackson's not alive any more. He's served his sentence, and it's time for Baseball to acknowledge his debt is paid; and the Hall of Fame Committee on Veterans to list him as a nominee.

To move things I have requested that Joe Jackson's name be placed on the ballot of the Baseball Hall of Fame and in support of my request have given the Hall a legal memorandum showing the reasons for that. It's time, and it's the right thing to do.

When I was younger, the Red Sox used to stop sometimes in Greenville, South Carolina—that's Jackson's home. And he was still alive. Oh, how I wish I had known that and could have stopped in to talk hitting with that man. It's too late, but it's not too late for him to come and join me—and all the other Hall of Famers—in Cooperstown

Come on in, Joe, I'd say, your wait is over. Let's talk hitting.

After David Pietrusza posted Ted Williams' essay on SABR-L, there was a quick flurry of reaction. It broke, essentially, into three parts: (1.) Common sense and sufficient information makes it clear that Jackson was involved fixing the 1919 World Series, so he should never be allowed into the Hall. (2.) It was never proven in a court of law that there was a fix. Since Jackson and his teammates were acquitted of fix-related charges, he should be allowed into the Hall, and (3.) Jackson was probably guilty of improper behavior, but he has been punished long enough and should now be elected to the Hall. What follows are a few representative samples of the passionate online debate.of Joe Jackson.

We thought all SABR members should have the chance to study Ted's essay. We expect to see more on this and related topics in the future.

—Ed.

John Coleman's 1883

James D. Smith III

In their 1993 book, *The Worst Baseball Pitchers of All Time*, Alan and James Kaufman provided a roll call of pitchers ranging from the consistently inept and unlucky to those of Hall of Fame caliber like Vic Willis, who in 1904 was 12-29 (the modern major league season loss record) while losing nine games by a single run.

In the process they touched on a figure who first fascinated me a decade ago: righthander John (12-48) Coleman, whose record in 1883 doubled the loss total of memorable Mets stalwart Roger (10-24) Craig, in a season schedule of less than 100 games!

John Francis Coleman was born in Saratoga Springs, New York, on March 6, 1863. Trained as a laborer/plasterer in his youth, he increasingly invested his energies in ballplaying. In 1882 his career was launched in earnest as he played on a Peoria team outside Organized Baseball.

On May 1, 1883, he was the starting pitcher in the Philadelphia "Phillies" first National League game at Recreation Park, at 24th Street and Ridge Avenue. After seven innings of shutout ball, the visiting Providence Grays scored four in the eighth, hanging on for a 4-3 win behind Hoss Radbourn. It was a portent of things to come. As the workhorse pitcher on a team that struggled to a 17-81 record, the twenty-year-old Coleman would lose forty-seven more games in his rookie season—allowing a stunning 772 hits in the pro-

Jim Smith *is pastor of Clairemont Emmanuel Baptist Church and adjunct professor at the University of San Diego and Bethel Theological Seminary-West. He wishes to thank John Coleman's late grandson, John III, and his wife Margaret, for biographical materials, and Bob Hoie for tracking the minor league data.*

cess—setting major league records never seriously challenged.

The following season, he was back for more, compiling a 5-15 mark in 21 games before moving to the crosstown Philadelphia Athletics (AA). There, with his strong throwing arm but mediocre mound success, he was converted into an outfielder. In a major league career concluding in 1890, he was a journeyman right fielder (510 games) on teams in both Philadelphia and Pittsburgh (in whose uniform he appears on "Old Judge" cards) compiling a .257 lifetime average.

In the minor leagues, seeing duty in 1889-90 with Toronto in the International Association, he also played with Pennsylvania teams based in towns including Lebanon, Danville, Harrisburg, York, and Philadelphia. Then, in his mid-thirties, his professional baseball career was over.

During the following years Coleman remained an active sportsman. He managed several billiard parlors in his adopted home state, doing some laborer and sales work as well, and lived for many years in Homestead. He and his wife, Maggie, also parented four children: Helen, Marguerite, John, Jr., and Betsy (who died young). But his love for the spotlight continued. This was evidenced in his activities as a boxing referee, but even more in his challenging of active ballplayers to exhibitions of strength or matches of Greco-Roman wrestling. Adding bulk to his sinewy 5'9-1/2" 170-pound frame, "Gentleman Jack's" exploits reportedly included lifting a billiard table with six men on it. His travels reached the Great Lakes area, were he was tragically killed by a hit-and-run driver in Detroit on May 31, 1922.

For the baseball historian, however, it is John Coleman's 1883 season record that remains most intriguing. To picture each decision on the way to his "bottom line" of 12-48, is to glimpse the mirror opposite of Radbourn's "iron man" 60-12 in the following 112-game season. With the invaluable help of Bob Tiemann, who provided the 1883 NL game sheets as raw material, here is the record of how the Phillies' original workhorse made his mark:

John Coleman's Astonishing 1883 Season

May	1	Prov. 4	at	Phila. 3	LP			29	Phila. 6	at	NY 7 (10)	LP
	2	Prov. 4	at	Phila. 1	LP		July	2	NY 7	at	Phila. 6	LP
	4	Bos. 11	at	Phila. 10	LP			4 (pm)	Bos. 17	at	Phila. 8	LP (relief)
	5	Bos. 5	at	Phila. 3	LP			6	Bos. 13	at	Phila. 6	LP
	7	Bos. 20	at	Phila. 8	LP			11	Phila. 1	at	Cle. 5	LP
	11	Phila. 9	at	Chi. 11	LP			13	Phila. 1	at	Cle. 10	LP
	12	Phila. 1	at	Chi. 6	LP			17	Phila. 6	at	Buf. 21	LP
	15	Phila. 4	at	Det. 3 (10)	WP			19	Phila. 5	at	Buf. 25	LP
	19	Phila. 10	at	Cle. 8	WP			25	Phila. 2	at	Chi. 11	LP
	23	Phila. 6	at	Cle. 8	LP			28	Phila. 6	at	Chi. 2	WP
	24	Phila. 4	at	Buf. 8	LP			31	Phila. 4	at	Det. 9	LP
	28	Phila. 3	at	Buf. 2 (11)	WP		August	2	Phila. 2	at	Det. 6	LP
	30	Chi. 15	at	Phila. 8	LP			4	Phila. 6	at	Det. 0	WP (shutout #3)
	31	Chi. 4	at	Phila. 3	LP			7	NY 4	at	Phila. 1	LP
June	1	Chi. 10	at	Phila. 1	LP			9	NY 3	at	Phila. 7	WP
	2	Det. 5	at	Phila. 2	LP			13	Phila. 1	at	NY 8	LP
	4	Det. 9	at	Phila. 3	LP			15	Phila. 4	at	Bos. 9	LP
	6	Det. 4	at	Phila. 20	WP			18	Phila. 4	at	Pro. 9	LP
	8	Cle. 8	at	Phila. 4	LP			22	Phila. 2	at	Pro. 8	LP
	9	Cle. 15	at	Phila. 1	LP			24	Phila. 3	at	NY 9	LP
	12	Cle. 3	at	Phila. 4 (12)	WP			28	Phila. 3	at	NY 9	LP
	14	Buf. 0	at	Phila. 2	WP (shutout #1)			30	Prov. 11	at	Phila. 5	LP
	16	Buf. 2	at	Phila. 4	WP		Sept.	1	Bos. 7	at	Phila. 0	LP
	18	Buf. 11	at	Phila. 2	LP			7	NY 9	at	Phila. 11	SV
	19	Phila. 8	at	Bos. 9 (11)	LP			8	NY 16	at	Phila. 6 (7)	LP
	21	Phila. 8	at	Pro. 13	LP			13	Cle. 1	at	Phila. 0	LP (Daily no-hit.)
	22	Phila. 9	at	Pro. 15	LP			14 (pm)	Cle. 5	at	Phila. 1	LP
	23	Phila. 2	at	Bos. 6	LP			15	Buf. 6	at	Phila. 5	LP
	25	Phila. 7	at	Bos. 15	LP			19	Buf. 8	at	Phila. 14 (8)	WP
	26	Phila. 4	at	Pro. 0	WP (shutout #2)			21	Det. 9	at	Phila. 3	LP
	27	Phila. 4	at	Pro. 8	LP							

A Photo, A Tour, A Life

David A. Hendsch

October 29,1927, was an exciting day for Fresno sports fans. Babe Ruth and Lou Gehrig were in town. Each major leaguer captained a team of local professional and amateur players, the "Bustin' Babes" and the "Larrupin' Lous." A crowd of 5,000 was on hand at Firemen Park to savor home run heaven. Babe and Lou were nearing the end of a nineteen-city barnstorming tour, and Fresno had been planning for this day for months.

Imagine the excitement of four young Japanese-American ballplayers having their pictures taken with these titans (below). All were members of the Fresno Athletic Club (F.A.C.), a Japanese-American organization that had recently completed a six-month baseball tour of Japan, Korea, Manchuria, and Hawaii. The team compiled a record of 50 wins, 9 losses and 2 ties. John Nakagwa and Harvey Iwata were the team's two best players. Iwata received a gold watch for being a "Champion" of left fielders, and he played a more consistent total game. If there had been such an honor, he probably would have been named the Most Valuable Player of the Fresno tour.

In 49 games, Harvey faced the best amateur and professional players in Japan, and it is clear from the record of the 1927 Japanese-American Baseball Tour that he was comparable to the best Japanese players.

Fortunately, the history of this distinguished team and of Japanese-American baseball is being preserved

through a fresh resurgence of interest in the Japanese-American experience. An effort is afoot in California to create a display of Japanese-American baseball for the Baseball Hall of Fame.

Genesis of the tour—1927 was a unique time in Japan's history. The legacy of Imperial Japan was being transfered to a new emperor, Hirohito. There was great enthusiasm and optimism. Baseball was at a high water mark. It was considered an important way to connect with the outside world, and also as a pastime that fit perfectly with national educational and spiritual goals to develop moral character in young men. Even the new emperor left his mark on baseball, offering a beautiful silver cup for the champions of the National High School League.

A team made up entirely of Fresno Athletic Club players had been to Japan to play before, and had demonstrated its skill with a 21-7 record. This was a very good team. The F.A.C. had won the California Japanese-American League in 1926, and had defeated local college and university teams, as well as Pacific Coast League clubs. To reach the top of the heap around Fresno, teams had to defeat the F.A.C. first—no easy task.

The Fresnans were enthusiastic about the possibility of another visit to Japan in 1927. They wanted to show again how well they could play, and some players looked forward to visiting family members. Ken Zenimura's cousins played for Meiji University in Tokyo, and this a gave him an inside track with baseball administrators. Also, Fresno was willing to pay its own traveling expenses, rather than holding out for a finan-

David A. Hendsch *is a retired public school teacher and a non-practicing marriage counselor. He is a writer, a video-maker, and a family tree ghost hunter. He has a strong interest in the baseball history of Fresno, California, especially the Nisei experience. He is married and lives in Oakland.*

cial guarantee. With all of this, it was still a profound honor for them—this time a squad made up of the best Nisei players in the California League, as well as three non-Nisei college-level players—to be invited back to play during the spring and summer months before imperial investiture ceremonies.

The J.A.B.T.—The touring team was officially called the Japanese American Baseball Team. The press tended to call it simply "Fresno," because it was primarily an all-star aggregation of Japanese Americans who worked in fields or in businesses around Fresno. Most were high school graduates from California or Hawaii, and several members had played on championship teams.

Iwata was from Dinuba. He worked on a melon-grape farm owned by his sponsor, Mr. Mayeda, who was a principal fundraiser for the local baseball establishment, and who encouraged Harvey's participation. On Sundays, baseball day, he played for the local Dinuba Japanese-American team and for the Fresno Athletic Club. At 23, this 5'5" lefthanded left fielder was in the prime of his baseball career.

Ken Zenimura, Fred Yoshikawa, Ty Miyahara, John Nakagawa, and Mike Nakano were all better known than Iwata and had been covered more fully in the press before the trip, but over the sixty-game grind, Harvey seemed to get stronger as the others tired. He thrived on the baseball diamond, and he seemed to possess greater stamina.

Among players who played 40 or more games in Japan, here is a list of selected team members. It reflected Harvey's comparative output .

Five Leading J.A.B.T. Hitters in Japan, 1927

Games		Hits	RBI	SO	AB	BA
49	Harvey Iwata	61	43	11	183	.333
50	Ty Miyahara	61	29	7	189	.323
50	Ken Zenimura	62	66	15	210	.295
50	Mike Nakano	74	66	14	192	.385
49	John Nakagawa	81	44	26	209	.388

Opposing pitchers were always in hot water with these hitters, and Japanese newspapers credit Fresno's solid fielding for supporting the effort. Harvey and others fielded 1.000 on tour.

A few Japanese teams walked off the playing field with a smile on their faces. A new generation of pitchers was developing in Japan, and they honed their winning skills against a highly publicized foe. Wakayama High School, the reigning holder of the Emperor's cup and "King of the Mountain" of Japanese schoolboy baseball beat the Californians, 2-1.

In Hawaii the tourists won eight of nine games. The chart below includes statistics for the eight games they played against other amateur clubs. The ninth game was lost to a professional team, and was not included in the record. Statistical information was published by

October 29, 1927 at Fireman's Baseball Park, Fresno, California. Left to right: John Nakagowa, Lou Gehrig, Ken Zenimura, Babe Ruth, Fred Yoshikawa, Harvey Iwata

Honolulu *Star-Bulletin* sports reporter, William T. ("Bill") Rapoza.

Five Leading J.A.B.T. Hitters in Hawaii, 1927

Games		Hits	RBI	AB	BA	FA
8	Iwata	9	10	26	.346	1.000
8	Nakagawa	10	6	36	.333	1.000
8	Nakano	8	4	32	.250	.978
8	Zenimura	7	7	33	.222	.962
8	Kunitomo	7	2	32	.217	.865
8	Yoshikawa	3	3	33	.090	.927

The Californians hit for a team average of .222, compared to .234 for opponents. J.A.B.T. made 14 errors as compared to 25. They fielded a .959 average, and their opponents .926.

Afterward—So Harvey Iwata was a fine baseball player, good enough to be the outstanding player on an international tour that competed with Japan's best teams. But his baseball career ended with his marriage in 1930, at the age of 26. Baseball had given him an identity as a young man, and had—along with his close-knit community, his religion, his work, his school, and his family—helped him develop elements of his character that carried through his life, but it didn't define him as a man.

In 1920 his father had died, leaving him the sole provider for his mother, sisters, and brothers He was forced to quit high school before graduation. He went to work for Mr. Mayeda, working on the farm and acting as a business interpreter during the week, and playing baseball on weekends. By the time he left for Japan in 1927, he was a respected member of the Japanese-American community. He developed such a positive rapport with local businessmen that he could successfully solicit hundreds of dollars for F.A.C. baseball functions.

His marriage is a story in itself. According to Japanese custom, his marriage was arranged between Buddhist priests and Mr. Mayeda. Akiko lived in a Buddhist boarding school in Guadalupe, California. She graduated from Santa Maria High School and was attending the local junior college. She dreamed of going to the University of California at Berkeley. But one afternoon she was asked by the local priest's wife to serve tea to two strangers—Mr. Mayeda and Harvey.

As a test of her worthiness, she prepared a dinner for them and sewed on a coat button, which Mr. Mayeda had cut off his coat. That afternoon Akiko's academic plans were scrapped, and she was committed to a marriage. Soon after, she was told by the priest's wife the wedding had to be in March because of the demands of melon growing. She quit school two months before graduating, and she and Harvey were married on March 6, 1930. He was 26 and she was 19.

After his marriage, Iwata focused his attention on his new family. Other members of the F. A. C. continued extending Japanese-American baseball into the 1950s, but Harvey used his organizational and management skills to became a full-time manager of the farm. He cut his formal ties with the game.

During the war Iwata and his family, like most Japanese Americans, were interned. In 1943 he was conscripted to use his knowledge of Japan and Japanese to work in military intelligence. He and his family were moved to Cleveland, Ohio, for military training. For the duration of the war, he served as a map reader at Cabin John, Maryland. After the war, he and Akiko were both employed by the Army Map Service. They moved to Alexandria, Virginia, where they raised three daughters and a son. His ties with his baseball past were severed.

Well-liked and respected, Harvey was active in Japanese-American affairs, being elected president of the Washington, D.C., chapter of the Japanese-American Citizen League in 1955. He taught himself to play the saxophone, to golf, and to swim. He was an accomplished public speaker. He read widely and voraciously, and many of the people he came into contact with assumed he had an advanced degree, despite his lack of even a high school diploma. He died of a coronary occlusion at work on January 19, 1959. Akiko still lives in Virginia.

Harvey's family did not know much about his baseball past. Only in the past year have they recaptured a partial picture of his brilliance as a ballplayer through the work of the Nisei Baseball Research Program.

Although Harvey gained local fame and self-satisfaction playing baseball, his family believes that his real distinction lies in his identity as a responsible family man known for his honesty and integrity. Clearly he was not a boastful man, or one who lived in the past.

The Harvey Iwata standing with Ruth and Gehrig was at the apex of his baseball career. He was 23 years old, a fine player just off a highly successful tour of his ancestral homeland. But for unknown reasons, he didn't play as the Larrupin' Lous beat the Bustin' Babes, 13-3. This little mystery could have a dozen reasonable solutions. It's safe to assume that Harvey Iwata, competitor, would have played if he could, and that he was disappointed that he couldn't appear on the diamond with these two great icons. But it's also safe to assume that Harvey Iwata, husband and father, didn't dwell on whatever misfortune sidetracked him on that October afternoon. He played ball as a young man, and applied his strengths to excel at this sport that connected his two countries. He enjoyed its pleasures, learned its lessons, then moved on to meet life's other challenges.

Tex Sanner's Big Year

Joe Murphy

Winning the triple crown stands high on the list of every batter's ambitions, and every pitcher strives to be a 20-game winner. Relatively few players achieve either of these objectives, but in 1948, in the Evangeline League, Roy (Tex) Sanner did it all in a single season. Pitching in 26 games and playing in 126, he led Houma to the league championship in a dominating all-around performance. He won 21 games and lost 2, for a league-leading .913 winning percentage, striking out 251 batters while walking 96. Playing in the outfield on days when he was resting his pitching arm, he hit 34 home runs and drove in 126 runs while batting .386, to lead the league in all three categories.

Sanner's spectacular season came roughly in the middle of a 17-year minor league career, during which he played in nine different leagues on twelve different clubs. In 1,426 games, his career batting average was .327 . In 305 pitching appearances, he won 138 games and lost 72, with an era of 3.61.[1]

Sanner was born on August 22, 1920, in Geuda Springs, a small Kansas town just north of the Oklahoma border.[2] His professional career began in 1941. After pitching a total of eleven innings with Topeka in the Class C Western Association, he was sent to Cheyenne in the Western League, where he displayed his versatility. Appearing in 22 games, he won 10 and lost 5, striking out 138 batters in 150 innings. As an outfielder, he played in 15 additional games, batting an overall .279 for the year.[3] Topeka welcomed him back

in 1942, and he led the league in games pitched (39), wins (20), walks (112), and strikeouts (204). As an outfielder that year, he came to bat in 34 games, and posted a seasonal .303 as a hitter.

This attracted the attention of the Brooklyn Dodgers, who, in those days, were always on the lookout for (1) pitchers, and (2) outfielders. They invited Sanner to their wartime spring training camp at Bear Mountain, up the Hudson River, hard by the Military Academy at West Point. They apparently had him targeted for their International League club in Montreal.

Sanner had an interesting spring in 1943. It may have been the first time that he had ventured out of the warm southern climes in the chill winds of March. In his memoir, *Every Diamond Doesn't Sparkle*, Dodger executive Fresco Thompson, recalled his first impression of the rookie:

> A young left-handed pitcher named Roy Sanner...reported to the Dodgers while they were training at Bear Mountain, New York, during the war. It was the dead of winter and Roy checked in wearing thin summer slacks and a lightweight jacket, the sleeves of which were several inches too short. He was also hatless.
>
> [Branch] Rickey saw the kid on the ball field and in the West Point field house where we worked out in bad weather, he instructed Buzzie [Bavasi] to take him to New York and outfit him properly before he froze to death. Buzzie was a fashion plate and when he went on a shopping spree, prices were unimportant.

Joe Murphy *is celebrating his sixteenth year as a SABR member. He spends his spare time updating the* SABR Index*, which is available at cost on disk or paper from SABR's executive office.*

He took Sanner to De Pinna's on Fifth Avenue and outfitted him from head to foot with a full complement of clothes along with accessories and extras. Sanner's old clothes could have been bundled up and mailed back…to use for scarecrows. When Sanner appeared in the lobby of the Bear Mountain Inn, the epitome of splendor and excellence, even Leo Durocher—himself one of the leaders in the dress parade—had to admire his appearance and run a finger over the luxurious cloth.[4]

Bavasi, some fifty years later, still recalled the occasion:

> Just before we got to the store, he looked up at the RCA Building and said: "Gee, you could store a lot of hay in that place." I told the clerk, whom I had dealt with before, to get Roy a new outfit, including suit, shirt, underwear, socks, etc. After an hour he came out of the dressing room looking like a new man. Nice blue suit, but I noticed his pockets were bulging. He had stuffed his old underwear, socks, and shirts in his pockets.[5]

In that 1943 spring, Brooklyn and Montreal were training together. Sanner pitched in an intersquad game in his first appearance, and Joe Medwick hit his first pitch for a home run.[6] Later in the spring training season Brooklyn played the Army squad at West Point, and the Dodgers loaned Sanner and Bob Chipman to pitch for the Army team. Sanner pitched the first four innings, giving up ten hits, including a first inning homer by newly acquired Billy Herman. Although he thus had the distinction of having surrendered homers to two future Hall of Famers, the Dodgers were not otherwise impressed, and that was the closest he ever came to appearing on a big league roster.[7]

After an undistinguished season in 1944, when he pitched in only 10 games for Montreal, winning 2 and losing 3, Sanner spent the last thirteen years of his career in six minor leagues, all situated south of the Mason-Dixon line. Dividing his time between the outfield and the mound, in 4,282 at bats between 1945 and 1957, he batted .331, while winning 96 games and losing 39.

But it was in 1948 that he realized his full potential. En route to his batting title, he hit safely in 31 straight games, establishing an Evangeline League record, collecting 48 hits in 113 trips to the plate.[8] On the mound his 251 strikeouts were exceeded only by Houma teammate Gene (Junior) Thompson, late of the Cincinnati Reds and the New York Giants, who fanned 259. His accomplishments resulted in a late-season sale to Dallas in the Texas League. Before reporting he staged a three-day walkout, claiming that Houma had promised him $3,000 of the $10,000 sale price. After accepting a $2,000 compromise settlement, he joined the Dallas Rebels, and played in seven games during the last week of the season. He pitched in two games, pinch hit in one, and played left field in the other four. He won a 10-inning decision in his first start, but five days later, gave up 8 hits and walked 8 in 6-2/3 innings. Perhaps the most memorable feature of his appearance that day was that he uncorked three wild pitches. He would have been credited with a fourth, but an errant pitch sped past home plate, rebounded from the base of the grandstand and returned to the catcher in time for him to tag out a runner trying to score from third. His week's work as a batter was more impressive, with eight hits in twenty-two times at bat.[9]

Without distinction, he spent portions of the next three years with Dallas. The balance of his career, ending in 1957, was spent mostly in the wide-open spaces of the sprawling Class B Big State League. At age 37, his final season was pretty much a typical one. He appeared in 74 games, batting .331. In 24 pitching appearances, he won 12 and lost 4, with an era of 2.80.

Roy Sanner died in Houston, Texas, on January 9, 1982.

Notes

1. *Minor League Baseball Stars*, volume 1, pp. 83-84

2. *The Minor League Register*, pp. 281-282

3. Joe Naiman, *Minor League History Journal*, vol. 2, no. 1, the 1941 Cheyenne Indians, p. 35

4. Thompson, Fresco, with Cy Rice, *Every Diamond Doesn't Sparkle*, New York, David McKay Company Inc., pp. 69-70

5. Bavasi correspondence with SABR member Richard Durrell, July, 1996

6. New York *Times*, March 29, 1943

7. New York *Times*, April 3, 1943

8. *The Sporting News*, June 30, 1948.

9. *The Sporting News*, September 15, 1948

A Happy Addendum

Viola Owen

Many baseball fans remember the 1934 Detroit Tigers-St. Louis Cardinals World Series. Real fans probably remember the Medwick-Owen incident at third base and the questions that remain. In my 1996 book, *The Adventures of A Quiet Soul*, eight pages describe the event with pictures, quotes, and questions. Every October during World Series time, the old 1934 films of the encounter are replayed, old timers argue who really had the ball, and at baseball meetings opinions are divided.

Shortly after Christmas, 1996, an eighty-something gentleman called me to say *The Adventures of A Quiet Soul* was his favorite Christmas gift. That, however, was not his main reason for calling. He had a story that made him wish we had known each other before the book was printed so that his story could have been included in the book. I agree with him.

In 1968, my caller, Bob Burton, was general manager of Class C Modesto, a farm club of the Atlanta Braves, and was at a night game at his club's Del Webb Field. At that time, Joe Medwick was a St. Louis Cardinals roving batting instructor and Marv Owen was a Detroit Tigers area scout. Bob knew that they were both at the game, Medwick seated at one end of the stands and Owen at the other. Bob told the PA announcer about the two celebrities, and the man behind the microphone introduced them to the crowd. Each stood up to be acknowledged. To the enjoyment of the fans who knew about the rough play at third base in 1934 and all that had flowed from it, Marv tipped his hat to Joe, and Joe, who never wore a hat, bowed in the direction of Marv.

Thanks, Bob Burton. The memory of that brief moment in 1968 gives me the kind of happy ending I love.

Vi Owen, *sister of the late Marv Owen, is a writer and editor living in Aptos, California.*

Remembering Mr. Brewer

David Davis

Long after his own bitterness had mellowed—indeed, long after Jackie Robinson had broken through and enabled him to convert some of his pain into a most generous love—the man told this story about the old days:

"There was a time when a colored man bugged the white man to let him play. And he bugged him and bugged him and bugged him. And the white man said, 'Boy, get outta this dugout before I call the police.'

"But the colored man wouldn't let him alone. So finally the white man puts him into a uniform, to embarrass him. Sent him in front of this big, mean relief pitcher and says to himself, 'This'll teach that boy.'

"Well, don't you know the first ball that big old white man threw, the colored boy hit into right field, with the bases filled. And as the colored boy takes off, the white man says, 'Well, will you look at that Cuban go!'"

The man who used to tell that tale, Chet Brewer, is no longer alive, but in the time when baseball ruled the land, he was considered one of the best pitchers in America. Trouble was, the 6'4", 200-pound righthander with the wicked curve ball was black and thus relegated to the Negro Leagues, where he pitched for such teams as the Tennessee Rats (purported to be the model for William Brashler's fictional barnstorming team the Bingo Long Traveling All-Stars), the Gilkerson Union Giants and J. L. Wilkinson's Kansas City Monarchs.

Brewer played with and against the best black ballplayers—guys like Josh Gibson, Judy Johnson, Oscar Charleston, Martin Dihigo—in every nook of

the United States and most of the Caribbean ports of call. He pitched a no-hitter against Satchel Paige in the Dominican League in 1937, but in Negro League annals Brewer is best known for his role in the infamous "Battle of the Butchered Balls." The 1930 duel between Brewer and the Homestead Grays' Smokey Joe Williams ended in a 1-0 Grays victory. Brewer struck out 19—Williams 27—in the 12-inning game, which featured the best spitballs and "emory balls" each pitcher could muster.

Toward the end of his playing career, Brewer was given a whiff of integrated ball when a couple of Pacific Coast League teams paid lip service to giving him a tryout and a contract. But this never materialized into an offer, and Brewer's resentment against major league baseball never completely disappeared. He once reminded a reporter about Pete Gray, who signed with the St. Louis Browns during the manpower-depleted days of World War II. "How do you think I felt when I saw a one-armed outfielder?" Brewer asked. "Shoot, the only thing a one-armed white man can do as good as a two-armed black man is scratch the side that itches."

Brewer retired and settled in Los Angeles, but he never left the game that treated him so shabbily. First, he organized a semipro team called the Kansas City Royals, which took on all comers (including white all-star teams) during the winter months. Among the players to wear a Royals uniform was Jackie Robinson, before he signed with the Brooklyn Dodgers. Then, after stints as manager in Mexico and in the California winter league, Brewer scouted for the Pittsburgh Pirates from the 1950s to 1980s, delivering to the Bucs

David Davis *is a freelance writer based in Los Angeles. This article first appeared in* LA Weekly, *June 6–12, 1997.*

the best talent in L.A.

He did this by organizing and funding a South-Central neighborhood team, known variously as the Chet Brewer Rookies and the Chet Brewer Pirates, that produced a generation of black major league superstars. The team was an inner-city version of the boys of summer: Reggie Smith, the Murray brothers (Charles, Leon, Eddie, Venice and Rich), Enos Cabell, Dock Ellis, Bobby Tolan, Dave Nelson, Willie Crawford, Leon McFadden, Don Wilson, George Hendrick, Joe Black, Ellis Valentine, and others tutored under Papa Chet.

While Brewer was still alive, several writers and former ballplayers campaigned to have him inducted into baseball's Hall of Fame—an honor Brewer himself thought he deserved. But after he passed away in 1990, at the age of 83, the crusade fizzled. Today, organizations such as Reviving Baseball in Inner Cities try to do the work that Brewer used to accomplish.

From the Negro Leagues to Jackie Robinson to the sport's present-day malaise, Chet Brewer's life is the story of baseball in the twentieth century. Here, four baseball lifers retell that story.

The Catcher—Sammie Haynes hangs up the telephone, and then with an exasperated sigh punches in a number before turning to a reporter. "Now we won't be disturbed," he says.

The phone's been ringing constantly for Haynes this year, the fiftiethth anniversary of Jackie Robinson's breakthrough with the Brooklyn Dodgers. *Everybody* wants the presence of a former Negro League player at their function. Haynes, 77, has made appearances all over the country, and is scheduled to be honored at the All Star Game this summer. In the fall, he'll help inaugurate the new Negro League Museum in Kansas City

Chet Brewer in his playing days.

Noir Tech Sports

with other alumni.

In the 1930s and '40s, Haynes was a catcher for the Atlanta Black Crackers and, later, the Kansas City Monarchs. He never played with Chet Brewer, but he vividly remembers having to bat against him when Brewer was pitching for the Cleveland Buckeyes. "Chet was a great pitcher—he probably won as many games as any pitcher in the old Negro Leagues," says Haynes. "He had a good fastball, a great curve ball and, above all, great control. I'd have to rank Chet up there with Bullet Joe Rogan and Hilton Smith. You get any of them two-three runs, you're gonna come away a winner."

At the time of their meeting, Haynes remembers, Brewer was at the end of his career. "I didn't see him during his heyday, and I'm very glad I didn't," he says with a laugh.

Brewer developed a reputation for throwing the spitball, but Haynes says that Brewer never deliberately threw the illegal pitch. "Chet wasn't a cheater, but he knew how to throw the spitter," he says. "See, in the Negro Leagues, we would only play with about a dozen balls for a whole ballgame—the fans would have to throw them back on the field after a foul ball. If Chet found that little scratch on the ball he knew what to do with it."

What also stood out was Brewer's ability to evaluate talent, even as a player. "Chet was a very brainy guy," says Haynes. "He could sit on the bench and observe guys and tell their weaknesses and strong points."

Haynes was forced to retire from baseball after glaucoma took his eyesight. He has lived in Los Angeles since 1948, and maintained a friendship with Brewer until his death. Haynes and other Negro League players would donate money so that Brewer could buy equipment for his Rookies, and they'd often show up at the games to talk to the kids. "Chet thought that segregation [in baseball] was an injustice, but he decided to make it his mission to help young kids develop into the major leagues, because he didn't have that opportunity," says Haynes. "Chet wasn't bitter about playing in the Negro Leagues, because he knew—we all knew—that we were playing with and against some of the greatest baseball players who ever lived."

In 1986, Haynes founded an organization called the International Society of Athletes to counsel at-risk students and dropouts. Like his old buddy, he believes that progress comes one person at a time, one conversation at a time. "There's nobody like Chet now to help kids with baseball and other things," says Haynes. "He loved the game and loved helping people. He was such an ambassador, such a gentleman." (Sammie Haynes passed away last year.)

The Scout—Phil Pote is slowing down. That is, if you can call scouting part-time for the Seattle Mariners, checking out anywhere from one to four games a day in the L.A. area, trying to sell his screenplay about a scout who finds a phenom with the world's fastest pitch ("but then, see, there's this twist to the plot…"), campaigning to launch a President's Council on Youth, seeking to establish a permanent place for scouts in baseball's Hall of Fame, and scratching his head about the state of baseball in the inner city slowing down.

Actually, the last one is easy. According to the 64-year-old Pote, baseball is no longer a priority in L.A. schools. "There's a lack of facilities and youth programs, while high school programs are under-budgeted," he says, ticking off a familiar list of complaints. "When I started coaching in the 1950s, to be a varsity baseball coach—whoa! That was a big deal. Now they almost have to hold a gun to pressure someone to go out and coach baseball."

Pote is entitled to his opinion. He spent many years coaching baseball here, first at Fremont, then at Locke, and finally at L.A. City College, and his teams won city championships back in the days when Willie Crawford was pure butter. Pote also scouted so many young players in the Southern California sunshine that the skin around his eyes is furrowed into a perpetual squint. "Basketball and football now offer a faster track for success than baseball," he says. "Look at the NFL—they built a youth workout complex and school in Compton. I don't see anything similar in baseball."

For many years, Pote traded information and stories about prospects with his friend and fellow scout Chet Brewer. Because of Brewer's team, says Pote, scouts had to make the desolate streets of inner-city Los Angeles a destination point. "When I first started coaching, I can look back and weep at the wasted talent that went through [Fremont] because no scout ever saw them," says Pote. "Chet provided a service to the community and for the youth, because it provided a spotlight for talented youngsters. Scouts tend to follow

the scent. If you start developing a few players out of an area, then they descend."

Brewer's ability to ferret out talent was exceptional, says Pote. "When you realize that 90 percent of the time you're wrong—because 10 percent or less ever get to the big leagues—then you realize what a daunting responsibility scouting is," he says. "No one can look inside a kid's head and heart at 17 or 18 and project what he's going to do 2,000 miles away when the going gets tough. Chet's program attracted the best. We'd all go down on Sundays and see who Chet had rolled out that week."

The lessons went beyond baseball basics. "He taught his players about life—about attitude, work habits, how to behave like gentlemen," says Pote. "He wasn't the in-your-face type, but you did it his way. Even around the bench, everything was done the way it's supposed to be done."

Like Sammie Haynes, Pote was impressed by Brewer's ability to take a negative and turn it into a positive. "He could've been very bitter over the fact that he had the ability to play many years in the major leagues—and perhaps have been a star—and yet he was deprived of that," says Pote. "Instead of withdrawing from baseball, you got the feeling that he said to himself, 'Maybe I can help some of these kids get to what was not possible for me.' In that sense, we were blessed by his presence."

The Phenom—The sun is burning bright on the Dodger Stadium infield as Reggie Smith steps from the dugout and heads toward his "other" office: the batting cage. There, the Dodgers hitting coach watches his charges go through their pregame paces. Smith is still somewhat peeved by an altercation the previous night, when Kent Mercker accused him of stealing signs from the first base coach's box, but his demeanor mellows when the name Chet Brewer is brought up. Or, as the 52-year-old Smith calls him—out of habit or respect or, more likely, both—"Mr. Brewer."

Smith was a 15-year-old Centennial High phenom with a Raul Mondesi-like throwing arm when Brewer first spotted him in 1960. "I was playing with the Compton Cardinals, and then I got an invitation to try out for Mr. Brewer's team," he says, his pale-brown eyes softening from their usual shade of intense. "Mr. Brewer asked my dad if I could play with his team on Sundays. My dad was a little reluctant to do that, because he figured I was too young to play with the older men, but he let me go after Mr. Brewer promised to pick me up and bring me back home."

In those days Smith lived on 132nd and Crocker ("It's now considered South-Central, but at the time it was known as 'Zone 61'," he says) and had to help his father with the family's egg-delivery business. That curtailed the amount of free time he had to play ball, but he always made it to the Sunday games. "Mr. Brewer was a great teacher, because he taught you all aspects of the game," says Smith. "He was well into his fifties, and he still used to throw batting practice. In fact, he taught me how to hit the curve ball."

Smith remembers that Brewer would oftentimes be joined by some of his Negro League cronies. "You'd hear about the hardships and the fun times they had," he says. "In the process, you'd learn about baseball situations and you'd start to anticipate and recognize those things when they came up in a ballgame."

Signed by the Minnesota Twins in 1963, Smith was then drafted by the Boston Red Sox. He spent 17 years in the majors with four different teams (including six seasons with the Dodgers) before retiring in 1982 with 2,020 career hits and 314 home runs. He's served as the Dodgers' hitting coach since 1994 and runs his own baseball development center in the West Valley. Teaching the game, it seems, is something else that Smith learned from Chet Brewer.

"Mr. Brewer knew baseball," says Smith. "He knew the strategy of the game, and he taught it to us. Playing for him was like going to baseball finishing school."

The Hitter—Leon Murray is hard to miss as he ducks into the Boulevard Café on Martin Luther King Boulevard. He stands 6'6", and he very much resembles his famous younger brother, Eddie, who finished up a Hall of Fame career with the Anaheim Angels. All five of the Murray brothers played for Chet Brewer, and all five went on to play pro baseball. (Besides Eddie, only Rich would make it to the majors.)

"I was exposed to great baseball players at an early age because of Chet," says Murray. "My oldest brother [Charlie] played for Chet, and so I became the batboy. We were out there early, playing catch with all of the guys from the time we were six and seven years old."

Learning from experienced players, the Murray brothers mastered the art of hitting. "See, baseball's funny," says Murray. "If you see good baseball played and you hear the ball hit the bat right, you understand that there's a correct way to hit the ball—there's a certain crack to the bat. After we'd go back to our high school teams and make contact—CRACK!—the other kids would be like, 'Hey, where'd you learn to hit at?' See, we'd learned to turn on the ball, and it was all because of this atmosphere that Chet Brewer created."

On Sundays, Murray remembers, crowds of fans and scouts would gather at South Park to watch the action. "It was something to see, because it was all about competition," he says. "At the games, there'd be two, three hundred people all lined up along the foul lines. And afterward they'd pass the hat through the stands to pay the umpires, and then Chet would take some of that money and give the kids hamburger money. He was a father figure for a lot of the guys."

Such leadership has disappeared, and Murray worries that baseball has lost its hold on today's youth, particularly African-American kids, who now flock to basketball and football in far greater numbers. In part, say Murray and others, baseball decided to concentrate its resources in other places (most particularly in the Dominican Republic) for one reason: money. It's less expensive to develop baseball talent outside the United States, where the sport doesn't have to compete against plentiful basketball and football scholarships.

"I think baseball got lazy," says Murray. "It started to take a lot of things for granted: 'We're America's pastime, we don't have to advertise, we don't have to try and attract kids.' And Nike and Michael Jordan snuck in and took over."

In 1989, former major leaguer John Young created Reviving Baseball in Inner Cities (RBI). Designed to give kids the opportunity to play, Young's grassroots program is now backed by major league baseball (and other corporations), and it's spread from L.A. to other cities. Leon Murray, now retired after a 20-year career as a cosmetologist, has begun working for RBI to help give back some of his baseball knowledge.

But if RBI's goals are worthy, Murray worries that it's too little, too late. "The RBI program does some beautiful things for the kids, but you can't get the community behind it," he says. "It used to be that the game was passed on—we passed it on from one generation to the next. Now, people laugh at baseball."

The Field—Several years ago the city of Los Angeles decided to honor Chet Brewer's contribution to baseball and Los Angeles by naming one of the diamonds at Ross Snyder Park "Chet Brewer Field."

Located at the intersection of Compton Avenue and 41st Street, just east of the Harbor Freeway and the L.A. Coliseum, Ross Snyder Park is a well-worn patch of green-and-brown used mostly by the students of nearby Jefferson High. Chet Brewer Field, however, proves impossible to find. The sign that used to indicate it has long been missing, and none of the Parks & Rec personnel seems to have noticed its absence. In reality, there is no Chet Brewer Field.

This shouldn't be a big deal. After all, a small placard can't possibly educate us about the breadth of a person's life. But the fact that it's missing is glaringly disrespectful to the memory of Chet Brewer.

He never got to play in the majors because of the color of his skin. He hasn't got a plaque in the Hall of Fame. Even so, he was able to transcend the pain of those snubs. At a time when nobody gave a damn about inner-city youth, he mentored and befriended many of them, using baseball as his language. At the very least, the man deserves his field back.

It Happened in Brooklyn

Bob Gruber

Bill Veeck, this issue's cover boy, once said, "If Jackie Robinson was the ideal man to break the color line, Brooklyn was the ideal place."

Why was Robinson so fervently embraced in Brooklyn? I'll attempt to portray the special feel and texture of Brooklyn when I grew up there in the 1940s.

Today, each year, from New York to Florida to California there are a growing number of reunions of middle-aged adults who attended Brooklyn high schools 40 or 50 years ago. These former students—no matter their station in life or distance from Brooklyn—will exclaim almost in unison, "Was I *lucky* to be brought up in Brooklyn!" To this day, when people ask me if I'm a native New Yorker, I reply, "Not really. I was born and raised in Brooklyn."

Historically, the heralded completion of the Brooklyn Bridge in 1883 opened Brooklyn for further expansion but, conversely, signaled the end of its independence. Exactly a century ago, Brooklyn, then the nation's fourth largest city, joined Greater New York. To many of Brooklyn's citizens, this was known as "The Great Mistake."

Brooklyn became known for its diverse and unsophisticated immigrant working classes. Most of its neighborhoods were ethnic enclaves, a kind of ad hoc segregation. A happy melting pot it was not.

In contrast to the worldwide popularity of Manhattan, Brooklyn was unfashionable and known for its zaniness. Brooklynites had a chip on their shoulder. They were different, as was their language, "Brooklynese." Two of early television's most popular

characters naturally came from Brooklyn, Ralph Kramden and Ed Norton. But being the butt of a national joke didn't bother Brooklynites—call it reverse snobbism. When we saw an offbeat character from Brooklyn on the movie screen, we'd feel a sense of pride. Our attitude was, "Hey, he's one of our guys. You wanna make something out of it?" And Jackie Robinson was to become one of our greatest guys.

The disappointing Dodgers added to the borough's greenhorn reputation. Under Uncle Wilbert Robinson, they were known as "the Daffiness Boys." Later they became "Dem Bums." But, of greater significance, the Dodgers anchored Brooklyn and the camaraderie of its wildly loyal fans united its insulated communities, long before Robinson and "the Boys of Summer." You can probably understand why many of us rooted against our former tormentors, the Yankees, in the 1996 World Series, even though their manager was a Brooklyn guy, Joe Torre.

Our family lived on Winthrop Street, off Bedford Avenue, about ten short blocks from Ebbets Field. Lying in bed at night listening to a Dodger game, I'd hear the roar of the crowd on the radio seconds before the cheering wafted through the bedroom window. My first Dodger hero wasn't Jackie Robinson. It was Dolph Camilli, the National League's Most Valuable Player in 1941.

We were to become Jackie Robinson fans even though the only blacks most of us knew were caricatures who visited our homes each week via the airwaves—"Amos 'n Andy." And the actors were white. The supreme black athlete of our youth was the reserved Joe Louis, always introduced as the "Brown

Bob Gruber *is an investor relations executive in New York City. He appreciates Jackie Robinson's heroic achievement even more today than he did as an adolescent a half-century ago.*

Bomber" and as "a credit to his race." How quickly did the assertive Jackie Robinson destroy many of our racial stereotypes! (I might add that the only real Southerner most of us knew was another radio personality, Walter Lanier Barber, the Ol' Redhead. He was born in Mississippi, raised in Florida, and beloved in Brooklyn.)

Demographically, in the late 1940s, Brooklyn's population was about 2.7 million. In this so-called "Borough of Churches," the largest single ethnic group was Jewish, numbering almost a million. The black population was about 200,000.

In the Brooklyn in which I grew up, doctors made house calls, teachers were held in esteem, and Chinese restaurants served only Cantonese food. Few of our parents had cars and most of our relatives lived within walking distance. On Sunday afternoons, all three generations would eat at Grandma's house. Marriage between young people of different religions was strenuously discouraged and I didn't know of any interracial couples. Drugs were not a problem and *I* can testify *personally* that there was no teenage sex.

Some memories of our youth are forever etched in our minds. When Hugh Casey's pitch eluded Mickey Owen in the fourth game of the 1941 World Series, we were sitting on a bench across the street from my grandparents' apartment on Ocean Avenue on a Sunday afternoon listening to my uncle's sizable portable radio. At that time, October, 1941, Jackie Robinson was playing semipro football for the barnstorming Los Angeles Bulldogs.

Two months later, on another Sunday afternoon, the family was gathered in my grandparents' living room. I was listening to the Dodger-Giant football game. The broadcast was interrupted with news of Japan's sneak attack on Pearl Harbor. It was the first time I heard some of my relatives curse. At that moment, Jackie Robinson was on a steamship two days out of Hawaii, sailing for home after having completed the football season with the renamed Honolulu Bears.

On October 21, 1944, President Franklin Roosevelt, running for an unprecedented fourth term, was campaigning through Flatbush. It was a cold, rainy day, but Roosevelt, wrapped in his big Navy cape, insisted on campaigning to dispel rumors about his health. His final campaign stop was Ebbets Field, the baseball season having recently ended. He began his speech, "I have never been to Ebbets Field before, but I have rooted for the Dodgers. I hope to come back here some day and see them play." At that time, Army Lieutenant Jack Robinson was coaching black athletic teams in Camp Breckinridge, Kentucky, awaiting his honorable discharge the following month.

Roosevelt, of course, never returned to Ebbets Field; he died on April 12, 1945. We were playing stickball in the P.S. 92 school yard when we received the news. We went home immediately. He was the only president we had ever known. On that same day, Jackie Robinson, a rookie shortstop with the Kansas City Monarchs, was awaiting a tryout in Boston with the Red Sox. It would prove to be a politically inspired sham.

After the war, Branch Rickey signed Robinson, who went on to a great season at AAA Montreal in 1946. On April 10, 1947, during the sixth inning of a Dodger-Montreal exhibition game at Ebbets Field, it was announced that Robinson had been promoted to the Dodgers.

A day later, on Friday, April 11, I was walking South on Bedford Avenue on my way to Erasmus Hall High School, where I was a freshman. As I passed Martense Street, a young black man in a late model car stopped and, in a distinctive voice, asked me, "Excuse me, fella, which way to Ebbets Field?"

I replied, "Keep going about a dozen blocks up Bedford. You can't miss it." As he thanked me, I realized that it was Jackie Robinson. He was to play as a Dodger for the first time that afternoon (in an exhibition game against the Yankees). As Jackie pulled away I was too excited to shout encouragement. When I told the story in the school lunch room that day, the few black kids there came over and shook my hand.

The season opener with Robinson at first for the Dodgers has been called baseball's finest moment. On hand were 26,623 fans, reportedly more than half of them black. "The Great Experiment" had its first success: Ebbets Field became a happy melting pot. (One sweltering day in the bleachers, Hilda Chester, with her ever-present cowbell, wouldn't let us kids take our shirts off because of the threat of sunburn. Hilda Chester, my first dermatologist.)

There was immense racial pressure—in the clubhouse, on the field, and on the road. But Robinson's play was extraordinary and his character was exemplary. As the 1947 season progressed, many white players on Brooklyn's sandlots adopted Jackie's bat-held-high stance and wore uniform number 42.

So why was Brooklyn the ideal place to break baseball's color line? Significantly, its citizens were not content with the status quo. They were strivers, hardworking, first and second generation immigrants. They were ridiculed outsiders. They were underdogs who could sympathize with an underdog. More than a third of Brooklynites were Jewish, with their tradition of social justice. Finally, frustrated Dodger fans wanted a winner and Robinson helped to bring them six pennants—and one world championship—in ten years. Winning can be a powerful force for tolerance.

It's been said that Babe Ruth changed baseball, but that Jack Roosevelt Robinson changed America. He also added to our pride in being from Brooklyn.

Tom Shea

Dick Thompson

The *Grandstand Baseball Annual 1996* reprinted an article titled "Baseball Research Before SABR," by Frank Phelps, which had originally appeared in the 1990 SABR membership directory. GBA's editorial comment stated that Phelps's article serves as the "definitive research road map," and that "all the big names are there who contributed to baseball's early foundation."

When SABR published Lee Allen's *Cooperstown Corner* several years ago, Steve Gietschier of *The Sporting News*, writing the introduction, felt Allen's greatest contribution was in collecting biographical data on the then estimated 11,000 major league players. Gietschier stated that Allen's effort "would grow into the first edition of *The Baseball Encyclopedia*," where Allen "labored with other pioneers in baseball research, including John Tattersall, S. C. Thompson, Frank Marcellus, Karl Wingler, Harry Simmons, Allen Lewis, Joseph Overfield, Clifford Kachline, and Paul Rickart."

Unfortunately, neither Phelps nor Gietschier made any reference to baseball's greatest biographical researcher, the late Tom Shea.

Shea remains the forgotten man among baseball's great researchers. He had been gathering baseball data since his graduation from Boston College in 1926. From then until the start of the Second World War, Tom worked as a traveling salesman for the Macmillan Publishing Company and later the Thomas Nelson Publishing Company. He sold textbooks to school systems from North Carolina to Maine, as far west as Pittsburgh.

Wherever he went he carried index cards and small scraps of paper in his pocket. While waiting for appointments with school administrators, he would kill time taking notes from the local newspapers of whatever small town he was in. During the evenings he would use his Macmillan expense account—these were Depression years—to buy drinks in an area establishment and steer the conversation toward local baseball.

Shea is less well-known than he should be because his best ideas and biggest contributions either didn't quite come off or were uncredited. Three examples:

His detailed proposal for a baseball reference encyclopedia in 1939 was sabotaged by Hall of Famer Eddie Collins' paranoia.

In 1941, Shea responded in detail and at length to J. G. Taylor Spink's plaintive requests for help in marketing the *Baseball Register*. His advice worked, but his only payment was a lifetime subscription—which was abruptly cut off when Spink died.

It is obvious from the materials in his files that Shea supplied a high percentage of the biographical facts for the Turkin and Thomson *Official Encyclopedia of Baseball*, first published in 1951. Tom trustingly thought he was a co-author, and the fact that he got only a brief credit in the preface turned him off baseball research for almost a decade. "Turkin and Thompson" should have been known as "Thompson and Shea," or at least "Turkin, Thompson, and Shea."

Cliff Kachline introduced me to Tom Shea at a SABR meeting in Boston in 1983, and for the next ten years I had the great pleasure of spending an afternoon a week

Dick Thompson's *chief interest is collecting biographical data on New England-born players.*

listening to an elderly man who could tell me the story of any major league baseball player from the advent of the game through 1950.

As our relationship grew, Tom decided I was a worthy successor to his research files. His collection consisted of about 125 shoe boxes crammed with index cards and newspaper clippings. Included in Tom's files were about 100 letters from Lee Allen, thirty-one from S. C. Thompson, thirteen from Hy Turkin, ten from Ernie Lanigan, two from Eddie Collins, and twelve from J. G. Taylor Spink.

Sampling these letters gives you a sense of how central Shea was in the development of the universe of biographical data we now take for granted when we turn to our favorite baseball reference works.

The two letters from Collins were both written on Boston Red Sox stationery.

May 18, 1939: "I received a letter from Mr. Harridge in which he indicated the American League would be interested in such a proposal as you [sic] suggestion."

June 13, 1939: "Thank you very much for yours of recent date enclosing brief analysis of the proposed work. I had planned to discuss this matter with Mr. Harridge at Cooperstown yesterday, but the opportunity was not presented. I have, therefore, forwarded all the material on to him to Chicago today."

Included with the Collins letters was a carbon of a letter from Tom to Collins with the outline for a prototype baseball encyclopedia. The book called for 743 pages: 150 for "history," 60 of "photos," 100 of "contributions," 156 of "statistical summary" and 277 of "biographical index."

Shea told me fifty years after the fact that Collins was interested enough in Tom's idea to run it by American League President Will Harridge. Collins swore Tom to secrecy about the deal, stating that he didn't want the National League to hear about the project. Several months into the project, Collins abruptly refused to respond to Tom's letters or answer his phone calls.

Tom approached his friend Moe Berg and asked him to find out the details. Berg returned with the following story. Tom had a friend named Andy O'Connor who had pitched one big league game for the New York Highlanders in 1908. Tom had been drinking one evening with O'Connor and had related some of the details of the deal he had going with Collins. Several weeks later O'Connor ran into Collins at Fenway Park and mentioned what Tom had told him. Collins, upset that a drunken ex-ball player knew of the plans, dropped the project on the spot. Berg attributed Collins' response to residual paranoia that Collins retained from his dealings with Charlie Comiskey and the Black Sox scandal.

Tom had begun his correspondence with Ernie Lanigan in the mid-1920s. Through Lanigan, Tom met S. C. Thompson sometime in the 1930s. Lanigan worked at the International League office which was in the Ruppert Building at 535 Fifth Avenue in New York City. Thompson, a musician by trade, spent a lot of time traveling with shows. Shea likewise was on the road a lot. Both called New York City their home base in the late 1930s. The International League office was their meeting spot, and they went there to exchange data and pick the brain of their mentor, Lanigan.

Unfortunately most of Shea's pre-World War II correspondence was lost. Tom left his files with a friend in Philadelphia, where he had been based in the early 1930s. The friend, thinking Tom was not going to return, threw out the files. Tom lamented that ten years of research done on Philadelphia area players was lost.

The letters from Lanigan were short and usually pessimistic.

October 23, 1941: "I took a terrible beating on revising Who's Who and doing the Baseball Cyclopedia."

December 12, 1941: "Thompson lacked some first names of players in the American League in 1900, that not being an American League. I got Irving Posan of the Sporting News to dig for them. He spent five hours and emerged with 15. No charge to Thompson and no dough to Posan. I think we-uns will have to take a course in accounting showing the hours spent in productive and unproductive labor."

July 31, 1946: "The Great Thompson gave me your address and I have told the Great Simmons [Harry Simmons] to send you the material you left at 535 when you departed for the wars. It is pretty well mixed up, but is intact. I came up here [Cooperstown] for the good of baseball and am making the mistake of my life. As I can sell everything I write I will not go into details. Have decided with Kipling that the fastest traveler is he who travels alone. I have been going at a snail's pace."

September 15, 1946: "I am taking a large sized and luxurious financial beating here, thanks for my fondness for doing something for baseball. I will recuperate. Nat Goodwin once appeared in a play called 'An American Citizen,' written by Henry Guy Carleton. In Act the first he discovers that his partner has absconded with the assets of the estate leaving him holding the well-known bag or portfolio or whatever you call it. He makes a speech to the effect that by observing a rigid economy until he is 93 years old he can pay off the debts and start life afresh. I am 73 now and have no debts, but I think I will start afresh at age 74."

April 2, 1948: "I plan a story on Mickey Cochrane and you ought to be able to tell me something about him that would appeal to the cash customers."

One afternoon in the late 1980's, Tom and I were in the cellar of his home on Bradley Hill in Hingham,

Massachusetts. In the corner of the room was a big stack of *The Sporting News*. Tom said that J. G. Taylor Spink had been sending them to him free since 1941. The issues were continuous until they abruptly stopped shortly after Spink's death in 1962. Some excerpts from Spink's letters:

March 22, 1941: "We are pleased to forward to you, under separate cover, a copy of the new edition of our Baseball Register, with the compliments of William J. Manley and Ernest John Lanigan of the International League. Will you kindly advise Mr. Lanigan of its receipt. Mr. Lanigan tells us that you have been following the publishing business for a number of years. As we have put a lot of time and effort into the Baseball Register, we would value your opinion as to whether it is a library book. Your views on this point, together with any suggestions you might care to offer regarding its distribution or sale, would greatly be appreciated."

April 12, 1941: "I just received your letter which Mr. Lanigan passed along to me, and I want to express my gratitude for the useful information you have given me…Thanking you for your fine co-operation, which we will be glad to reciprocate whenever we can be of service."

April 21, 1941: "In your recent helpful letter, you indicated that if we wanted any additional names that might help us in getting library distribution for our Baseball Register, you would be able to send them to us. I trust that you will not feel that I am unduly persistent, but we are very anxious to get such names and I will appreciate any further information you might be able to give us."

May 25, 1941: "I want to thank you very much for additional list of libraries received, which we will follow up at once. Note letter I had from Baker and Taylor. If there is anything you can suggest in this connection, I would appreciate hearing from you."

May 31, 1941: "After using the lists you sent us, we now have about 250 circulars similar to the attached we would like to send to libraries and I wonder if you might have some list that you might forward to us, or advise us where we might obtain."

The earliest letter from S. C. Thompson was dated July 26, 1946, and it reads in a familiar, reacquainting fashion, probably the first correspondence the two had exchanged since the start of World War II. The last was dated July 20, 1951, after *The Official Encyclopedia of Baseball* had been published. Most of Thompson's letters were undated and they usually consisted of narratives of varying lengths attached at the ends of longhand rosters and biographical data. A typical Thompson letter would be about fifteen ledger-sized pages. He would list players he lacked birth or death data on alphabetically, Tom would then make notations

on each name: "Resident of Altoona, Pa. May still be living there." Or, "From around Sunbury, Pa. A noted judge in Pennsylvania." After making an entry on each of Thompson's queries, he would send the entire letter back to Thompson who would then send out inquires to players or local vital statistics offices based on Tom's tips. There are hundreds of these pages, and I came to realize they were the true guts of the "Turkin and Thompson" book.

The Thompson letters are the most fascinating, but also the most disturbing.

July 26, 1946: "Surprised but glad to get your letter of June 21st but notice it was dated July 15, 1942. I heard you were in the service but it is a mystery about the date of the letter. I also notice it was mailed in a very old envelope of mine. What have you been doing and all about it? Ernie is now the curator of the Baseball Museum at Cooperstown, N.Y. and Harry Simmons has his job at the International League office."

Undated: "You certainly know where the body is buried in a lot of these cases. Don't know how you do it or how you keep them all in your noodle."

Undated:"Received your stuff but haven't time to dig into it yet. Thanks for the mass of new data and leads. It will take me a little while to get it all digested."

Undated:"Am sending out letters by the score, sent out over 100 last week. As soon as replies start coming in I will keep you informed as usual."

Undated:"I guess this is quite a letter but then you wrote a little hunk of epistle yourself. I wish you could arrange to drop in if you are going to be in New York soon. I have a lot of new stuff that I would like to discuss with you…trusting to hear from you especially on your ideas on how we can squeeze info on these Conn. League boys out of the old Conn. League."

Undated:"Having finished your latest and most interesting letter piece by piece and paragraph by paragraph, let me say that you sure gave out with a lot of very valuable data and clues which I shall follow up and advise you of the results."

Undated:"We are filling them up slowly but surely thanks mostly to your clues. I think you carry more data under your hat than J. G. Taylor Spink carries in his files."

Undated:"Your big mass of data on hand today. Will send this on now as it will take several days to digest your latest effort."

Undated:"Hope to hear from you again soon with some more good dope and leads to follow up."

Undated:"Thanks a million for your fine letter and mass of data which I received this past week. I am enclosing information wanted lists of 'C's' and 'D's', also complete data list of New England players thru 'C's' and 'D's'. Also returning information wanted list of 'A's' and 'B's' per your request."

Undated: "I am definitely interested in collaborating with you on a book such as you suggest if I can be of any help. I think your idea is a good one. I thoroughly agree with you that no one cares about a history of the American League."

Undated: "Just got thru checking your last three letters. Comment (if any) enclosed on my new dope list. Just got two more from you this a.m."

Undated: "I have picked up your cards from the International League office as you suggested and have them here at the house so if you ever want them, you will know where they are. I will keep them in good condition and separate from my files. I haven't had the opportunity to open the boxes and examine them yet as I just picked them up about a week ago."

Undated: "Looked over your cards. It was the first time I had opened the boxes since I brought them over from the International League. They are in pretty much of a mess, I am sorry to say. They have been packed in several cardboard cartons and have been pretty well scrambled in the process. As soon as I can get around to it, I will sort them out. It is going to be a job. What are the little sheets done up in rubber bands? Do they belong with the cards?"

Undated: "Yes, I had the Clipper annuals here about a year ago but like a dope, I never took down places of death. I'll try to get them again from Laurie who lives across the street and who had them before 'Variety.' I have combed the Swales card files in the book stack at the public library and got all I need from them."

Undated: "Thanks a lot for your last letter. Many clues which I am following up. Will keep you advised weekly as usual."

Undated: "Looking forward to another good mass of data soon. I finally wrote to everyone you gave me an address on. Took a little time as there were a lot of them. Where did my last "A" and "C" list stop? I think I was up to the "H's" but I forget."

Undated: "Thanks for all the new dope—too numerous to mention each case. Hope I am doing the same for you. Looks like you will get to see a World Series. My pal Turkin is coming up to Boston this week. I told him to phone you if he has the time. He's one swell guy and is helping us a lot so if he calls you, show him the ropes."

July 20, 1951: "The book [*The Official Encyclopedia Of Baseball*] is doing well. I haven't had any reports on it lately but at last report it had sold over 30,000 copies and was 8th on the non-fiction best seller list. I am a little disappointed in that the book did not bring forth any appreciable information from the players or their relatives. As far as I know not a single one has written in to offer anything in the way of missing information. So I guess we will just have to go our own way doing business as we always did…Don't take our friend Hy too serious. He is a good Joe but inclined to get into

your hair with his grandma tactics. He is one hell of a writer though as I believe you will agree if you have looked over the book. He has gotten a fellow writing to him now and this jerk is a specialist in finding out that a certain player died on August 5th instead of August 4th as we have him etc. etc. etc. ad nauseum. Nothing new or startling. Just petty junk like that until it got into my hair and I just had to tell Hy off. There is never any full data on some guy who is blank. Just a rehash of stuff we have gone over thoroughly. So I finally wrote this jerk and told him off. I hope he shuts his mouth. Ernie is the other sniper. He has a funny system. He never writes to me but sends Marcellus notes that he "don't think" so-and-so is right. We only have these two snipers so I guess we are lucky. I told Hy if we changed the data in the book to conform we would lose all prestige and respect of the sports writers as well as that of the publishers. It is my idea that once you go into print, you simply can't bring out a new edition with a million petty changes like one or two days difference in a player's birth or death without damaging your prestige beyond repair."

This was the final letter from Thompson. Tom was shocked that he was not listed as one of the authors. He believed that he and Thompson were co-authoring the project. While there is no doubt that S. C. Thompson was the driving force behind *The Official Encyclopedia of Baseball*, the only credit Tom got from Turkin and Thompson was an acknowledgement in the preface along with Lanigan, Frank Marcellus, Allen, Phil Redelheim, and Harry Simmons.

In retrospect this seems naive on Tom's part as he had spent so many years in the publishing business, but he had been living in Massachusetts, and by the time the book was published, had not seen Thompson face-to-face in almost a decade. Suspicions aroused, Tom started to hold back material. Tom told me that Turkin was upset when he realized the full extent of what Tom had provided.

The dated Turkin letters all came in 1950 and 1951. Like the Thompson material, there are also many pages of raw data. Turkin would send on whatever biographical data he had obtained and ask Tom to review, correct, or simply okay them for admission to the database.

March 9, 1950: "I have received quite a few new middle names, birth data, etc., as soon as I transribe them to the rosters, I intend to keep up Thompson's habit of sending you copies of the agenda. There seems to be some difficulty about the Hengle brothers. Thompson lists only Edward S. (nickname Maxie), and mistakenly lists him as both playing second base for and managing Chicago UA in 1884. The fact is there were two men, brothers. One is Edward S., but that is probably the manager. The other was E. J. Hengle, and Harry Simmons says he thinks that this is the second baseman who later popped up with the St. Paul club of the Northwestern League, full name Emory J. Hengle. Can you enlighten me on this?"

October 27, 1950: "If you get the info, would you please shoot it to me on the enclosed self-addressed postal? I am in the proof-reading stage of the Encyclopedia, so any last-minute additions will have to come in the next few weeks...the sooner the better...or else miss the first edition."

February 23, 1951: "I do hope that last missile I forwarded from Marcellus didn't scare you off. He was just in a crotchety mood, though generally he's very genial, helpful and responsible. Lee Allen writes me that he heard from you re Charles Marvin (Pop) Smith. Would appreciate your sending me the data, too."

April 5, 1951: "Thought I would be seeing you by now, but the old family bus burned out two bearings, stayed in drydock three weeks, and just burned out another. I'm marooned indefinitely, till the jalopy straightens out and flies right. Thank goodness, the book is going much better than the car. In fact, a second printing is imminent. Hence this letter. Could you please send me as soon as possible all the additions and corrections you found for the Encyclopedia? I have found many typos. When I round them all up for the printer's benefit, I promise to send a copy of the complete batch to you."

May 28, 1951: "Your last 'letter' overwhelmed me. I'm plowing through it carefully. Am piling up a load of material, and will faithfully send you the complete list of corrections for the next printing."

December 20, 1951: "Please forgive my not writing earlier, but I've been bogged down tracing more than 1,000 claims about missing players. Your leads alone would take a year of research. Since $100 reward was the top amount offered, you are being sent the full Century note, which you so rightly deserve many times over. Fine Christmas present."[In 1951, *The Official Encyclopedia of Baseball*'s publisher, A.S. Barnes and Company, awarded $50 to each person who furnished the name of any major league player who was missing from the encyclopedia, with a $100 maximum. Tom sent in four names,and received $100 for himself and $100 for Frank Bruno, a Boston librarian who knew nothing about baseball but to whom Tom owed money.]

The letters from Lee Allen ran from 1950 to 1951, and then again from 1960 until Allen's death. From 1951 through 1960 there are no baseball letters. Tom told me he was so put off by the Turkin and Thompson in-

cident that he gave up baseball. It was Allen who resparked his interest. Most of the Allen letters read like a column from *Cooperstown Corner*, and justice can only be done by reading them in their entirety. While Turkin and Thompson were more task-oriented in their research, Shea and Allen clearly took delight in the details they discovered. Both were master storytellers.

October 13, 1950: "I have heard S. C. Thompson and Hy Turkin speak of you so frequently I almost feel I know you, and I wonder if you could help me out with something. I have for years been trying to find out something about Robert S. Clack, who played the outfield for Cincinnati in 1876...would you be kind enough to tell me what you know about Clack, and where I might go to trace him further."

October 22, 1950: "Many thanks for the kind words about my work in your letter of October 18. I appreciate them, because the book was not a great financial success...extremely grateful for such tips. I'm trying to improve my writing, and think that the next book will be a better job...I'm sure that S. C. Thompson, who delights in every mistake I make, will rejoice if Borden's game was a phony. I am absolutely at a loss to understand Thompson's attitude. Last winter, for instance, I received a letter saying that Charles Wesley Jones died in 1910 when struck by lightning. I reported the matter to Turkin and we listed Jones as having died then. When I thought about the incident and decided to check on it, I went to considerable expense and made a trip to Princeton, Indiana, and consumed three days before proving the death notice erroneous. When I then asked Hy to erase the Jones death in his records, Thompson considered the whole thing very amusing and proof that I was irresponsible. You figure it out; I can't. Lord knows there are few of us interested in this sort of thing, and I don't see why we can't stick together.

"Thompson has done a lot of good work, and we all owe him a great deal, but he seems to feel that the research he did years ago is final. I am always open to correction, knowing how tough it is to get accurate data on obscure players from the long ago, and he should feel likewise...thanks a million for the tips on Clack. You bet I'll follow up every one of them, and then let you know what happens.

"I think you probably agree with me that the early players' records should be reexamined to prove their data. I know Turkin and Marcellus feel that way too, although it is a nuisance sometimes to erase something you gathered painfully."

February 28, 1951: "Many thanks for straightening me out on Charles Marvin (Pop) Smith. I will certainly follow your leads and complete the data I need."

March 11, 1951: "I read your recent letter with great interest. There are so few people in the world who have studied baseball history to the extent that we have that it is a real treat to find one."

Excerpts from the second run:

March 5, 1960: "I have often wondered why I never heard from you again, and wondered if I could have possibly offended you. I hope not. I wrote to Thompson and he reported that he hadn't heard from you for a long time either. Are you well? If you are, and if you are in a position to resume corresponding, I would appreciate hearing from you."

March 11, 1960: "Thanks for your long letter containing all that information. As time permits, I will pursue some of the leads you have given me…If you ever locate the data on Frank McLaughlin, I'd surely appreciate receiving it."

August 22, 1960: "That was a dandy job you did on the McLaughlins. There is a lot still missing, but you dug up much I didn't have."

November 16, 1960: "What a wonderful job you did in turning up William J. Tiernay after all this time. I knew he was a Boston lad, but somehow never got around to doing any research concerning him. He played the opening day of the 1882 season for Cincinnati, their first AA game, and the papers took very little notice of him."

June 30, 1961: "Thanks for your good letter about 'The National League Story,' and all the priceless data you enclosed. First of all, it was not flattery that prompted my mention of you in the book. Although you may not have contributed anything specific to that one volume, it was an acknowledgement of my general indebtedness to you for enriching my study of baseball and enriching my life.

"Sam Wright. I'm delighted that you have finally cleared up this most baffling of cases. Some years ago I visited Harry Wright, Jr. in Mt. Holly, N.J. He remembered Uncle Sam but had no idea where he died or where he was buried. I think one of two things happened. First of all, Harry and George Wright were the sons of Samuel Wright and Mary Love Wright. Shortly after George's birth his father either re-married, his bride being Ann Tone, or Sam was born out of wedlock. I would imagine that Ann Tone was a Catholic which would account for Sam's burial in St. Patricks. So Harry and George Wright would be English and Sam would be English-Irish. I think it would be more logical to believe that Sam, Sr. re-married than to have had a son out of wedlock, inasmuch as the maiden name of Sam Jr.'s mother was known at the time of his death, and George took charge of the funeral. There was a lot of hatred in the Wright family, due, I think, to the fact that George's branch became wealthy and Harry's did not. George's sons have been most uncooperative over the years about their father's baseball achievements."

December 16, 1961: "Meanwhile, can you put me straight in regard to the various John Farrells? It seems to me that obituaries confused Hartford Jack Farrell and Providence Jack Farrell. The latter was well known player, and the former a bum. I seem to recall that Hartford Jack was often jailed, and newspaper accounts would say it was the Providence player, and then the Providence player would write in and deny it."

January 13, 1962: "I certainly enjoyed the latest fat envelope from you and have studied the material. My American League book is out of the way now, so I have time to write you the letter of a length you deserve."

January 19, 1962: "Coincidence piles upon coincidence. Shortly after receiving your letter about Honest John Kelly being the Syracuse-Troy performer in 1879, I ran into a long account in The Sporting News for 1889 describing an incident in which Honest John created a scene in a bawdyhouse, throwing beer bottles at the girls and cutting up much in the manner of Fred Lewis or Lew Dickerson."

February 16, 1962: "I picked up many heights and weights, bats and throws from your latest, and for which many thanks. In confidence, the American League has just read the manuscript of my history and refuses to make it the "official" history because of references I made to drinking by Ruth and Waddell and the suicide of Chick Stahl."

April 14, 1962: "In my Sporting News column this week I had occasion to mention Daniel R. Ryan, and of course gave you credit for the information I had about him. Thanks to your informing me that Burrill (apparently it is Burrell) is still alive I was able to give that information to Bert Abbey, who, strangely, is an old battery mate of Buster's."

October 24, 1962: "For some time I have been embarrassed and pained by the possibility that at our meeting, after inviting you to be my guest, I may have left without having paid the check, thus sticking you with it. Lord, I hope not. But if this did happen, would you please let me know the amount so I can send it to you and ease my conscience. Such excursions have been very rare for me in the past few years, and I beg your indulgence."

January 7, 1963: "Your letter made me feel better than anything that has happened in many weeks. I want to write at length about this some day, but not right now, so I will confine myself to baseball material. But I still am upset because of the possibility that you had to pay that bar check, so please let me know if this is the case, as it has bothered me for weeks."

January 21, 1963: "As for separating the Quinns and Morgans, I'm afraid it is beyond my powers. I think the Morgan with Washington in 1884 was William Morgan, a Brooklyn boy and that the one with the Virginias was Henry W. Morgan, of Baltimore.

"Another erroneous date of death in T&T is that of Robert M. Barr, who did not die on 11-14-93. That was the date of death of some amateur from Philadelphia.

Turkin slipped a lot of those deaths from the Clipper Almanac into T&T and didn't seem to care to check them out in his anxiety to get data. Robert M. Barr died in Washington, D.C., his lifelong home, on March 11, 1930."

"Another wrong death date in T&T is that of Jimmie Woods, or Wood. T&T says he died 11-3-86. The Clipper almanac shows plainly that the man who died on that date was Burr Wood, a pitcher from Canastota, N.Y. So Turkin lists the player as James Burr Wood and kills him in 1886."

March 28, 1963: "Thanks to you, I today received a wonderful bunch of stuff from Wilfred Hamill about his father's career, including pictures of a Union Association game, the first I have ever seen."

April 8, 1963: "What you say about Frank Whitney is extremely interesting. He must have been the last survivor of the 1876 boys. When the Golden Jubilee dinner was held at the Astor on February 2, 1925, the following players were present: Bond, Bradley, Burdock, Holbert, Knight, Manning, Morrill, Deacon White and York. I don't know why George Wright was not included in this group. I believe all the deaths of 1876 players in the Encyclopedia are correct except for that of Thomas John Carey, who is shown as having expired on Feb. 13, 1899. The Clipper Almanac identifies the man who died on that date as John Carey, an infielder who died in Los Angeles. Turkin probably saw that and leaped to the conclusion it was Thomas John."

May 30, 1963: "Your opinion that Thayer was Fair makes sense to me. Game in which he appeared for Mutuals, July 29, 1876, was played at Boston. I wonder where T&T got that 'Mechanic Falls, Maine' bit for him?"

January 7, 1965: "If I have offended you in any way, I am very sorry about it. It has been so long since I have heard from you, I felt that this must be the case. However, I'm at a loss to know what it could have been. In any event, you may be happy to learn that I went back to AA last January, and am about to complete my first year and am very happy about it."

May 20, 1966: "You really started something with the business about 'Sis' Hopkins. First of all, a curiosity, *The Sporting Life* shows that the Pittsburgh 1902 player made two hits in four trips in the second game of two on August 24, 1902 at Cincinnati, a Sunday. In its coverage of the same game *The Sporting News* also runs the name as Hopkins but gives him two-for-two, including a double. To settle the matter I went down to our basement where we have an original volume of the 1902 Cincinnati Enquirer. There was a note that said something like this, 'When Zimmer left the second game and was replaced by Hopkins, a friend of Wagner's from Carnegie, the boys in Rooter's Row all screamed "Sis".'

"So you were right. But apparently his name was Mike Hopkins and not Hawkins, although when the press box sent word down to the field the name could have come back from the bench as 'Hopkins' when 'Hawkins' was intended.

"But there were two different Hopkinses, just as you said, just as there were two different Bradys."

May 28, 1966: "Thanks for straightening me out on John and Cozy Dolan and John T. Fitzgerald."

June 28, 1966: "Your booklet on nicknames gave me something I never knew, a VPI connection for Wally Shaner, one of my favorites. Maybe I can trace him now."

August 15, 1966: "Thanks very much for the collection of notes, which, as usual, contains much information that delighted me. Let's start by taking up the year of 1874."

August 23, 1966: "I am haunted by what you wrote about Connie Mack telling Magee's son-in-law to 'lay-off, let sleeping dogs lie'."

January 28, 1967: "I know it isn't always easy for you to drop what you are doing and reply hurriedly to something, but I would appreciate it greatly if you could help me out at once in straightening out the two Quinns of the 1870's...You also once told me that the T&T sketch of Henry William Morgan was the combined record of at least three players...The death date on Rooney Sweeney in T&T is also erroneous. Rooney was alive and kicking in 1887."

March 24, 1967: "Bollicky, Boozing Billy Taylor could not possibly have been the player with Baltimore in 1874, Hartford in 1877 and Troy in 1879...Now, you have established that James B. (Sandy) Taylor was definitely the Troy man. That leaves at issue the identity of the players with Baltimore in 1874 and Hartford in 1877...But who could the Taylor be who played with Baltimore in 1874?

"As for the Hayes matter, I consider Michael Hayes, born Cleveland, to be one of Hy Turkin's flights of fancy."

Undated: "I have the exact date on Anson at Notre Dame. He entered December 3, 1866, when he was 14 and remained two years, attending with his older brother, Sturgis R. Anson. So it was an academy as I suspected, high school level, and Anse was not a collegian, Baby."

Undated: "James Niels Peterson runs the swankiest restaurant in Palm Beach and he told me a couple of weeks ago that he handled Connie Mack's personal correspondence for 20 years and that the 1914 World Series was fixed. He named Bender, but I do not believe it. Bender was a good friend of mine, which is meaningless, but he was coaching for the Athletics and Connie was still alive. I'm sure he would not have taken the Chief back if Peterson had the right dope."

April 9, 1966: "I am very much amused at your discovery that Carrie Nation died of paresis. When it was not known what caused paresis, newspaper obits often listed it as cause of death. The only ballplayers whose death certificates I have seen that list syphilis as the direct cause of death are Rossman, Claude and that strange person, Charles Leander Jones, no-hitter in his first start.

"Even more amusing than the Carry Nation cause of death, however, is the 'image' that Christy Mathewson has. Never smoked or drank, but he could handle the women. Tom Swope, the retired Cincinnati baseball writer, has always disliked Mathewson because he (Swope) saw Matty coming out of a whorehouse on Christmas Eve."

January 23, 1968: "I was thinking of you last Saturday morning, for I was sitting in the living room of Edith Hanke, who is the youngest daughter of James H. (Orator Jim) O'Rourke. I had searched for her for many years and finally learned she was living at Madeira Beach, near Clearwater...I told Edith about you and what you had written me about O'Rourke's fatherless childhood and the strong Christian character of his mother, all of which she verified. She also told me that John O'Rourke never married, got very fat, was an enormous eater and died of acute indigestion."

March 10, 1968: "The announcement of our Encyclopedia will be coming in a couple of weeks. Could I induce you to look at some proofs in about a year to make certain we have the right club connections for Morgans, Taylors et al?"

June 25, 1968: "Also, I think you will be amused to know that Waldo Ward Yarnall denies having died in 1934 as T&T claims...I think you ought to read a galley of our Encyclopedia for a good fee and have so recommended that you be asked to. We may have some wrong club connections. But we will have some things right too, and I think it will be a big step ahead of T&T."

July 16, 1968: "One time on the telephone you told me to disregard VPI's claim that Skinny Shaner did not attend the institution. You are so right. Shaner says he went to VPI three years. He is now stage manager of the Lido show at the Stardust in Las Vegas, of all things."

August 15, 1968: "Did I tell you I turned up the date of death at Philly of George Stacey Davis? 10-17-40, of paresis. The widow refused to tell any of the Davis side of the family even that he had died and they didn't find out until several years later."

Lee Allen's death in 1969 was a heavy blow for baseball researchers. SABR was formed shortly after his death and it's been said that SABR's biographical committee was an extention of Allen's biographical research club.

The biographical committee has been ably chaired over the years by such researchers as Cliff Kachline, Joe Simenic, Rich Topp, and Bill Carle. It has continued to solve some of the most baffling cases.

The flow of letters to Tom Shea did not stop with Allen's death. Researchers continued to flood Tom with requests for clues on long-dead major leaguers. Some of the most interesting were from Simenic and Bill Haber, both of whom had become mesmerized by Tom at SABR's founding meeting in Cooperstown. Excerpts from the Simenic letters are as follows.

September 23, 1971: "Many thanks for your 'fat envelope' of September 13 with data on Cleveland players. You certainly will keep me busy for many months to come tracking down all these leads but I will enjoy every minute of it."

January 22, 1972: "Among the many notes I made the night of our dinner in Cooperstown was to let you know when and if I got a questionnaire for Raymond Benjamin Mowe, the 1913 Brooklyn shortstop. You were of the opinion that he came from Earlham College. Earlier this week I received his questionaire from his daughter-in-law who lives in Sarasota, Fla. She said that he was athletic director at Earlham College, Richmond, Ind., from 1917-1923."

March 31, 1973: "The last time we were in touch was when we solved the Gonzzle-Gouzzie riddle thanks to your excellent tip. Now thanks to another of your excellent tips I am happy to report the solution of another puzzle. You may recall you sent me a lengthy list of players who attended Ohio colleges. One of these was Elisha S. Norton, the 1896-97 Washington pitcher, you said attended Ohio State University. I recently wrote to the Ohio State Alumni Assn. and today I received the enclosed information from their monthly bulletin showing that Norton died in Aspinwall, Pa., March 5, 1950."

April 11, 1973: "What an interesting letter from you (as usual). So full of nostalgia but more important some excellent leads to follow up. You had so many tips I don't know just how to begin my reply."

May 21, 1973: "In your letter of April 4 you were telling me about all the players who came up from the small western Pennsylvania towns along the Ohio River, and 'one of them was Dr. James S. Darragh, out of the Univ. of Pennsylvania, who practiced as a dentist—I suppose all his life—and died in Rochester, Pa., not in N.Y.'

"A few weeks before I got your letter I had written to the New York State Dept. of Health requesting Darragh's death certificate but they wrote back saying they could not locate it.

"Acting on your tip I wrote to the Pennsylvania State Dept. of Health and in today's mail I received his death certificate. Darragh died in Rochester, Pa. (as you said), Aug. 12, 1939."

November 26, 1976: "It has been much too long since

I was last in touch with you and I wish to apologize for my tardiness. Some months ago you were kind enough to send along a lot of little 'tid-bits' on pre-1900 players and though I have done a little digging I regret to say that my efforts so far have been fruitless. I have not given up and will continue to bear down on these 'toughies'."

November 15, 1977: "I recently decided to concentrate my research efforts on players who made their major league debuts prior to 1900. It is this group that is the most difficult to trace and presents the greatest challenge. Do you realize that in this pre-1900 group there are over 700 players for whom we have no death data, and that of these 700 there are about 100 for whom we have no first name? Our young friends, Bill Haber and Tom Hufford, are more or less concentrating on the 1900-1915 group and are meeting with a fair amount of success."

Excerpts from the Haber letters:

October 12, 1971: "Trust all is going well with you. I was hopeful that by this time I would've heard from you concerning some of the 'missing' players we were discussing at Cooperstown. I recall your saying for instance that Frederick H. 'Klondike' Smith died in Massachusetts some six to eight years ago. Cliff Kachline tells me that you've provided Joe Simenic with enough leads in the Ohio area to keep him busy all winter long. I am hopeful that you'll be good enough to do the same for me in the New York City area."

January 10, 1972: "Thanks a million for sending me all those leads—they're beautiful and I only hope that some players are found as a direct result of those leads.

"Tom, my main request this time around is that I'd like you to go through the Encyclopedia from C to Z as you did with A&B and send me similar lists as you did from time to time. I hope you'll be able to do this in your leisure time—I realize this is quite time consuming, but perhaps you can do a little at a time. I feel you'll be able to provide us with countless clues on missing players and also straighten out errors of which we're not aware."

October 22, 1972: "Thanks so much for your letter received, I've got some good news to pass along as a result of your letter. I've been able to verify the data on Varney Anderson. He was born at Geneva, Illinois, June 18, 1866, and as you said, died at Rockford Illinois, November, 1941."

February 8, 1973: "Tom, I hope you don't feel I 'bug' you too much, but I know for a fact that you have a good deal of information which will help us locate a good number of the players we list as missing."

November 16, 1978: "Rich told me that you've repeated that Ernie Courtney ended up in Buffalo, so I wrote there. The library had nothing so I wrote to Vital Statistics and don't you think they found his death certificate. Courtney was listed as a hotel keeper and died in Buffalo, February 29, 1920. So, I've just written to try and find a surviving relative, but in any case, that's another one we can chalk up to you—thanks a million.

"I recently had occasion to locate Charles A. Armbruster with your help. You had suggested that he may have ended up in Salem, Oregon, so I wrote to Oregon Vital Statistics and they sent me his death certificate. You were close, he ended up in Grants Pass, Oregon where he died in 1964."

March 16, 1979: "Well it took long enough, but I finally found the elusive Walter W. Thomas. If I recall correctly, it was in August of 1976 when my brother-in-law and I visited you at your home, when you first told me that Thomas was from Altoona, Pennsylvania.

"Since that time, I've been fighting a battle of sorts, trying to locate an office in Altoona, where I could write for information. I found a young woman at the Altoona Public Library who traced Walter Thomas into the 1940's. At the same time, she referred me to a genealogist in Hollidaysburg, an Altoona suburb, and he did some digging. Enclosed please find a copy of the letter I've just received from him. It turns out that the name of the player was William Walter Thomas, he was born April 28, 1884 and died June 6, 1950.

"So, that's another one I can chalk up to you. Thanks again for the lead on Thomas. Even though it took the better part of 3 years, it ultimately paid off and I'm grateful to you for the information you provided."

The letters with research requests continued into the 1980's. Soon Tom had me answering the letters and eventually the requests came addressed to me, not Tom. But whether the letter came from Haber, Simenic, Topp, Carle, Bob Richardson, Tom Hufford, Cappy Gagnon, Bob Davids, or some other SABR member, the letter always said, "what does Tom think," or "can you check Tom's files."

Tom Shea passed away in March of 1995. Bill Haber followed less than three months later. Shea and Haber, along with Allen and S. C. Thompson, were baseball's greatest biographical researchers, just as Joe Simenic is the dean of those still living. One thing, though, is certain. Whenever Haber, Allen, or Thompson had a tough nut to crack, the man they turned to was Tom Shea.

The 1921 AL Race

Paul Warburton

Babe Ruth enjoyed his greatest season in 1921 as he led the New York Yankees to their first pennant. This is how the season is normally remembered. But that year's pennant race was one tremendous battle. The Yankees needed all the production they could get from Ruth's mighty bat to outdistance Tris Speaker's defending world-champion Cleveland Indians. By the end of June both teams had pulled away from the rest of the field and during the frantic stretch drive the lead changed hands at least a dozen times.

Nobody in major league history ever put together a season to equal Ruth's performance in 1921. He hit .378, rang up 204 hits, 44 doubles, 16 triples, and clouted 59 home runs. He scored 177 runs—the all-time record. He drove in 171 runs. He walked 144 times, including an estimated 50-plus intentional passes. His slugging percentage was one point behind his 1920 record at .846 and he was good for another record: 457 total bases.

Still young and slender, he was a complete player, stealing 17 bases and throwing out 17 runners from his position in left field. Newspaper accounts described him often as taking an extra base because of an outfielder's momentary bobble. It wasn't rare to see him make a fearless tumbling catch on the dead run.

But the 1921 Yankees were not a one-man team. First baseman Wally Pipp hit .296 with 97 RBIs. At second base Aaron Ward enjoyed a career season batting .306. Shortstop and team captain Roger Peckinpaugh put up a .380 on-base percentage, scored 128 runs, and

starred on defense. Veteran Frank "Home Run" Baker and Mike McNally produced 95 RBIs at third base. Baker, who missed the entire 1920 season due to the illness and subsequent death of his wife, Ottalee, was especially effective driving in 71 runs in 330 at-bats. Switch-hitting catcher Wally Schang socked 30 doubles and batted .316.

New York's outfield possessed another tremendous slugger, too. "Long Bob" Meusel hit .318 with 40 doubles, 16 triples, 24 homers and 135 RBIs. At 6'3" Meusel cut an imposing figure in right field, and he had a gun for an arm. He tied for the league lead with 28 assists. In center field significant time was shared by an unlikely trio—Braggo Roth, Chick Fewster, and Elmer Miller. In 592 at bats the platoon combined for a .292 average, with 37 doubles and 114 runs scored.

Bad blood—The ace of the New York pitching staff was Carl Mays. Mays, who had a tough submarine motion and a longstanding reputation as a beanball pitcher, was notorious for throwing the pitch that killed star Cleveland shortstop Ray Chapman the previous season. The Indians won the 1920 pennant and wore black armbands in memory of Chapman while beating the Brooklyn Dodgers in the World Series. Mays pitched a shutout just one week after the fatal beaning, but did not accompany the Yankees in their last crucial series in Cleveland that year. Yankee co-owner Cap Huston explained Mays's absence this way: "Not because we think there is danger of any trouble, but out of respect to the feeling of the people there. We don't want to offend them. It is largely a matter of sentiment."

Paul Warburton *is a former sportswriter for Wilson Publishing who now works for Metropolitan Home and Auto Insurance Company in Warwick, Rhode island.*

A contingent of the Indians, meeting without player-manager Tris Speaker, circulated a petition shortly after Chapman's death calling for American League teams to refuse to play the Yankees whenever Mays pitched. Boston, Detroit, St. Louis, and Washington supported the petition, but the A's and White Sox did not. Eventually nothing came of it.

Mays always maintained that he was not trying to hit Chapman, but many players didn't believe him, and even those who did felt that he never showed an appropriate degree of remorse. His comments a half-century later to Jack Murphy of the San Diego *Union* are representative. "I fooled them," Mays remembered. "I went out and pitched the rest of the year. Why should I let it ruin the rest of my life? I had a wife and two children, and they had to eat. I had to make a living. I had to provide for them."

Mays was at his peak in 1920 (26-11, 312 innings, 3.06 ERA) and 1921 (27-9, 337 innings, 3.04 ERA). In 1921 he even hit .343 with 22 RBIs. The other two workhorses on the Yankee staff were Waite Hoyt (19-13, 282 innings, 3.10 ERA) and Bob Shawkey (18-12, 245 innings, 4.08 ERA).

Early days—Opening day, April 13, 1921, turned out to be a rousing success. The Yankees were the tenants of the Giants at the Polo Grounds in those days, and a capacity crowd of 37,000 saw the Yankees humble the A's, 11-1. Mays spun a three-hitter while Ruth ripped five

Bob Meusel

hits. New York's American League fans expected something special from this team, and they crowded the park all season to see their astonishing phenomenon: Babe Ruth.

Manager Miller Huggins' team invaded Cleveland for the first time on May 14. The Indians were leading the league with a 16-9 record, two games ahead of New York. Speaker's club had scored ten or more runs in six of their wins, including a 23-hit, 18-5 thrashing of the Tigers and a 20-hit, 17-3 rout of the White Sox. Just about the only pitcher Cleveland wasn't hitting freely was Chicago's Red Faber, who had tossed a pair of two-hit shutouts at the Tribe.

In the opener, Ruth belted a three-run homer into League Park's center field bleachers in the eighth inning to propel New York to a 6-4 win. The next day, an overflow crowd of 28,000, expecting to see Mays pitch, required temporary roped-off accommodations. Hoyt appeared instead, and shackled Cleveland, 8-2. Mays won the third game, 6-3, powered by Meusel's three-run inside-the-park homer off Duster Mails. Cleveland averted a sweep in the final game, 4-2, behind the hurling of George "the Bull" Uhle.

Despite the early setback Cleveland would prove to be a game foe. Speaker hit .362 with 52 doubles and juggled his lineup effectively enough to produce what was then a record 355 doubles, a .308 team batting average, and 925 runs scored—just 23 fewer than the

Yankees. Among the Tribe's talented batsmen were Joe Sewell (.318), Larry Gardner (.319), Steve O'Neill (.322), "Tioga George" Burns (.361), Riggs Stephenson (.330), Charlie Jamieson (.310), Elmer Smith (.290 with a team-leading 16 homers), and former pitcher "Smokey Joe" Wood (.366 with an eye-popping 60 RBIs in just 194 at bats).

In early June the Indians came into the Polo Grounds sporting a 2-1/2-game lead. The Yankees won the first two games, 9-2 and 4-3. Ruth missed half of the second game because he was arrested for speeding in his maroon sports car and spent part of the afternoon in a Manhattan station house. The Indians regrouped to pound the Yankees, 14-4, in Game 3. In the fourth game Cleveland knocked out Mays with three runs in the ninth inning to tie the score at 6-6, and won it in the eleventh, 8-6, on Gardner's homer.

Ty Cobb's Tigers followed the Indians into the Big Apple and Ruth destroyed them. Rarely was his sheer power more evident than in this series. In the curtain raiser, Ruth's three-run homer in the seventh inning tied the game and Peckinpaugh's ninth-inning RBI single won it, 7-6. In Game 2, Ruth doubled twice and rocketed his 19th homer to pace a 21-hit New York assault in a 12-8 win.

In the third game, the Babe went both ways in a 13-8 victory. He pitched one-hit ball through the first four innings and fanned Cobb before being relieved by Mays in the sixth with New York up, 10-4. He also homered twice, one of his prodigious wallops being the first ball ever hit into the center field bleachers at the

Tris Speaker

Polo Grounds, some 500 feet from home plate. On June 14 the Yankees completed the sweep, 9-6, with the Babe bombing two more homers—one of them again landing in the center field bleachers. This magnificent clout was reported to have outdistanced the shot from the day before, and it brought an amazed gasp from the crowd.

On July 2, New York swept a doubleheader from Boston, 5-3 and 5-1, with Ruth homering in both games against his former team. This gave him 30 homers and put him 17 days ahead of his 54-homer 1920 pace. The Yankees celebrated the Fourth of July by whacking the A's, 6-4 and 14-4, before a capacity Polo Grounds crowd. Meanwhile, in Cleveland the Indians swept the White Sox, 6-4 and 11-10, winning the second game after falling behind 10-0 in the second inning. The Indians led the league at 46-26. New York was 1-1/2 games back at 45-28.

In July the Babe hit a shot during a 10-1 win at Detroit that groundskeepers measured at 560 feet. After leaving the Motor City, Huggins' ballclub split a four-game set with their toughest rivals, in Cleveland. One of the Indians wins was especially sweet, as the Tribe drove Mays from the box with seven runs in the third inning on the way to a 17-8 rout.

Cleveland was getting solid pitching from Stan Coveleski, a former Pennsylvania coal miner who would win 23 games with a 3.36 ERA in 316 innings. A big boost to the Indians' pitching came with the acquisition of Allen Sothoron from Boston on waivers. Sothoron was a flop in both St. Louis and Boston early in the season, but he won 12 of 16 decisions for Cleveland, not allowing a single home run in 179 innings. In addition, Guy Morton, nicknamed the "Alabama Blossom," was giving the Tribe stingy relief pitching. He ran off a string of 22 consecutive scoreless innings in July and finished the season with a 2.75 ERA in 30 appearances and 108 innings. And when the Indians did not get good pitching, their hitters often bailed them out. In a series in St. Louis against George Sisler's Browns, Cleveland swept four straight by scores of 12-6, 11-9, 10-8, and 12-5, racking up 45 runs in four days.

When the Indians came into New York for another big series on July 30, they still held a two-game lead over the Yankees, with a 61-34 record. They arrived at the Polo Grounds with a bang, clobbering the Yankees, 16-1. Coveleski's shutout was spoiled by Ruth's 37th homer. The next day the Yankees turned the tables as Mays threw a two-hitter and whacked a bases-loaded double in a 12-2 Yankee win. Ruth singled, tripled, and homered again. The rubber game of the series saw Hoyt stymie the Tribe, 5-2.

The Yankees made their last trip to Cleveland in late August. Ruth hammered a pair of two-run homers in New York's 6-1 win in the first of three. Hoyt out-dueled Coveleski, 3-2, in the second game, and the Yankees moved into first place. A near riot took place in the final game when Yankee hurler Harry Harper hit three consecutive Cleveland batters with pitches. The third batter to get plunked, O'Neill, picked the ball up and fired it back at Harper. Mounted police came out on the field when the game ended, protecting New York's players from an unruly and threatening crowd. The Indians won the game, 15-1, retaking the league lead with a 73-46 mark.

As September opened, the Yankees swept six straight from the Senators. Mays won the final game, 9-3, with Ruth swatting his 50th homer. The Babe tied his 1920 mark of 54 homers in a three-game set in Philadelphia a week later. The Yankees won one of the games, 19-3, showing no mercy for the hapless A's by scoring nine runs in the ninth inning.

Head to head—The ultimate showdown between the Yankees and Indians took place at the Polo Grounds from September 23 to 26. Cleveland came into the four-game series leading the Yankees by mere percentage points—.631 to .629. Ruth slashed three doubles and scored three times as Hoyt bested Coveleski in the opener, 4-2. Uhle came back to whitewash the Yankees with a four-hitter in Game 2, 9-0. On September 25 an estimated 100,000 fans tried to get into the Polo Grounds to see the hottest show in town. Meusel singled, tripled, and homered as New York opened up a 15-4 lead after four innings and thrashed the Indians,

21-7.

The fourth game was a thriller. Speaker tried Coveleski again on two days rest, but he was gone by the third inning. New York started spitballer Jack Quinn, but he was knocked out with three runs in the first. Ruth crashed a solo homer in the first inning and shot a two-run missile over the roof in right in the fifth. Hoyt relieved Quinn and pitched until the seventh, when he injured his hand trying to stop a smash line drive off the bat of Speaker and was relieved by Mays.

Yankee center fielder Elmer Miller played a major role in the game. In the seventh he threw out Sewell at third base, killing an Indian rally. In the eighth, his diving grab of a dying quail off Speaker's bat with runners on second and third saved two runs. Mays finally nailed down an 8-7 Yankee win by fanning O'Neill on a 3-2 pitch with two on and two out in the ninth. Yankee co-owner Jacob Ruppert became so worked up with the tension of the contest that he left his post in the press box and missed the dramatic ending.

The Yankees never relinquished first place. They clinched the pennant when Mays gained his 27th victory, 5-3, in the first game of a doubleheader on October 1 against the A's. Ruth came in to pitch in the eighth inning of the second game, with the Yankees leading, 6-0. The A's scored six runs, but Huggins left him in and he eventually got the win after pitching shutout ball in the ninth, tenth, and eleventh frames.

Ruth hit his 59th homer in the final game of the season, a 7-6 win over the Red Sox at the Polo Grounds. Owner Harry Frazee's Red Sox finished in fifth place with a 75-79 record. Their leading home run hitter was Del Pratt with five. The team as a whole hit only 17 homers. During the past few years the Red Sox had supplied the Yankees with Ruth, Mays, Schang, and Hoyt. Indians Speaker, Gardner and Wood had also been Red Sox.

The 1921 Yankees won 98 games, lost 55, hit an even .300, scored 948 runs and led the league in pitching with a 3.79 ERA. Ruth hit .404 at the Polo Grounds with 32 homers and a .929 slugging percentage. (His highest slugging percentage for a season at Yankee Stadium was .805.)

The all-Polo Grounds World Series against the Giants would prove to be anticlimatic for the Yankees and for Ruth. The Babe scraped his elbow while stealing third base in the second game and the wound became infected. He was warned by the team doctor not to continue playing and he sat out Games 6 and 7 as rumors of blood poisoning and possible amputation circulated. The Yankees lost both games in the best-five-of-nine series, and the Giants clinched the world title in the eighth game as Art Nehf beat Hoyt, 1-0. Ruth pinch-hit in the ninth inning and grounded feebly to George "Highpockets" Kelly at first base, a sad way for his greatest season to end.

Mr. Foster Comes to Washington

Lyle K. Wilson

It's April 5, 1914, and Rube Foster's Chicago American Giants (CAG) take the field in front of a standing-room-only crowd of 10,000. The lineup includes Smokey Joe Williams on the mound, Ben Taylor at first, John Henry Lloyd at shortstop, Bill Monroe at second base, and Pete Hill in center field—a lineup full of actual or potential Hall of Famers. Pitching for the opposition is Wheezer Dell—after Pete Schneider the second major leaguer this club has thrown at the Giants in the past three days.

The location of this game? Chicago?…No. Somewhere in the East?…No. The Midwest?…Guess again. Try Seattle, Washington. Pacific Northwesterners are treated this day to a one-hit, shutout performance by Williams, who enters the game during the first inning with the bases loaded to relieve Pat Dougherty.

The start of the game had been delayed half an hour because the crowd had swamped the box office. Some enterprising youngsters broke a window and sneaked in, while some others pried off a board in center field to gain entry. Long lines or lack of funds were not going to keep these lads from joining the record crowd.

Williams had also prevailed against Schneider just two days earlier, allowing only one run over nine innings. With just four hits that day, CAG had managed a 2-1 win.

Seattle *Post Intelligencer* sportswriter Royal Brougham interviewed Rube Foster during this sojourn in Washington. Because of the significance of Foster's comments about the breaking of baseball's color line, the entire interview is reproduced here:

"Before another baseball season rolls around colored ball players, a score of whom are equal in ability to the brightest stars in the big league teams, will be holding down jobs in organized baseball."

This is the statement of Rube Foster, who travels around the country in a special car with a bunch of ball players that has beaten the strongest major league teams. He believes that the time when a player can be kept out of baseball because of his color is past. Rube is manager of the American Giants, colored, which team is now touring the Northwest.

"The Feds [*i.e.*, the Federal League] are going to force it," says Foster.

With five men on his team that baseball experts have proclaimed as good as any big leaguer of the present day, Foster believes that the new league has made players, [good] players, scarce, and that soon the colored ranks will be invaded, and the best talent picked to fill the breach. He thinks that the magnates will overcome the prejudice which has kept the black man out of baseball, and that the bars will be let down, because there is no other way out of it.

Taking on Cubans.

"They're taking in Cubans now, you notice," Rube says, "and they'll let us in soon. Remember last year when there was so much fuss raised because the Cubans were trimming the

Lyle K. Wilson *is the author of* Sunday Afternoons at Garfield Park, *a history of Seattle's African American baseball teams. With appreciation to Merl Kleinknecht and Jim Riley.*

major league team? Well, listen." Rube showed a row of even white teeth, and his 262 pounds of flesh shook in a chuckle. "There were more negroes on the team than there were Cubans."

"And when they let the black men in," he added, "just watch how many present-day stars lose their positions."

Foster tells how organized baseball planned to form a colored league, with teams in the towns which the Federals were playing, to take the crowd. It was last year, before the new organization had cut so much ice in baseball, that several big fellows got together and decided to put the league on a basis the same as a big league. The players were to have the same privileges and be governed by the national body. The black teams draw enormous crowds in the East, Foster says, and the idea would have been a good one if it had been carried out. But last fall, when things slowed up in the new league, and it was not thought that anything could be feared from the Feds, the magnates gave up the plan.

We Wouldn't.

"A few months later," Foster grinned, "when Gilmour and the rest of the live wires began to shout, I received a message from one of the party which mentioned the colored league last year. He was very anxious to go through with the thing, then. But we"—and "we" seems about to control things in colored baseball—"had our schedule arranged for this tour, and it was too late. I would not consider the thing. But at that, I would not be surprised if the league is organized next year."

Foster is positive that he has the greatest player in the world in Lloyd, the 200-pound shortstop.

"If you don't believe it, wait until he gets into the big league—then watch the Barrys, the Wagners and the Tinkers sweat to keep their jobs."

In an article published the same day as the interview, April 5, 1914, the *Post Intelligencer* went to great lengths to describe Lloyd's tremendous hitting, fielding, and speed.

This was the not the first, nor the last, visit of Foster's team to Washington. In the years 1913-1916, it appeared in the Pacific Northwest.

1913—The first visit was in 1913. Starting in November, 1912, CAG played in a California Winter League, comprising four teams. The other three teams were white teams made up of Pacific Coast League and major league players. On opening day, there was a parade, complete with an African American band, and speeches by several local mayors.

Foster's opening day lineup was:

Jess Barbour, rf
Pete Hill, cf
Frank Duncan, lf
Candy Jim Taylor, 3b
Bill Pierce, 1b
Bill Monroe, 2b
Bruce Petway, c
Pat Dougherty, p
Fred Hutchinson, ss

First baseman William Parks and pitchers Bill Gatewood, Dicta Johnson, and Bill Lindsay were also with the team.

One of the highlights of the opener was a throw by Petway, picking off a runner who had taken a lead at second. For a long time, the runner refused to believe that he was out, maintaining that no catcher could throw him out with only a four-foot lead.

In the third game that winter, Pierce had two unassisted double plays and a two-run home run. Lindsay pitched well, striking out 10, walking none, and allowing only four hits.

Foster inserted himself as a pinch hitter in the ninth inning of the next game, with CAG down 5-1, two men on and two outs. Like "Mighty Casey," Rube went down swinging. The L.A. *Times* reported that the 1,000 African American fans in the stands "gasped" with each mighty swing by Rube.

Though the *Times* did not report the results of every game, it appears that the Giants won about two-thirds of their games, and they were reported as being the champions of the league. It was also reported that in March, 1913, they won four out of five games from the Portland Beavers of the Pacific Coast League.

Continuing up the coast in their Pullman car, the Giants made their first appearance in Seattle, April 4, 1913, prevailing over Pete Schneider, 10-5. The *Post Intelligencer* reported, "There is not the slightest doubt about their being of major league caliber."

Two days later, third baseman Candy Jim Taylor hit two consecutive home runs to lead the way in a rain-shortened, 5-3 win. Declared the *Post Intelligencer*, "It is unfortunate that the visitors cannot stay longer, because they are undoubtedly the greatest colored club in the world, and qualified to battle on even terms with the best in the National and American Leagues. In the two games they have played here, they have shown their class in many ways, yet the conditions have been such that they could not play the kind of ball the fans like to see." The conditions, of course, referred to the damp weather which would prevail generally during all of the years that the Giants visited Seattle. The idea of a retractable dome had not quite caught on yet.

In their final game against Seattle in '13, the Giants racked up 17 runs on 20 hits, giving up 7 and 12 to the opposition. Five thousand fans, half of whom were women, attended the game. Hill, Taylor, and Gatewood all hit home runs in the game and each had three hits. Gatewood, pitching and batting ninth, hit the first ball pitched to him over an apartment house at the southeast corner of the field. It was foul. On his next swing, he hit the ball out fair, clearing the "Orpheum" sign in right field.

Venturing into Canada, the Giants dropped two games, 2-1 and 5-1, to the Vancouver Beavers. Vancouver's pitchers, Bob Ingersoll, Bert Hall, and Rex Dawson, were all former or future big leaguers. Beavers manager Bob Brown "was all smiles when the game was over," proclaiming, "Let Portland talk about this now…I guess we are ready to start the race now."

The Giants fared better after a short ferry ride to Victoria, defeating the Victoria Bees, 4-1 and 7-2, facing down another major league pitcher, Erv Kantlehner, in the first contest. The Giants chalked up at least two more wins, against the Tacoma Tigers and the Portland Pippins, before heading east.

1914—The West Coast tour the next season, which would include the overflow crowd in Seattle on April 5, started with a series in Santa Maria, California, against the Portland Beavers. A number of new faces had been added to the lineup, including Williams, Lloyd, Ben Taylor, Billy Francis (3b), Jude Gans (lf), Lee Wade (p), and Peter Booker (c).

Unlike the previous year, the Giants did not fare well against Portland, losing three and tying one. Again facing big league opposition like Harry Krause, the CAG pitchers gave up a lot of hits, and there were not quite enough runs to prevail. Rube even took the mound, pitching five good innings in the fourth contest, but could not sustain the effort, eventually giving up four runs.

The next stop was Seattle, then the team continued north to British Columbia. In a game in Victoria on April 8, the Giants tried out a local battery, Lee and Gilbert. The *Post Intelligencer* reported "neither made good. The former was as wild as a March hare." CAG managed to win, 8-7, despite the futile effort of the local hurler and catcher.

1915—The next year, 1915, saw the Giants in the Northwest again, after starting out in California in March. Sadly, though, Bill Monroe had passed away on March 16. The *Oregonian* reported:

> Saddest of all, Monroe contracted the cold that later caused his death while touring the Pacific Northwest last spring. Despite a bad

cough, he held down his customary job at second base for the Giants last summer, and not until a few weeks ago did his friends learn of his serious condition.

> …Monroe's particular specialty was poking fun at the opposing pitcher. Last spring the Giants defeated Nick Williams' Portland Colts in a no-hit-no-run game at Santa Rosa, California. Williams used his Indian flinger, Battiste, against the Negroes for five innings and Monroe had the time of his life "kidding" Battiste.

> After the game it was tipped off to him that Battiste was deaf and dumb, and the joke was so good that Monroe bought the treats for his entire crew.

As with the previous year, there were a number of new faces in the lineup, including Harry Bauchmann (2b), Hurley McNair (rf), Frank Wickware (p), Richard Whitworth (p), Horace Jenkins (p), Walter Ball (p), and Louis Santop, the great catcher.

The Giants had left Chicago on March 4 to train in New Orleans. Rainy weather had allowed only six practice games there. Out to the Coast they came, arriving in Fresno for another series with Portland.

Although the Giants would improve on the '14 series, they still ended up short, with two wins and four losses. The series almost ended in a tie, with the Giants dropping the final contest, 1-0, in 12 innings.

During the series they again faced some major league caliber pitchers, Krause, Tiny Leonard, and Stanley Coveleskie. On March 27, the Giants racked up 14 hits against Coveleskie, including two home runs (Gatewood and Barbour) and three doubles. A third home run by McNair in the ninth was lost when rain shortened the game, the score at the end of eight innings standing at 9-1.

The preceding game had been marred by a near brawl. It started when Wickware hit Derrick who responded by throwing his bat at the Giants' pitcher. When Derrick arrived at first, second baseman Bauchmann went after him, and both benches had to step in to calm down the potential combatants.

From California, Foster's crew headed north again, this time stopping to defeat the University of Oregon, 9-5. A game against an all-star team in Portland was rained out, but the occasion gave Foster the opportunity to comment on the Portland team, as reported in the April 2 issue of the *Oregonian*:

> Owing to an excess of moisture Portland ball fans were not able to size up "Rube" Foster's famous Chicago colored Giants yesterday against an All-Star City League cast. "Rube" was here with his dark horde, however, and before he submerged for the run to Seattle the

240-pounder let drop the interesting remark that the Portland Coast club is the strongest [owner W alter H.] McCredle has opened with in three years.

And "Rube" ought to know because he has met the Mackmen in a special camp series every Spring within that period.

"I told you last Spring your team was weak," said the negro McGraw. "If Mack hadn't strengthened he would never have won the pennant. But I like this 1915 club. Mack has a bunch of good pitchers. Of the youngsters I like Coveleskie best, because he has all the natural requirements. Leonard beat us 1-0 in the final game, but, even so, I don't believe he will ever become a Coast Leaguer. He pitches only one way. Callahan is young and promising.

"Stumpf at second base, in my judgment, will prove even superior to Bill Rodgers," added Manager Foster. "That is a strong statement in view of the fact that Rodgers is now in the big leagues. Stumpf looks to me like a comer. I have some of the greatest infielders in the world on my club and yet they couldn't accustom themselves to that rough Fresno diamond like Stumpf. He fields much better than Rodgers and I really believe he will hit just as well, although Rodgers is a great pinch hitter.

"Portland's catching staff is 50 percent stronger than it was last season. Carisch is a better catcher today than Chief Meyers, of the New York Giants. I know because we were in the Southern California Winter League two years ago, when Meyers and Carisch caught for the San Diego club, side by side. Carisch isn't as strong at the bat as Meyers, but he is a wise man behind the windpad.

"They were all shaking their heads at Fresno about Shortstop Murphy, but he looked all right to me."

Foster is in close touch with the big league ball situation and he does not think the Federal League will ever stick as a third major. If it does not go broke it will be merged with the American and National, in his opinion.

The Colored Giants left early last night for Tacoma and Seattle.

The interview was conducted by Roscoe Fawcett. If Foster had read some of Fawcett's reports of the games in California over the years, I wonder if he would have consented to be interviewed by him. Fawcett had referred to the Giants as "pickanninies," said the pitchers included Rube "hisself," called Lloyd, "a huge ape-like Negro," and called the players "buffs."

In 1916, he would write that pitcher, Edgar Washington (father of Kenny Washington, the great football star), was having "the time of his young shoe-shining life." Fawcett's blatantly racist language stood in contrast to almost all of the rest of those who reported on the Giants during these years when they played in California, Oregon, and Washington.

The Giants arrived in Seattle in early April, hoping for enough sunshine to get in a few games with the Seattle Giants. Articles announcing the games again gave the Chicago nine the accolade of being of major league strength.

Before playing Seattle, CAG traveled an hour north to Everett, where they defeated the Aberdeen Black Cats, 3-0. The Sunday, April 3 game was scheduled for 10:15 A.M. so the Giants could catch the noon train back for their Seattle opener.

In the two previous years, Seattle had been unable to defeat CAG. But behind a brilliant pitching performance that afternoon by Walter Mails—another pitcher who would go on to play several years in the major leagues—they finally won a game, 3-2. The next day Seattle again prevailed by one run.

A return engagement in Everett was scheduled for the following Sunday morning, and the Everett *Herald* primed the local fans by advertising that the game would be preceded by the famous shadow-ball routine.

The Giants delivered on all counts, defeating Aberdeen again, 9-3, and captivating the audience with their comedy routine. The Everett *Herald* reported it this way on April 12, 1915:

> The one big hit of the day with the fans was the "shadow ball" game pulled off by the Colored Giants just before the regular game began. Francis, the diminutive third baseman, who is about as tall as half a minute, was placed on first and the other players were scattered around the bases promiscuously. Without using a ball the players went through the performance of fielding practice, and their antics kept the fans in a constant uproar, Francis easily being the star in the comedy line with his almost inhuman leaps into the air for imaginary "high ones."

The Giants would beat the Black Cats one more time, 3-1, completing a sweep. On April 6 they had finally beaten Vancouver for the first time, 4-3, behind Whitworth's six-hit performance on the mound.

On their way back to Chicago, the Giants stopped in Spokane for a series against the Spokane Indians. In the opener, CAG came from 10 runs down to win, 14-13, in a game that totaled 41 hits. In the second contest, Foster pulled his team off the field to protest a pinch hitter who was allowed to come into the game after